Praise fc
STREET SMAR
for
Wome

T0014089

"*Street Smart Safety for Women* is filled with wisdom that every woman should have to better situate herself for security and safety. There is so much about the life skills that women can employ/develop/learn to maintain their health and well-being. I really enjoyed the well-researched information and the personal stories of the authors. Sharing their personal perspectives gives the reader a clearer perspective on the importance and the suggestions that are made throughout the book."

—**Dr. Robin Larson, PhD,** retired Broward Sheriff's Office Captain

STREET SMART SAFETY

for Women

STREET SMART SAFETY for Women

Your Guide to Defensive Living

JOY FARROW, Retired Deputy Sheriff
and **LAURA FROMBACH**

Health Communications, Inc.
Boca Raton, Florida

www.hcibooks.com

Authors' Note: Unless referenced as endnotes or related as personal experiences by the authors, all events and people depicted within have been completely changed for anonymization. Any correlation to actual people or events is strictly coincidental.

Library of Congress Cataloging-in-Publication Data

Farrow, Joy, author. | Frombach, Laura, author.
Street smart safety for women : your guide to defensive living / by
   Joy Farrow and Laura Frombach.
  Boca Raton, Florida : Health Communications, Inc., [2023] |
   Includes bibliographical references.
LCCN 2023023740 (print) | LCCN 2023023741 (ebook) | ISBN
   9780757324932 (trade paperback) | ISBN 9780757324949 (epub)
LCSH: Women—Crimes against—Prevention. | Women—Violence
   against—Prevention. | Self-defense for women.
LCC HV6250.4.W65 F383 2023 (print) | LCC HV6250.4.W65
   (ebook) | DDC 362.88082--dc23/eng/20230613

LC record available at https://lccn.loc.gov/2023023740
LC ebook record available at https://lccn.loc.gov/2023023741

Publisher: Health Communications, Inc.
          301 Crawford Boulevard, Suite 200
          Boca Raton, FL 33432–3762

Cover, interior design, and typesetting by Larissa Hise Henoch

For Women Everywhere

Contents

Introduction

The motivational speaker Tony Robbins once asked half of his audience: "Men, raise your hand if you've felt unsafe in the last week." Out of the thousand or so men in the audience, a few hands went up. Then he asked the other half: "Ladies, raise your hand if you've felt unsafe in the last week." A thousand female hands went up, surprising only the men in the audience.

Every woman in that audience felt unsafe at some point—over the period of just *one* week. And yet, the men were surprised.

Are you surprised? We aren't, either. We would have raised our hands as well.

Maybe you would have too. If so, this book is for you.

Now, the audience participants weren't *attacked* within that last week. However, they did perceive a threat of some type. And that week wasn't any different from any other week. No prison breaks had occurred nearby. No serial killer was reported to be on the loose. It was just an ordinary week. Another week in a series of weeks. In other words, women perceive threats to their personal safety almost *all* the time.

There's no way of knowing how many of those audience participants were actually victims of violence at some point in their lives. But it's safe to say that their response was based on *some* point of reference.

The United Nations (UN) Women website estimates that 736 million—almost one in three (30 percent of women age fifteen and older)—women across the globe have been subjected to violence at least once in their lifetime.[1] The lives of almost a billion women have been shattered. Because the mental and emotional impact of violence can last a lifetime.

We believe that as staggering as these numbers are, they don't reflect reality.

We think that they're too low.

For one thing, the UN also notes: "Less than 40 percent of the women who experience violence seek help of *any* sort, and less than 10 percent of those seeking help appealed to the police." [2]

And as staggering as *those* numbers are, they are even higher for Black, Latina, Indigenous, and increasingly, Asian women in the United States.

For another, many women whom we've personally spoken with have indicated that they have been the victim of some type of attack or attempted attack in their life.

We agree with Angelina Jolie[3] and Chantal Mulopea,[4] special advisor to the president of the Democratic Republic of the Congo, who made the same statement within days of each other:

> **Violence against women has become normalized.**

Violence against women has become normalized.

According to FBI statistics, 77 percent of violent crime offenders are male.[5] So those who protest, "Not all men," are technically correct. But 77 percent definitely points to the source of the issue.

Consider if the tables were turned: What if women suddenly began attacking men at the same rate? Or if this violent crime wave of attacks was occurring against any other group of people? There would be an international law enforcement task force dedicated to solving the problem and bringing the perpetrators to justice.

It's important that we as a society, but especially women, understand the true extent of this public health emergency, and we'll address some of that in this book. Because without understanding and acknowledging the actual scope of the crisis, it will continue to be minimized, as violence against women has been traditionally dismissed for centuries.

One other point that we'd like to make right away is that we don't fault all men for aggression against women, nor do we think that all men are out to "get" women. In fact, almost anyone may find some of our information useful, not only for the women they love, but themselves as well. And we hope that they do.

All are welcome here, including all genders and identities. And although we've tried to make our descriptions gender-neutral because they do apply to all, there are occasions when the majority of predators are cis men, and the language reflects that.

The gist of this book is geared toward cisgender women because, as such, we are taught to think differently. We're trained from infancy to attend to everyone else before we pay attention to ourselves. It's important for women to be aware that this attitude is dangerous to their own personal safety. We can say this with conviction because, well, that's how we ourselves have been raised and conditioned. We're both nice girls who were hardwired since birth to *be* nice. We're also both aware of the toll that can and has taken on our own safety. It's taken many years for both of us, and Joy's law enforcement training, to get in there and adjust that wiring.

We believe that a large part of the reason that violence against women is normalized is because most men, like those in Tony Robbins's audience, have no idea that this *is* a global health emergency for women. This includes judicial systems and law enforcement, which is composed, of course, primarily of men. Another contributing element is that many predators don't present themselves in public the way that they do privately. In other words, most men will never see the side of other men that women do, which can lead them to not believe women.

This leaves a global systemic failure to protect women and to prosecute perpetrators to the full extent of the law.

No one is coming to save us. There is no 9-1-1 for this.

So we have to save ourselves.

What can you do to save yourself? How can you help keep *yourself* safe so that you don't become one of these statistics? And if you have been a victim, where can you find resources to help you recover?

That's what this book is about.

Why We Wrote This Book

To our observation, the world has reached a dangerous inflection point regarding women's safety. Given the ancient history of violence against women, this rising trend in threats can be attributed to one thing:

The weaponizing of misogyny enabled by the technology revolution.

And make no mistake, it *is* a revolution, unprecedented in human history. Laura spent almost forty years of her life as a technologist and, as such, observed firsthand the rapid rise and acceleration of technology. For ten years, she evaluated the power and capability of each subsequent generation of servers, consulting with engineers and Fortune 500 customers of Hewlett Packard (now Hewlett Packard Enterprise) on those findings. The acceleration of technology over those ten years was amazing.

It has become breathtaking. And it moves faster every day.

For example, just since 2016, the miniaturization of computers has enabled your car to have an onboard computer that allows your car to practically drive itself yet is small enough that you don't even notice it. In other words, it doesn't need to fit in your trunk, which it would have even ten years ago.

Sensors surrounding the car communicate with the central processing unit to notify you if you're about to back into a grocery cart, of cars approaching on either side, and it even automatically slams on the brakes if the car in front of you suddenly stops, whether you're distracted or not. And all these features are readily available in even "basic" cars, lowering your car insurance because insurance companies know that you'll have fewer accidents with this technology onboard.

But that same miniaturization has also enabled the development of tiny video cameras that fit inside devices masked as deodorant or smoke detectors that can be used to take nude videos of women and children without their consent and then easily sell those images on the dark web.

One would think that—with the massive advances in computing power, artificial intelligence, data mining, and more (especially since the price point of accessing technology is affordable to virtually everyone in the civilized world)—these tools would be harnessed to improve the safety of half the world's population.

But, on the contrary, the tech revolution has *accelerated* threats to our safety. In addition to the age-old dangers of assault, rape, and murder of women, tech has provided those who would harm us with a veritable arsenal of powerful weapons. Online predator schools, violent anonymous communities, the rise of the dark web, and other horrors have cropped up and are increasing with dizzying speed.

In fact, it could be argued that the threat posed by the digital revolution to women and our safety is unprecedented.

The world has been revolutionized and changed in the digital age, and our judicial system is still no closer to addressing violence against women. Law enforcement and legislators have barely acknowledged *physical* gender-based violence that has always existed, let alone recognized the additional threats to women's safety that the digital age has brought. If authorities even acknowledge online incidents, they often treat each attack as an isolated event instead of recognizing the systemic savagery that it is.

And without that recognition, the legal framework needed to charge and prosecute these crimes is practically nonexistent and shows no signs of developing.

The success of many predators and cons, including domestic abusers, depends heavily on the initial ignorance of their victims to their ultimate aims. They bank heavily on their ability to rapidly develop trust and rapport.

Joy has seen this countless times over her twenty-eight-year career as a deputy sheriff. And, after caring for her sister through her illness and subsequent death, she is present to do what she's always wanted to do: educate women to what she's learned about predators and cons.

To be clear, *anyone* can be attacked or conned.

Being financially scammed can ruin your life as well. And although most attackers are men, that certainly isn't the case with con artists. The art of the con isn't exclusively a male domain. But we'll show you how you can protect yourself from many frauds as well.

The Irony of Men Teaching Women's Safety Classes

Now there *are* good men who are trying to help us keep ourselves safe. Some of them teach women's safety classes. Their intentions are *so* good.

Laura attended a number of those safety classes in neighborhood rec centers over the years. Joy, of course, has had extensive law enforcement training over the course of her career.

Those neighborhood women's safety courses are typically instructed by big, gruff guys who inevitably resemble Smokey the Bear. The instructor is typically a deputy (or retired law enforcement officer) who sincerely wants his female audience to learn how we can reduce our probability of becoming the next crime victim.

Frequently, the instructors encouraged us to buy a gun and toughen up a little in order to blast the perp. They basically consider a gun to be the equivalent of a Swiss army knife: the solution to every problem. But that solution assumes a single scenario: that every assault against a woman will be the result of walking alone at night. And to instill this knowledge, Smokey has two basic strategies that he barks over and over at the audience, emphasizing a different word with each iteration: "Ladies! Don't walk alone at night! Be aware of your surroundings!"

Ladies! *Don't* walk alone at night! Don't walk *alone* at night! Don't walk alone at *night!*

After beseeching us to just say no to solitary night strolling and then assuring us that if we insist on doing so, we should be on the alert, Smokey has an arsenal of war stories to fill in the rest of the hour, each story illustrating how this two-pointed game plan with a gun will protect every woman in the room, every time, in every situation.

The implication is that rapists, muggers, and other predators are boogeymen, strangers who only attack women after dark in public places. So if you don't wander around alone outside your home at night, you'll be safe. But if you must, then your awareness and your weapon will prevent an attack.

Problem identified; problem solved.

Oh, sir. If *only* it were that easy.

First of all, it appeared that many of those instructors were un-aware of the actual data surrounding violent crimes. Rape is one of the most brutal crimes against women and the one most alluded to in their safety classes. Yet, according to the latest FBI statistics,[6] 70 percent of reported rapes occur inside the victim's home, not on a street.[7] And half of all homicides (irrespective of gender) also occur within the victim's residence. So it appears as though we ought to be more protective of who gets *inside* our home as well.

Second, we are not unappreciative of the intentions and personal time that Smokey and his friends are devoting to women's safety. It's just that the poor guy is missing the forest for the trees (pun intended). Because in addition to contradicting actual crime data, that simplistic yet oft-repeated advice overlooks the most important point:

None of these men have a clue how it feels to be a woman in an unsafe world.

Remember the different responses of men and women in Tony

Robbins's audience? The guys were stunned, which is the response of almost every man when they realize the personal safety dangers that women navigate every day. And that isn't even taking into account that many women also have the safety of their children to consider, so whipping out a gun and blasting away isn't always the best solution. Especially if you're holding a child.

In fact, it would be extremely surprising if any of those safety instructors gave their personal safety a second thought after they left their audience. And we'd bet that 99 percent of them have never gambled the safety odds of going to the grocery store after dark, juggled the challenges of traveling solo with children, or prayed that the handyman isn't psycho.

Laura once sat next to a blind woman and her Seeing Eye dog on a flight. The flight attendant stopped by before the plane took off and assured the woman that she'd be back for her in an emergency. The woman chuckled after the flight attendant left and said to Laura, "If there's an emergency, follow me. Who do you trust during a blackout, someone who is used to navigating in the dark or the person who took a couple of classes?"

Joy is accustomed to navigating the dark of women's safety. Smokey has effectively taken a couple of classes.

A Female Cop Who Knows How You Feel

When Joy was in uniform, she got the respect from the public that goes with wearing the badge and the gun, along with the challenges of being a woman in a male-dominated profession. But when she wasn't on duty, she got treated the same as every other woman does. This means that she is also subject to predators and knows how it feels to be unsafe just because you are a female in this world. So, unlike her male colleagues, she is acutely aware of her personal safety, no matter where she is.

Throughout her career in law enforcement, Joy always wished that someone would write about safety from a woman's perspective, from someone who's been on the street and has actual experience. She couldn't find a book that reflected the reality of what she saw every day, so she decided to write it herself. This book provides safety information for women by a woman who knows what it's like to feel unsafe every day.

As a result of her twenty-eight years as a cop on the street, Joy is particularly aware that predators come in all types, and that women's safety is at risk *everywhere*: outside/inside, day/night, rich/poor. And that there are no one-size-fits-all solutions to reducing your risk of becoming a victim. So while not walking alone at night remains solid advice, it doesn't guarantee your safety.

And although most women instinctively sense when we're not safe, society programs us to override our built-in safety mechanism. For generations, our global framework has been built on women's deference to others. And although that is slowly changing, it is still hardwired into millions of women.

However, Joy's colleagues *are* right about one thing: Increasing your awareness of your surroundings *can* help you stay safe. And although Smokey keeps barking about it, he doesn't provide the women in his audience any guidance in *how* to increase their observation skills in this area. Namely, because he doesn't know himself. He can't since he's never been in that situation. He doesn't have firsthand knowledge. As a man, he doesn't live with the constant uncertainty of his own safety, so he doesn't have the experience of designing his life around being defensive.

But we do. And that's what this book is going to show you.

Your Guide for Defensive Living

As mentioned earlier, few will dispute that the world is an unsafe place and becoming more so, especially for women. And when you factor in the increasing ability of technology to amplify anonymous digital attacks on women, it almost seems overwhelming at times. However, the response of most women seems to be an elevated but vague sense of fear without a specific strategy to maintain personal safety. We'd like to change that.

In defensive driving classes, motorists are taught specific principles and techniques to avoid accidents, which saves lives, time, and money. Many of us drive every day, safely maneuvering among thousands, tens of thousands, or more unpredictable drivers yet rarely being involved in a traffic accident. And the key to the safest driving records is fairly basic: awareness and a few essential strategies.

In this book, we're proposing a similar strategy for defensive *living*: Use the same level of awareness and confidence in your daily life that you do behind the wheel of your car, and we'll provide you with some crucial strategies that we've developed, both from a law enforcement perspective and the perspective of a civilian who grew up with daily violence.

If you drive on a daily basis, you confidently get into your car every day and get behind the wheel without a second thought, let alone contemplating that you may get into an accident. Consider that you get into a two-ton virtual tank every day and unhesitatingly maneuver at great speed in and among thousands of similar vehicles. In fact, a lot of the driving public barely pays attention, talking, texting, drinking coffee, even applying makeup and watching videos! You watch the news that often depicts traffic disasters that may include casualties, and while you feel badly for the victims, it doesn't terrify you in the same way that apparent random or even targeted acts of violence seem to because you've developed confidence in your defensive driving skills. We'd like you to have that same level of awareness and confidence in your defensive living ability.

If there's anything that Joy has learned from her years of professional training, it's that internal preparation and how you live your everyday life is the best way to practice for a crisis. To that end, your daily mental training is your best predictor of how you'll respond in an emergency—which is why we'd like you to implement a defensive living mindset immediately.

We don't want you to live in the "red zone" and to be on edge all the time, anticipating an attack. We want you to remain alert but relaxed and curious about your surroundings, knowing that you can avoid problems before they begin and that you know what to do in the event of an emergency.

Not only will you be calmer under pressure, but you'll be more confident overall.

Keep in mind that a display of confidence in and of itself can be a deterrent for predators because all predatory animals are attracted to weakness. And just like predators in the wild, criminals are more likely to attack those that they think can be overcome easily.

The goal of this book is to equip you with knowledge of how predators operate in a changing world, and to provide you with street smart safety strategies to help *you* recognize some of their traits and tactics. We want to arm you by teaching you why you should trust yourself instead of others, thereby developing your safety intuition, your personal early warning system of sorts.

Now this doesn't mean that you can't still be a kind and compassionate person. We encourage you to be the nice person that you are; the world certainly needs you! However, for women, it seems to have become an either/or proposition: You're either considerate to a fault or you aren't a nice person. We maintain that you can be warm and benevolent but still keep your boundaries and protect your personal safety.

Trauma expert Dr. Gabor Maté, MD, clarifies some of the confusion the world has had regarding women's natural safety instincts in *The Myth of Norma: Trauma, Illness and Healing in a Toxic Culture.* Dr. Maté, a physician for forty years, notes that there are two essential needs in every person: attachment and authenticity.

Attachment is defined by child development psychologist Dr. Gordon Neufield as "the drive for closeness—proximity to others, in not only the physical but the emotional sense as well. Its primary purpose is to facilitate either caretaking or being taken care of." He continues, "For many people, these attachment circuits powerfully override the ones that grant us rationality, objective decision making, or conscious will." For women, you can feel the thumb of society on the scales of this one. The world demands: Take care of us. To the exclusion of everything else.

But we also have another core need: authenticity. Dr. Maté describes it as:

> The quality of being true to oneself, and the capacity to shape one's own life from a deep knowledge of that self. Authenticity is not some abstract aspiration, no mere luxury for New Agers dabbling in self-improvement. Like attachment, it is a drive rooted in survival instincts.
>
> At its most concrete and pragmatic, it means simply this: Knowing our gut feelings when they arise and honoring them. Imagine our African ancestor on

the savanna, sensing the presence of some natural predator: Just how long will she survive if her gut feelings warning of danger are suppressed? A healthy sense of self does not preclude caring for others or being affected or influenced by them. It is not rigid but expansive and inclusive. Authenticity's only dictate is that we, not externally imposed expectations, be the true author and authority on our own life.

From childhood, most women are programmed to be nice, to be a good girl, to be polite. But that inclusion comes at the cost of our safety.

Because here's the truth: That niceness can get you killed. Read this part again: "Imagine our African ancestor on the savanna, sensing the presence of some natural predator: Just how long will she survive if her gut feelings warning of danger are suppressed?"

It's as true today as it was on the savanna.

Your safety is more important than being polite.

This is also the truth: Your safety is more important than being polite.

If even one person has been saved from the lifelong trauma of being the victim of a violent attack or losing her hard-earned money, we'll have accomplished our goal.

When you finish this book, it is our hope that you've realized along the way that you can trust yourself and your safety intuition and that you'll feel more confident in your ability to protect yourself and your family.

You can bring the hammer down, if needed, and still be a kind person.

Because that's who you are.

Chapter One

Design for Defensive Living

eputy Joy Farrow pulled a car over for running a red light. Two middle-aged Caucasian males were in the car, and the driver obligingly provided his license when asked. She glanced over at the passenger. At this point in her career, Joy had several hundred traffic stops under her belt. So she knew something about this passenger was off. He wasn't combative or belligerent, nor did the vehicle smell of weed or booze as could be the case when drivers blew through red lights.

There was just *something about that.*

With a professional tone in her voice, she asked the passenger, "Sir, may I see your license also?"

"Um, I forgot it at home. Why do you need it? I'm not driving." He stared at her. Hard.

She looked back at him, unblinking. "Well, in the event that the driver can't drive because his license is suspended, you'll be permitted to drive the vehicle if you have your license. So not only does the law allow me to verify that you are licensed to drive, but it's to your benefit so that you don't need to wait." As luck would have it, he suddenly remembered that he *did* bring his license.

She ran both of the licenses. The driver's license came back clear, meaning that it wasn't suspended, nor did he have any warrants. But it turned out that the passenger *did* have a lengthy criminal history and an outstanding warrant for a felony. What was it about the passenger that caught Joy's attention?

Laura's cousin Sue had a new boyfriend, and the family was thrilled because Sue's life had been so difficult since her husband had passed away from cancer several years prior, leaving her with a young child and little money. She was in her late twenties, so young to have fate deal her such a cruel hand. But it seemed as though the heavens were finally going to balance the scales; something good had finally happened to her.

Sue's mother gushed to Laura, "I can't wait until you meet him! He's so handsome and funny! He treats her like a queen. She deserves it after everything she's been through. Can you believe it? When are you coming home?" Laura was also happy for Sue and could *not* wait to meet Mario.

Finally, when she couldn't take the wait any longer, Laura flew home. She'd arranged to spend the weekend at Sue and Mario's to get the most out of her time with the happy couple. When she arrived at their home, Mario was working, so Laura and Sue happily chatted about Sue's new life and how wonderful Mario was to her daughter. Finally, Mario's 'vette roared in the driveway, and the big moment was here.

He walked in. Everyone was right. Mario was a presence. Laura felt him from across the room. She has rarely been so moved by a person in her life. He kissed Sue and moved toward Laura with a huge smile. Waves of nausea hit Laura like a tsunami. What the hell was *this*?

Instinctively, Laura backed up and then slowly willed herself forward for the obligatory hug. She shivered at the physical contact as though she'd just hugged frozen evil. Her rational mind went blank. She had no idea what had just happened.

Laura forced herself to endure a perfectly repugnant evening with them by hammering down so many gin and tonics that Tanqueray probably had to fire up their second shift to refill stock. That might have been the night that she crossed over the one-way bridge into alcoholism. The first thing in the morning, she mumbled some excuse and took her hangover to stay at Sue's mother's house for the rest of the weekend. Laura couldn't articulate to anyone, even herself, what had happened.

On the flight home, she contemplated a letter to Sue. But what to say? Your idyllic boyfriend creeped me out, so please leave him? In the end, Laura had no answer, so she convinced herself to forget the entire situation.

Six months later, Sue's mother called Laura, her words jumbling together. She was crying so hysterically that it took several attempts to understand her words.

"Mario. Put. Put. Sue. In. The. Hospital. Broken. Ribs."

Laura's blood ran cold. How had she known? It would take her decades to answer that question.

We All Have Intuition

Both of us have backgrounds in violence and are intimately familiar with it but not as abusers. We belong to separate populations that have developed the ability to immediately react to situations without conscious thought to potentially save our lives. Joy is a retired law enforcement officer (LEO), and Laura is a survivor of childhood domestic abuse. These two groups, along with combat military vets, often know what we know without knowing how we know it.

This type of perception is often called intuition—knowledge that we seem to instantly have access to without mental processing. But we don't have this awareness because we're extraordinary people. On the contrary, we're regular folk. We both developed this as a result of being ordinary people in extraordinary situations. Neither of us are magical, can predict the future, or conjure lottery numbers (sadly). The intuition we developed is the result of being in life-threatening situations. Intuit or die.

However, we believe that every one of us has the same ability because the intuition we're referring to is not a supernatural or emotional superpower. The type that we're talking about is the kind that harnesses your subconscious as it communicates through your intuition. As you'll see shortly, the variety of intuition that we're discussing is biology based; it is simply accessing the power of your subconscious as it rapidly processes data from your five senses and attends to it. We call it safety intuition.

We both have *had* to learn to pay attention to our subconscious in the form of safety intuition because of our circumstances. But everyone has this ability because every human has senses and a subconscious.

The difference is that we have both learned to listen to our own subconscious, *regardless of anyone else's opinion*. And this is a very important factor for women as you'll soon find out.

It's our observation that women's overriding concern about being so consumed with everyone else's comfort before being aware of their own safety is a false narrative that they tell themselves. It's a belief that's been told/sold to women, which then becomes the stories women tell themselves, often in very subtle ways.

When our colleague Olivia heard about this book, she commented, "This has happened to me. I can immediately think of some potentially dangerous situations that I have put myself in by trying to be too polite. And in every instance, I knew better; I knew I should get out. But I wound up telling myself stories about not being rude so that I would remain."

Olivia readily provided an example: She detailed an instance where she told herself a lot of different stories when she was in a potentially dangerous situation at a rodeo. Here is her story in her own words.

My husband, Tony, and I were staying with friends, and they had invited us to attend the Fourth of July rodeo in a small Midwestern town in the USA. I was disturbed at the violence of the rodeo and decided to wait for Tony in the car and read until it was over.

I'd been there about ten minutes, engrossed in my book, when somebody knocked on the car as if they were knocking on a door.

It was a friend of our friends who we'd met the night before when we'd all had dinner together. I knew that he was a doctor working at the town's medical practice, and that he was married with a young daughter. He was probably in his mid-thirties, some twenty years younger than me.

He said to me, "It's really hot here. You could come and sit in the medical practice in the cool if you'd like. It's only a few minutes' walk from here. I can take you there."

This was two days into our big adventure. Tony and I had sold, given, and lent everything we owned in New Zealand and were on our way to live in Spain. Here was another adventure in front of me. I thought this would be more interesting than sitting in the car reading my book. So, I said yes.

On the way he started to tell me about his marital troubles. That should have been a red flag. And the medical center was more than a few minutes' walk; it was more like twenty. Another red flag. But I skated right past them. I was having an adventure, meeting new people, having new experiences.

We arrived at the medical center, and he unlocked it. He said I could sit in the waiting room or in one of the doctors' surgeries, where the chairs were more comfortable. I chose the doctor's surgery. I was about to get out my book, but he sat down in another chair and carried on talking about his marital troubles. I'm a good listener, and I went straight into my listening/coaching mode.

But as this carried on, I realized that I'd got myself into a situation. Tony didn't know where I was. Nobody knew where I was. I was alone in a deserted building with a man I hardly knew. Everybody else was having fun with Fourth of July celebrations. I had initially trusted him because he was a friend of a friend, and because he was a doctor, and he knew I was married. He was twenty years younger than me; surely, he wouldn't try anything! But none of these things meant very much if he had bad intentions.

What if Tony decided to leave the rodeo to look for me and went to the car, and I wasn't there? He would panic. I went through an internal dialogue:

Me: I must text Tony.

My Inner People-Pleaser: It will be rude to interrupt this guy.

Me: But I must tell Tony where I am.

My Inner People-Pleaser: The guy might feel insulted. He might think that you're insinuating that you feel unsafe with him.

Me: I am feeling unsafe with him. It's imperative that I tell Tony where I am as soon as possible whether I insult this guy or not. And I need to get out of here.

I texted Tony, and I said to the guy, "I'm going to go back to the car." And walked out without a problem. I will never know whether this guy had bad intentions or not. What I'm appalled by is that my initial reaction was to ensure that I wasn't rude to the guy, that I was polite and pleasant, that I didn't insult him. My comfort and safety came way down the list.

Olivia continues, "We need to practice being rude, being impolite, so that we are not caught in situations like this. When somebody makes you uncomfortable and you don't speak up and be honest, you're holding onto all that discomfort when they should be the ones who should be feeling uncomfortable." You are under no obligation to allow someone to be comfortable in making you uncomfortable.

Like Olivia, many "nice" women rarely consider the implications of being so polite on their own safety until it's often too late. The authors have spoken with so many women who have dozens of stories like Olivia's. Chances are pretty good that you know some women who do too.

Olivia didn't want to "hurt the feelings" of a man she barely knew. Many women put their safety at risk because they don't even want to take the chance of "hurting the feelings" of a stranger! When you believe your safety is at risk, challenge those internal beliefs. When your safety intuition alerts you, it doesn't matter *who* the potential predator is.

Can you think of a time when you challenged those beliefs right away and followed your own safety intuition? Can you remember a time when you didn't?

In this book, we dare you to challenge those assumptions about being polite all the time *immediately*, instead of waiting until it may be too late to save yourself.

Tips **FROM A COP:**

When your safety intuition alerts you: Act. It doesn't matter who the potential predator is.

Your Safety Intuition

During Joy's law enforcement career, she interviewed many women who were victims of predators. Most of them said they were embarrassed because they didn't listen to their intuition and were persuaded by someone against their better judgment. Joy could relate to the victims she questioned, having had a similar experience as a teen, when she was coaxed into a stranger's car against her own better judgment. More about that in a minute.

Just what is safety intuition?

Here's what it is not: As mentioned earlier, it isn't woo-woo. Or mystical. Or that only certain people have it.

It's your five senses and your unconscious. Your safety intuition comes from what Dr. Timothy D. Wilson calls your "adaptive unconscious" and is like your own supercomputer. It is constantly processing data that it takes in from your five senses 24/7.

At any given moment, your five faculties are taking in eleven million pieces of information *per second* and feeding them to the supercomputer: your unconscious. But your conscious mind can only process forty bits of data per second. Forty. Forty versus eleven million.

As Dr. Wilson notes in his book *Strangers to Ourselves*:

> Scientists have determined this number by counting the receptor cells each sense organ has and the nerves that go from these cells to the brain. Our eyes alone receive and send over 10,000,000 signals to our brains each second. Scientists have also tried to determine how many of these signals can be processed consciously at any given point in time, by looking at such things as how quickly people can read, consciously detect different flashes of light, and tell apart different kinds of smells. The most liberal estimate is that people can process consciously about 40 pieces of information per second.

To put that in context: If you lay forty pennies side by side, it will go from the floor to about your hip. But if you lay eleven million pennies side by side, the trail will go one hundred and thirty miles. That's the half the width of the state of Florida.

So your safety intuition can see, hear, and process information far faster than your conscious mind can keep up. And because it's so fast, you often don't recognize the signals it gives you, and we as women tend to ignore them. Ignoring these signals is like ignoring a flashing red emergency light on a nuclear reactor: Ignore it at your own peril. And many of us do.

Maybe you have had a few of these signals at some point:

- A gut feeling about someone? You know, the feeling in the pit of your stomach?
- Or the hair on the back of your neck stands up?
- Maybe just an odd sense that something is off?

Those are just some of the signs of your unconscious alerting you to danger. They're the way that it tries to blink red at you, like the light on the nuclear reactor. Or tries to scream at you to get your attention, the way that we scream at the characters in a movie, the minute before something terrible is going to happen to them: "Don't open the door!" We know that they shouldn't do it and we try to warn them, but they do it anyway!

There are a couple of important things to recognize about how your safety intuition works. The first is that your unconscious can notice people's micro-expressions. Micro-expressions (ME) were discovered by Paul Ekman, PhD, in the early 1970s while analyzing facial expressions in order to recognize concealed emotions. MEs are short facial expressions (with a duration between 1/5 and 1/25 of a second) that usually occur when people try to hide their feelings (either consciously or unconsciously).[1]

Micro-expressions have also been found to be universal[2] across cultures, meaning that whether you're being lied to or conned in New York or Beijing, the emotions are revealed in the same kinds of micro-expressions. Neither Joy nor I had any idea what we were doing when we recognized the danger of those two people who were described earlier; we had learned it through hard, cold experience.

And those experiences had become part of our own adaptive unconscious, below the level of awareness.

Which brings us to the second point about safety intuition: It builds on experience. Hopefully, you haven't found yourself in some of the situations that either one of us has, but you can learn from our experience, and that is what this book is about. We want you to learn from our experience so that if you find yourself in a potentially dangerous situation, you will immediately recognize it for what it is and be able to respond immediately—instead of talking yourself out of it, just to be polite.

Your safety intuition is the foundation to your defensive living and will be covered throughout this book. It's another name for situational awareness, being aware of your surroundings and people as you move around in your life. However, as we mentioned before, women in particular are trained to pay attention to everyone else around us, even strangers on the street, before we pay attention to what our instincts may be telling us (even going so far as trying to silence our own inner warnings) and before we pay attention to ourselves.

There is nothing wrong with being polite and concerned citizens, but for the love of God, ladies, you're not the solution to everyone's problems. You're not the world's Swiss Army knife!

You *can* continue to be a nice person and to be helpful. But not at the expense of potential danger to yourself.

You're not the world's Swiss Army knife!

Defensive Living Strategies

Without getting into a lot of fearmongering, few will dispute that the world is an unsafe place and becoming more so, especially for women. However, the response of most people seems to be an elevated and generalized sense of fear without a specific strategy to maintain personal safety. We'd like to change that.

Our strategies, the strategies that we live by ourselves, are not based on fear. We are not looking around every corner of every day, frightened that the boogeyman is going to jump out at us. That would be a terrible way to live. And that is *not* what we're suggesting here.

What we are suggesting is a heightened awareness when you're out and about and a little bit of a different mindset if you are approached. And we'll get into exactly how you can do that in this book. It has been our observation that women and men respond differently to requests, and much of that has to do with what we're taught.

All that said, there are five basic concepts behind the design for defensive living, shown in Figure 1.1:

Design for Defensive Living			
Persuasion-Proof	Daily Safety	Tech Vigilance	Victim Recovery
Safety Intuition			

Figure 1.1: Design for defensive living.

As you can see, the concepts are pretty straightforward: We want you to raise your awareness by listening to your safety intuition, listen to yourself instead of someone who wants something from you, by being persuasion-proof, follow some safety tips from a cop, and help yourself heal if you have been victimized so that the trauma doesn't severely impact your relationship with yourself and others for the rest of your life.

Now that you understand safety intuition, we'll break the rest down so you understand exactly what we're talking about.

Be Persuasion-Proof

On a scorching day, thirteen-year-old Joy was walking the country road back to her house from town. A car slowed next to her, and the dark-haired driver gave Joy a big smile. She thought he was cute; it seemed like he might be in college. So she smiled back.

"Hey, do you need a ride?" he asked.

"No, thank you. I'm not going far."

"Are you sure? It looks like the heat is getting to you. Oh, come on!"

Well, that midday sun *was* horrible. So Joy got in. Then, he hit the gas and laughed. "I can't believe you got in a car with a stranger!"

Joy said to herself, *Whoa. That's a* weird *thing to say.* She felt the oddest feeling in the pit of her stomach. So she said, "I'm not far," pointing slightly off in the distance. Silence.

So she leaned out the open window and yelled, "Hey, Dad!" And waved to a guy working on his lawn. He waved back. "Hey, stop! Pull over! That's my dad!"

He stopped. She flew out. He sped off.

Joy was relieved. The lawn mowing man wasn't her dad, but she knew that she needed to do something quickly after that eerie feeling she got from the guy. The neighbor was relieved that he didn't have a long-lost daughter.

That same year, Janice was twenty-three. She was ready for a day at the shore. She found her spot on the crowded beach. Minutes later, a good-looking, dark-haired guy with his arm in a sling sat down next to her. His tennis attire seemed out of place on the beach. But she let him stay, and they chatted. After a short while, he asked her to help him put his sailboat on his car. Barely concealing her annoyance, she reminded him that she had just sat down. He coaxed her, and she was persuaded. She reluctantly got up and followed him. An off-duty DEA agent was at the beach that day and overheard her saying, "I can't believe I'm doing this" as she shook her head at herself.

Janice Ott was never seen again.[3]

Also that same year,[4] eighteen-year-old Phyllis encountered a well-dressed, polite, twenty-something man on her college campus. They chatted on the steps of the library. Then he pleaded with her to help him get his car started. She was unsure and hesitated. But his charm and persuasion helped. She glanced at his crutches and felt sorry for him. As they walked along, she was surprised that his car was parked so far away. She thought to herself that it was an odd request under the circumstances but kept going.

When they finally got to his car, he told her to look under the steering wheel for wires to start the car while he was at the engine in the back of the Volkswagen Beetle, directing her. After a few seconds, she suddenly got a strange feeling that made "the hair on the back of her neck stand up."

With that, she bolted from the car saying, "I gotta go!" Phyllis Armstrong will remember that day for the rest of her life.

What do these three stories have in common? *All* the women knew better than to accompany the men, but they all allowed themselves to be persuaded against their better judgment. Joy had no idea who the driver was that picked her up on that country road. But the other two women encountered the notorious serial killer Ted Bundy early in his spree.

Phyllis Armstrong escaped and lived to tell the story. Tragically, Janice Ott was murdered by Ted Bundy.

How many times have *you* thought something was odd about a request but didn't listen to yourself?

Remember some of the signs of your safety intuition mentioned earlier? Now let's look at them in the context of being persuasion-proof:

- A gut feeling about someone? You know, the feeling in the pit of your stomach? *Like Joy had with the weird guy driving the car.*
- Or the hair on the back of your neck stands up? *Like it did for Phyllis Armstrong at her college.*
- Maybe just an odd sense that something is off? *Like Joy did at the traffic stop.*

In the almost fifty years since the Ted Bundy murder spree, predatory behaviors haven't changed, unfortunately, and neither has our response to them. The reason they haven't changed is because women are *still* more easily persuaded—primarily because we're *still* conditioned to be. A large part of our society has a vested interest in persuading us to act against our own self-interest. We also live in a world that puts a lot of stock in influencers and hustle. In this book, we'll discuss the spectrum of persuasion, influence, manipulation, and their more dangerous cousin, coercion. How can you recognize the difference? We'll discuss all these. And we'll also show that these patterns can be perceived early in a dating relationship, long before they become one of the most dangerous situations a woman can be involved in: domestic abuse. But keep in mind that attempted persuasion can come from *anyone* in your life—a stranger, a friend, family member, or someone whom you're dating or involved with.

It isn't *always* bad, but it's your responsibility to ensure that you aren't persuaded solely because someone else is pressuring you.

Where are *you* in the equation? Do they want something from you that benefits them more than it does you?

Part of a defensive living strategy is to be persuasion-proof.

Being persuasion-proof doesn't mean that you stop being generous, loving, and kind. It means to look at every situation and to at least ask yourself, "Why is this person *still* trying to persuade me when I've already made my wishes clear?"

And just as importantly, listen to yourself and act accordingly.

Tips **FROM A COP:**

Women are still more easily persuaded— primarily because we're still conditioned to be. Part of defensive living strategy is to be persuasion-proof.

We wholeheartedly agree with Clarissa Pinkola Estes as she states in her classic book *Women Who Run with the Wolves*: "One can protect one's territory, make one's boundaries clear yet be available, accessible, engendering at the same time. One can be fierce and generous at the same time." I believe that is how we are hardwired, to be fierce and generous simultaneously; they aren't mutually exclusive. But society got in there, messed with our circuits, and activated that damn auto-yes switch.

Tech Vigilance

Misogyny has weaponized technology.

It is not an overstatement to say that the power of technology to extend the reach of predators to harm women is unparalleled. This means that in addition to threats from the age-old dangers of physical attacks to women, there is now further danger to women and children's safety from the massive strides that technology has made since 2008.

The rapid expansion and capability of networks, computers, social media, and technology's ease of use is not only unprecedented in power but also the changes and speed with which they have shifted society. We will explore many of these and show why awareness of these shifts is key to your recognition of how they're reflected online, in the news, and your ability to keep yourself safe.

Unfortunately, although tech is increasing the danger to our safety, many women don't consider themselves techies, as men do, so may not be aware of the power and perils it poses. And tech advances so rapidly that a lot of women don't have the time or inclination to keep up with the changes, or understand them, let alone the ramifications.

You may have thought that what happens online stays online, much like the Vegas tagline. If a bunch of people want to play video games online, who can they be hurting? You may also be under the impression that porn is porn. What can change about people having sex? You may believe that the kid who looks like he's sitting alone in his room *is* doing exactly what it looks like—just sitting there by himself without a social life and no friends.

If that's the case, you couldn't be more wrong. All those scenarios can pose real-life, physical dangers to women and children.

But there are some things you can do to protect yourself. And in this book, we'll provide you with some easy-to-implement technical safety tips that will enable you to keep yourself safer.

Personal Safety

Taking measures to ensure your personal safety is certainly something every woman should do. Being able to defend yourself is another thing. But how much is enough? How much is too much? How do you know?

Should you carry a gun? If so, what kind? What if you don't know whether you could ever shoot someone, no matter what the circumstances? Then what? Are guns your only option for self-defense?

Of course, these are very personal decisions, and you're the only one who can decide what's right for you and your family. In Chapter 11, Joy guides you in how to decide what measures you should take and to stick to your guns, no matter what your decision is.

But personal safety is not a one-and-done decision on whether to carry a weapon. It's a series of small decisions we make that can have a significant impact. We all make these decisions every day, so a great deal of it has to do with your safety intuition and having a persuasion-proof mindset. Consider a decision as seemingly small as deciding whether to ever open your car window when you are approached by a stranger.

When Joy was shopping on her off time, she was in her car getting ready to leave the mall when two women approached her car and one tapped on the driver's side window.

"Excuse me?"

"Yes?" Joy said.

"Well, can you put your window down?"

"No," said Joy. "I can hear you. What do you need?"

"If you could just roll your window down for a second?"

Joy thought to herself: *This is odd; they're obviously not in distress. So why are they adamant that I open my window?*

After this went back and forth a few times, Joy said, "Back up, because I'm pulling out!" and then did so.

Laura was surprised when Joy told her the story. "What did they want?"

Joy replied, "To get me to open my window! Everyone on the

planet has a cell phone. But if they didn't, they could have easily asked me to call. I certainly would have called someone to assist them, including 911. But they didn't ask for help. They could have had a gun, or knife, or pepper spray. Then where would I be? Fighting off two attackers and trying to stay alive. Your car is your safe space. Do not roll your window down and violate that space for anyone."

Your car is not a drive-thru. You're not required to open the window because someone knocks.

She continued, "Here is the P.S. to the story: I drove a little way away and watched them. They kept wandering around until they approached another woman who just got into her car."

So this seemingly trivial decision never to roll your window down for a stranger under any circumstances may have larger implications for you someday. It certainly changed Laura's viewpoint, and several people have approached her since and asked her to roll her window down.

That was *one* lesson that Laura didn't have to learn the hard way.

Another, larger aspect of personal safety that may seem odd in a book on women's safety but is crucial to many of your decisions in life is financial security. Women are forced to make terrible decisions in life as a result of financial insecurity. From where they live, who to live with, whether to leave a relationship or not, whether they can postpone having children, *if* they have children, whether they can afford childcare, and on and on. Both Laura's mother and grandmother were trapped in loveless, abusive marriages that threatened their

 **FROM A COP:**

Your car is not a drive-thru! Do not ever roll your car window down because a stranger wants you to.

personal safety for years because they couldn't afford to leave. Laura learned to be financially savvy from her grandmother, who lived in a time when women didn't have a lot of financial independence and paid a high price. She taught Laura well, and Laura shares some of the things that she's learned along the way as well.

From Victim to Victor

If you've been the victim of an assault, abuse, or financial scam, you've been traumatized. This trauma can have a long-lasting impact on the rest of your life. It can even rewire your brain. And when you've been affected to this degree, it can disproportionately affect the decisions you make because you make them out of pain, confusion, and fear.

If your decisions are free from that pain and emotional turbulence, you'll make far better decisions regarding your personal safety and, in fact, your life. You won't settle for less than you deserve because you'll know that you are worthy of more.

So many women who have been damaged think that they must have done something to warrant whatever happened to them and then begin to punish themselves. This can lead to some horrible consequences and downward spirals.

Know that if this has happened to you, you did *nothing* to deserve what happened to you. Please don't continue to punish yourself. You need kindness, not more suffering.

Imagine that you have an infection on your hand and someone bumps into it; you will jerk your hand away to protect it. You may even lash out. But if the infection heals and you just have a scar, you wouldn't give it a second thought because you aren't in pain.

How can you help yourself heal from trauma? How can you shorten the healing process? What are some helpful resources? We aren't therapists or professional healers, but both of us have taken steps to heal from our own ordeals and can provide some resources for you that may be constructive for your own recovery.

We look forward to seeing you on the journey.

Chapter Two
Victimization and Trauma

Being attacked or being the victim of a crime can be a traumatizing experience.[1] Trauma can be defined as any experience that overwhelms a person's ability to cope. It is actually a normal reaction to an abnormal event. Violence isn't acceptable and it should never be normalized. So if something like that has happened or does happen to you, you have more than likely been traumatized by it. It is a highly individual response that you have no control over. Being traumatized does not mean that you are weak.

But if you have been a crime victim or become one in an unfortunate situation in the future, it's important to remember that it isn't your fault.

We've both been attacked or victimized in various ways, which is why we're writing this book—to help you learn some methods that you can use to avoid potential victimization and subsequent trauma.

And as trauma survivors ourselves, we want to encourage you to do whatever is necessary to help you cope and ease your mind and feelings. It's also important to understand that trauma can take a long time to manifest and, sometimes, an even longer time to heal. As you go through this book, you may recognize some situations that you've been in but may not have even realized that they were crimes, or that you are a victim. In other words, you may be triggered. We want you to know this beforehand, to prepare you, in the event that you do have unresolved trauma.

But to resolve it, you have to acknowledge it. As Bessel van der Kolk, MD, notes in *The Body Keeps the Score: Brain, Mind and Body in the Healing of Trauma,* "People cannot put traumatic events behind until they are able to acknowledge what has happened and start to recognize the invisible demons they're struggling with."

Unresolved trauma lives in almost everyone but most especially the population of women. First of all, because of the sheer number of women who have been the victims of sexual attack but also because women often minimize their own injuries at times, ignoring them until they reach a point where they boil over—coming out sideways and injuring ourselves and others. As the adage says, "If you don't heal what hurt you, you'll bleed on people who didn't cut you." Including yourself.

How We Know About Trauma

Laura stared out the window of her therapist's office, fervently wishing she were anywhere else. "When will it be over?" Laura asked Teri rhetorically. Laura was just getting warmed up for another self-flagellating diatribe and went on for the next ten minutes. Disgusted and angry with herself as usual, she was tired of therapists and weary unto death searching for "the fix"—the magic bullet that she was certain would make her "normal."

Teri smiled but remained silent and allowed Laura to finish ranting. Laura had come to Teri recently, after relapsing on vanilla extract after sixteen years of sobriety, waking up all those years later with her face on the bathroom floor one more time. Most people don't know that vanilla extract is 35% alcohol, or 70-proof, almost as much as bourbon or vodka.

But alcoholics know.

After relapsing, she hated herself even more than usual, which she didn't think was humanly possible. She thought she had finished with this therapy stuff years ago, yet here she was, back for yet another round of therapy with yet another therapist. Wasn't twenty-seven years of it enough? Who in the hell could be this messed up?

Back in therapy. Again.

There was no other way to stay alive. The cravings and compulsion to drink had already kicked in—the tiger was out of the cage again. She knew from experience that if she didn't get help, then she'd find herself on a different horse—the merry-go-round of around-the-clock drinking. Laura recognized from her family that an early and painful death is the only result of substance abuse. Both of her parents died of it, and the consequences also killed her sister, Mary Pat.

Alcoholism is just what they say it is: cunning, baffling, and powerful. And she could see its specter in its ghostly rocking chair on the front porch of her life. Waiting and rocking patiently for her to mess up so it could kick in the front door again. She was acutely aware that active alcoholism is suicide on the installment plan.

That hadn't bothered her in the past. In fact, she'd often wondered why she was still alive. But this time around, she had a concern that hadn't occurred to her before: her dogs. Who would take care of them if she died? So, for their sake, Laura traipsed back to therapy to try to figure out why she relapsed. She knew it had to do with her upbringing, but that had been over many years ago.

Would it *ever* end?

Joy, on the other hand, didn't grow up in a violent family. But almost every day of adulthood, she dealt with the worst of human cruelty and barbarism. First responders rush from call to call, often with no break in between. Police and other rescue personnel must cope with any savage situation that comes up, focusing on the current emergency, simultaneously aware that others are waiting, just as urgent. Sometimes with backup, sometimes without. A typical morning's call log could read: Child abuse, burglary in progress, vandalism, suicide, disorderly intoxicated person, multiple vehicular crash with injuries, domestic violence, maybe lunch, then back at it. Exhausted and traumatized themselves, first responders may handle anywhere from ten to twenty or more calls a day. Each a separate crisis.

On the day of the Fort Lauderdale–Hollywood Airport active shooter incident in 2017, Joy's morning started at 5:00 AM. The shooting occurred at 12:53 PM. Joy worked with her colleagues to secure the crime scene in baggage claim, assisted surviving passengers who had just witnessed a mass shooting, calmed panicked airline personnel, searched for additional shooters, and she can't remember what else. She also has no recollection of when she got home at 10:00 PM.

She does recall that she was back again at 5:00 AM the next morning. On the way to her morning shift roll call, she had to pass back through baggage claim with its blood-soaked carpet, body outlines, and yellow crime scene tape. There was no visit by county executives, law enforcement brass, or thanks from anyone. Just another day with calls to be answered.

In another incident, as Joy drove to work one freezing morning, she encountered a scantily clad young woman ballet dancing on the guardrail of a bridge that overlooked a busy highway. Joy called for backup as she pulled over.

She exited the patrol car and calmly began conversing with the woman. Suicidal people can be dangerously unpredictable, so Joy continued talking to her while backup rushed on-scene and fire rescue set up a perimeter below the bridge, blocking traffic and on-lookers. Joy had been talking to the woman for a while, delicately trying to find who she is and letting her know that Joy was there to help her. As the woman continued her bizarre ballet dance and recited Bible verses, Joy hoped the woman would let Joy take her to safety. Then, without warning, almost in slow motion, the woman raised her arms above her head as she faced Joy, yelled a biblical name, and flung herself in a backward swan dive off the bridge. Joy watched in horror, powerless to help her as she ran over to the bridge railing. Still in shock, Joy was saddened to hear over the police radio that the young woman had ended her life.

When Joy went to the office and updated her sergeant, he flippantly said, "It's not gonna take you too long to finish the report, is it? We're short today."

Joy's day had just begun.

For twenty-eight years, Joy went from call to call never stopping to think about trauma being an issue. She did what all first responders do: They crush those emotions into an imaginary vault in the dark underbelly of their brain. Never to be opened. New data to be slipped in daily. That's just what had to happen so one call did not bleed on the next one. Police officers can't go to their next complainant or victim whining about how bad their day has been. Joy is sure they would love to sit and chat with someone, but there's no time for that on duty.

Amazingly, that little vault seems to hold a lifetime of emotions. Or should we say the quiet part—trauma—out loud?

Joy never considered that the imaginary vault's hinges could come loose one day, and the data would seep into her brain. Or that being on *red alert* for nearly half her life in a stressful career could have any ill effects. Well, surprise, surprise! To no one but Joy.

Joy is learning we are all a work in progress.

The World Breaks Everyone

> The world breaks everyone and afterward many are strong at the broken places. But those that will not break it kills. It kills the very good and the very gentle and the very brave impartially. If you are none of these, you can be sure it will kill you too but there will be no special hurry.
>
> **—Ernest Hemingway,** *Farewell to Arms*

Everyone in this world has been broken in some manner. We have all been traumatized: some physically, others emotionally, mentally, or spiritually. Many, especially women, have been crushed in every way.

Human society has always been a vicious and sadistic overlord with a voracious appetite that feeds on the broken. It seems as though every woman we know has been preyed on in some way, providing fodder for the beast. If you've been victimized, you've been traumatized.

But Hemingway also offers hope: Many are strong at the broken places. However, the strength doesn't come automatically. Like a broken bone that will heal in its deformed state without assistance, you will have to consciously work with your psyche to help yourself heal. But you can do it. It is the most important gift you'll ever give yourself.

The damaged areas will not only grow back better than before, but your entire spirit will be transformed. The pain your psyche may be enduring now will heal over into a scar and it will be like a physical injury that is excruciating when bumped but then heals into a scar. This wound will heal, as well, into a scar. You'll know it's there, but the pain will be gone.

We know from experience.

If we can do it, so can you. The good news is that the world is rapidly becoming more trauma informed. As a result, new resources and information become available almost daily. Some are traditional, like talk therapy. Others are less traditional. Some are expensive; others are freely available online. We hope that if you have been damaged and are suffering, you'll embark on the journey, one step at a time. And even if you don't remember being damaged, if it seems as though you repeat the same mistakes or attract the same type of people over and over, you may have been so traumatized that you don't remember. It can't hurt to investigate. It may become more evident as your journey unfolds. You may be able to treat the symptoms before you discover the cause.

It was that way with us.

We aren't therapists or counselors, so we aren't qualified to diagnose anyone or guarantee that anything specific will work for you. But we are survivors and, with some discovery and work, have come out the other side.

And we learned some things along the way.

What Is Trauma?

Addiction and trauma expert Dr. Gabor Maté, MD, defines trauma as "an inner injury, a lasting rupture or split *within* the self, due to difficult or hurtful events." In *The Myth of Normal: Trauma, Illness and Healing in a Toxic Culture*, he emphasizes, "Trauma is not what happens to you, but what happens inside you. It is a psychic injury, lodged in our nervous system, mind and body, lasting long past the originating incident(s), triggerable at any moment."

Trauma can be emotional or physical, but the lasting impact of every trauma is an emotional breach within us. Dr. Maté notes that the essence of trauma is a "fracturing of the self and of one's relationship to the world." In other words, it separates and disconnects us from the world and often from our own bodies.

How many women are severed from their own selves due to trauma yet don't or can't seek treatment? More so, how many have been so traumatized that they've blocked out even the memories of it? It was that way with Laura for over twenty-five years. She had the symptoms of trauma but not the memories, as hard as she tried. Perhaps it is with you as well. We're not suggesting that you invent a memory if it isn't there, but at least keep your mind open.

Experts have learned that *trauma changes your brain*. To put it into computer terms, not only has your behavior (operating system) been affected, but your physical body (hardware) has been altered as well.

Listen to your instincts and observe your own feelings, body, and behavior. Is there something there? You may not remember, but your body does. In *The Body Keeps the Score*, Dr. van der Kolk notes, "Trauma produces actual physiological changes, including a recalibration of the brain's alarm system, an increase in stress hormones activity, and alterations in the system that filters relevant information from irrelevant."

He continues, "Trauma, by definition, is unbearable and intolerable. Most rape victims, combat soldiers, and children who have been molested become

Trauma produces actual physiological changes.

so upset when they think about what they experienced that they try to push it out of their minds, trying to act as if nothing happened, and move on. It takes tremendous energy to keep functioning while carrying the memory of terror, and the shame of utter weakness and vulnerability."

Not only are these experiences themselves devastating, but society perversely blames the victims for their own trauma. As described in Chapter 7, when American POWs returned from being held captive in Korea, many in the military and federal government believed that they collaborated with their captors, revealing an alarming weakness on the part of the soldiers. Rape victims are re-traumatized by the court system. And the buried memories of child molestation are often mocked and minimized when they finally come to light and the victims face their accusers.

As a result, it is actually in the social best interest of victims to act as though nothing happened, twisting their psyche even further. They look around at how everyone else is behaving and believe that they themselves are the only ones when the truth is that we have all been damaged in some way, and we're all pretending. That is, until our energy runs out, and we can't pretend anymore.

There are four categories of trauma that could impact you.

- **Acute trauma:** One-time traumatic event, such as rape;
- **Chronic trauma:** Cumulative trauma that creeps up on you over time, so you may not notice it at first;
- **Complex trauma:** Combination of acute and chronic trauma; for instance, growing up in a violent home, suffering ongoing abuse or a tour of combat; and
- **Secondary trauma:** Studies have shown that observing someone else being traumatized can impact you almost as much as it impacts them; for instance, a child watching their mother in a domestic violence situation.

PTSD

As with women who have been traumatized, some military veterans haven't recognized the long-term effects that war has had on their psyche. These psychological impacts, also known as post-traumatic stress disorder (PTSD), have existed since ancient times, with some literary accounts describing symptoms in the *Iliad,* around 762 BC. However, it wasn't officially listed as a diagnosis in the *Diagnostic and Statistical Manual of Mental Disorders* (DSM) until 1980.[2]

Until then, it was considered a personal weakness. Women are all too familiar with that viewpoint.

Van der Kolk notes, "Feeling out of control, survivors of trauma often begin to fear that they are damaged to the core and beyond redemption."[3]

Does this mean that we all feel that we're beyond being redeemed?

Since the world has traumatized and broken all of us in some way, then it stands to reason that we're all suffering from PTSD. This means that it is not an aberration but is a common human challenge.

In our experience, trauma and its aftermath created suffering and dysfunction. And through our recovery work, we've observed several patterns that we found enlightening.

Addiction

Addiction afflicts almost all of us in some form or other: alcohol, drugs, food, sex, shopping, porn—the list of opportunities for us to lose ourselves is endless. And it isn't until we suffer catastrophic consequences, known as hitting bottom, that we're willing to deal with our addiction. And even then, it can be a long road back, littered with difficulties such as vanilla extract bottles.

Why is that? Are we a society of addicts because we're all suffering from trauma?

Dr. Maté, who worked for over a decade in Vancouver's Downtown East Side with patients challenged by drug addiction and mental health, provides the answer. His bestselling book *In the Realm of Hungry Ghosts* notes, "Not all addictions are rooted in abuse or trauma, but I believe they all can be traced to painful experience. A hurt is at the center of all addictive behaviors. It is present in the gambler, the Internet addict, the compulsive shopper, and the workaholic. The wound may not be as deep and the ache may not be as excruciating, and it may even be entirely hidden—but it is there."

"Not all addictions are rooted in abuse or trauma."

We were fortunate to work with Dr. Steven N. Gold, PhD, who founded the Trauma Resolution Integration Program (TRIP) at Nova Southeastern University (NSU). TRIP offers a unique model, pairing trauma-trained clinical psychology doctoral students with trauma clients while providing mental health services at an affordable price point. HealthPoint, a similar program, is also currently available in Renton, Washington. In this brilliant model, everyone wins. The client is provided with affordable access to trauma-informed mental health care, and the students win by gaining experience with actual clients. Both student and client are aware that progress is carefully supervised by the student's PhD advisor.

Dr. Gold is one of the most talented and compassionate therapists with whom we've had the privilege to work. His early work began with individuals struggling with substance abuse, and he began to notice that the stories many of his clients told were very similar. They spoke of lives spent in traumatic households and the negative impact that the trauma had on their lives. This correlation was the turning point for his work, and he began to focus on the source of addiction in many cases: trauma.

This recognition was also a turning point for us. Although Laura was aware of generational alcoholism, domestic violence, and trauma in her family, she was completely unaware of the correlation. She became aware of it when Dr. Gold mentioned his early work. And when she began to understand how each one caused the other in a vicious circle, it transformed her life. It wasn't her fault; she wasn't a failure, it was all part of a pattern—a family template that stretched back for generations. By realizing that, it not only took the weight off her but also assuaged the bitterness that she felt toward her parents because it wasn't their fault either. As we'll see in the following pages, they had been victims before they had been persecutors. Laura also finally understood that despite everyone in her extended family "acting as though nothing happened," as noted by Van der Kolk earlier, a lot had happened. And every person in the family had been terribly affected. No one emerged unscathed.

Generational Cycle of Addiction/ Trauma/Rage/Abuse

Although these correlations are well-known in the mental health field, we find the following model, illustrated in Figure 2.1 below, helpful in understanding the generational cycle and how each response continues to impact one family member after the other.

The abuser is almost always the father or male head of the house.[4] His ongoing violence and coercive control cause trauma in the rest of the family. The family members are understandably angry, which causes rage within them, which is either internalized or externalized. Unable to manage their internal rage, the family turns to various types of addiction in an attempt to manage their feelings. As the children mature, their internalized rage can be exacerbated by their substance abuse, resulting in abuse of their own families—generation after generation.

Figure 2.1: Generational cycle of trauma and addiction.

The Drama Triangle

The drama triangle is a dysfunctional relationship dynamic that women often get involved with; not only because of the world's expectations of us but also because we're reluctant to leave anyone in peril. And, as women, we may also romanticize being saved, but some women find themselves attracted to relationships where they are continually rescuing others.

> **As women, we may also romanticize being saved, but some women find themselves attracted to relationships where they are continually rescuing others.**

But the triangle can occur in any relationship, even within us. Especially if you've been sucked into or brought up with the victim triangle. The victim triangle is a model that demonstrates the dysfunctional (and often shifting) roles that people take on in a conflict. The triangle can be maddening because you can't put your finger on the cause of the constantly shifting dynamics. But even just being aware of it can go a long way in allowing you to disengage, retain your sanity, and take your power back.

Here's how it works.

Developed by Steven Karpman, MD, in the sixties, the drama triangle maps out conflict or drama-intense relationship transactions. In *A Game Free Life: The Definitive Book on the Drama Triangle and Compassion Triangle*, Karpman identifies the three roles that define these dynamics within the triangle, shown in Figure 2.2: persecutor, rescuer, and victim (PRV).[5]

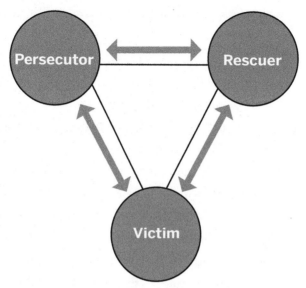

Figure 2.2: The drama triangle.

In the role of the persecutor, the person wants to be in control of the situation and can use a variety of tactics to achieve their status as the boss. According to *Breaking Free from the Victim Trap* by therapist Diane Zimberoff, persecution can take place in a variety of abusive ways: physical, psychological, or sexual. It could also be a withholding: love, money, or sexual gratification. Persecutors typically display anger and aggression to get their way. But Zimberoff notes that "there are many different ways to persecute, some more subtle than others." But you get the idea.

As Karpman's drama triangle demonstrates, the role of the victim is at the bottom, with less power as seen by the other two roles, who feel the power in the dynamic.

The victim role is on the receiving end of the persecutor's bullying. But here's the thing: The victim is getting something out of it. You may feel helpless and sorry for yourself. But in a weird way, you enjoy being a professional victim. In *The Karpman Drama Triangle Explained: A Guide for Coaches, Managers, Trainers—and Everybody Else*, Chris West describes this role succinctly, "You take it to heart. Somehow you get sustenance from it; it makes you feel good, in a strange way that you don't quite understand. Note that if you are on the receiving end of persecution but don't take it to heart, then you are not playing victim."

The superhero rescuer role wants to take care of everyone else. Like Mighty Mouse, their motto is: "Here I come to save the day!" Zimberoff notes that an example of a rescuer's background may be "the child who grew up in that dysfunctional family who thinks that it is her responsibility to solve the family's problems or to take care of her alcoholic father. But underneath that helpful exterior, they feel like victims."

But here's where it gets good: The roles shift within the conflict! In real time! Let's use a family example.

Mom (persecutor): "Barbie, get those dishes done. Now. Or else."

Barbie (victim): "You're always on my back."

Grandma (rescuer): "Give the kid a break. She's had a hard day at school."

Mom (new victim): "Well, Mom. You never gave me a break growing up."

> **But here's where it gets good. The roles shift within the conflict of the victim triangle!**

Grandma (new persecutor): "You've always been lazy; look at your messy house."

Barbie (new rescuer): Cleans the entire house.

The variations within roles are always on the move, which is why the victim triangle is so maddening when you don't know what's going on. But you don't even need to enlist others to participate. Zimberoff notes that you can play it by yourself: Say you're unhappy with your weight (victim), so you decide to rescue yourself by going on a diet. Then, if you aren't happy with the results, you persecute yourself, which then turns into another diet. And around it goes. But the good news is that once you recognize the pattern, you can quit playing. Just like that. It may take a while to unhook yourself, but you'll at least be on the path to stopping the insanity.

Note that the drama triangle only applies to interpersonal games; it does not apply to criminal acts, such as rape or assault or unprovoked domestic violence, but perhaps innocence in dangerous situations could have PRV motivations.

And it's important to keep in mind that the triangle maps out roles that people play in a conflict situation; it isn't who they are.

Disassociation

Many women who have been sexually or bodily assaulted disassociate from their body. The mind fractures completely from the physical body to protect itself. It is a coping mechanism to protect the psyche from the horror that is occurring to the body. But if the trauma isn't rapidly addressed, disassociation becomes a way of life, particularly in the case of repetitive and ongoing trauma.

Growing up in a violent home, Laura considered her long-term disassociation an indicator of strength. After many years of therapy, she finally understood the enormity and impact of family violence. For so long, she had just taken it for granted as a way of life.

If you find yourself spacing out when you feel overwhelmed or anxious or that you often feel numb, chances are good that you're disassociating. There are different levels of disassociation, the most extreme leading to dissociative personality disorder (DPD), formerly known as multiple personality disorder (MPD). Those suffering from DPD may be told that they did things that they don't recall or with unfamiliar objects that they don't remember acquiring. This can be a response to prolonged trauma. Laura's mother may have been suffering from DPD due to extended domestic violence.

But disassociation responds to treatment, so if you believe that you may disassociate, find a qualified trauma professional who can assist you in recovering. There is far more to life than living on an emotional flatline.

The Four Fs

There are four human responses to traumatic events: fight, flight, freeze, and fawn. Known as the four Fs, a term coined by therapist Pete Walker, depending on their complex nervous system, people generally gravitate toward one or the other. In *Complex PTSD: From Surviving to Thriving: A Guide and Map for Recovering from Childhood Trauma*, Walker describes the following:

- *Fight* response is triggered when a person responds aggressively to a threat;
- A person launches into *flight* response by fleeing or launching into hyperactivity;
- *Freeze* response is triggered when a person realizes that resistance is futile, gives up, numbs out into disassociation, and collapses, accepting the inevitability of being hurt; and
- Someone demonstrates a *fawn* response to a threat by trying to be pleasing or helpful in order to forestall an attacker.

Most people are familiar with the first three, but we believe that fawning isn't discussed often enough. Maybe because it's a survival response particularly demonstrated by women. Insightfully, Walker describes the childhood origins of fawning: "Many fawns survived by *constantly* focusing their awareness on their parents to figure out what was needed to appease them. Some became almost psychic in their ability to read their parents' moods and expectations. This then helped them to figure out the best response to neutralize danger."

Although this certainly doesn't describe every woman, it describes how so many women have been socialized to betray ourselves in our relationships. Before recovery, Laura used to say that she saw the slightest change in a person's mood coming from three blocks away.

Nice girls go along to get along.

In response to these societal expectations, a lot of women have become black belts at fawning. This default behavior of many women is so ingrained that it seems almost hardwired into our world—as even the *absence* of female fawning can be interpreted by some men as a lack of respect, which can turn into a dangerous situation.

However, it doesn't mean that women have to be one or the other: fawners or non-fawners. We can be ourselves without turning our psyche inside out to proactively appease others. We agree with Walker when he notes that we don't need to suppress our empathetic attunement when it is genuine. Setting boundaries and being your own person doesn't turn off your empathetic switch. Walker describes the balance of being empathetic without losing ourselves in the process. He notes: "We can be there caringly without abandoning our own feeling of contentment."

We can be there caringly without abandoning our own feeling of contentment.

If you have been traumatized, know that you can heal. Also know this: No situation, no person can force you to abandon yourself forever. And even if you think that you have, it's just temporary, no matter how long temporary has been.

Starting now, you can find your way home.

Chapter Three

Can You Recognize a Predator?

I t is important for you to recognize the predator/criminal mindset, so you'll understand the reasons behind our recommendations and tactics in the following chapters. Some of our recommendations may seem harsh if you don't understand who you're really dealing with.

You may even find this chapter difficult because you might not even want to consider yourself in a life-or-death crisis with a predator. Many of the women that we talk to shut down during these difficult conversations. If you find yourself doing so, know that it's okay. Give yourself some space, even several days, and then come back. As difficult as some of these topics are, we'd like you to be aware of the characteristics of these predators before you encounter one so that you'll be better equipped to save yourself.

Just ignoring that such situations or people exist won't keep you safe. But knowledge of their thinking will.

The most important thing for you to know is that they don't think like you do.

Nor do they hold the same values. Because the only values they have are what benefits them.

It is vital for you to know this so that you'll suspend your default trust of people who initially seem very charming, and we'll discuss this more in this book. Because it bears repeating: *predators/criminals do not think like normal people.*

Which raises the question: Who *are* all these attackers? Statistics don't lie. And according to the latest available FBI Crime Data Explorer statistics,[1] most—though not all—are men. As shown in Figure 3.1 below, men comprise the majority of violent offenders:

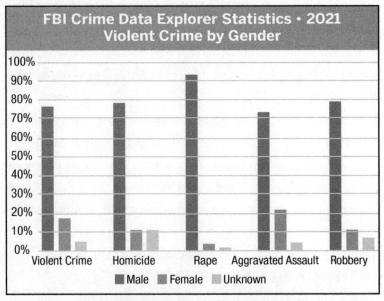

Figure 3.1: FBI crime statistics—violent crime by gender.

We note this *not* to be sexist but because much of this book is focused on male predatory behavior. So it's important to establish that the concept of most predators being men is true. However, it's just as critical to note that not *all* violent and predatory behavior is exhibited by men, so you shouldn't trust someone just because they happen to be or present as female.

In fact, you shouldn't automatically trust *anyone*. Period.

Many predators are criminals—because they commit crimes—whether they're caught or not. The crimes they commit are taking something from someone, whatever it might be, for nothing. They believe that they're entitled to whatever they want, and acquiring it gives them a thrill. These crimes are not accidental, and those who commit them have a certain mindset, a type of thinking unlike that of a normal person—a predator mindset.

What is a "normal" person? Normal people just want to live their life, mind their own business. We typically have jobs, seek relationships, have friends and hobbies. We give and take and are basically responsible, ordinary citizens who, for the most part, don't want to habitually hurt people or take anything from them.

It doesn't mean that normal people are saints. We all act selfishly sometimes, dead set on getting our own way at the expense of others. We lie and sometimes cheat to obtain our own ends. And, of course, the world isn't simplistically divided into good and evil.

But predators, on the other hand, those who have a predator mindset, have their *own* agenda.

The most important thing for you to know is that predators don't think like you do.

Experts on the Predator Mindset

Joy has encountered and arrested many criminals over her long career. She's also encountered and *not* arrested many noncriminals who may have had a situation that forced an encounter with law enforcement but didn't intend to harm anyone.

As a law enforcement professional dealing with tens of thousands of tense situations over the years, Joy's instincts were finely honed. Lives depended on her ability to quickly detect whether a person was a professional with a criminal mind or just someone caught in a bad situation. She didn't want to ruin someone's life with a criminal record or a traumatic stint in jail if it could be avoided. But she also didn't want to allow predators to remain unpunished or to roam the streets preying on people if it could be helped.

Joy was handling an injury accident one night. The driver didn't have a license and gave her a name that she found to be one of his aliases. He made excuses for not having his license on him. It wasn't the first time Joy had heard this story. If Joy had believed him, she could have just written him a ticket for not having a license and gone on her way.

But his demeanor indicated that he was lying. He was sweating, stammering, and nervous. Joy knew that he was hiding something. After she ran a quick computer check on him from her squad car, records indicated that he had a warrant for murder. In addition, she subsequently found out that he was fleeing from the scene of a domestic battery. From her years of experience, Joy's safety intuition told her that his nervousness came from something more than just a traffic stop. All those years of experience taught her to recognize the difference between the simple nervous response of a stopped motorist and someone deliberately trying to conceal their identity.

Joy's skill in dealing with criminals taught her that there is a real difference between the average citizen and a habitual lawbreaker. In other words, a criminal mindset does exist. As an afterword to the incident, Joy successfully took the wanted murderer into custody.

As a result, Joy is an expert on predators. And it is her professional opinion that there is definitely a predator mindset.

Two doctors who focused exclusively on studying criminals for many years reached the same conclusion: a criminal personality does exist.

Dr. Samuel Yochelson, MD, began **A predator** studying criminal/predator personalities **personality does** in 1961 with the sole objective of under- **exist.** standing the mind of the predator. He worked one-on-one with predators at St. Elizabeth's Psychiatric Hospital in Washington, DC. Dr. Yochelson's patients had committed every crime imaginable, violent and nonviolent: homicide, rape, child molesting, and more. Some of these predators had been remanded to the hospital instead of prison because they'd been found not guilty by reason of insanity (NGBRI). Dr. Yochelson's observations had no bearing on the patient's legal outcome, nor did he share his observations with the hospital or legal staff.

His goal was not to discern what type of crime they committed but to *determine how they thought.* Dr. Yochelson's Program for the Investigation of Criminal Behavior remains the longest research treatment program of offenders conducted in North America.[2]

He was joined in 1970 by Dr. Stanton E. Samenow, PhD, a clinical research psychologist who carried on Dr. Yochelson's work after his death in 1976, and who has continued evaluating and working with offenders well into his seventies.

It is important to note that these two doctors were not "armchair theorists," those who have little or no actual face-to-face experience with the people whom they research. They interviewed and interacted with the people whom they were studying on a daily basis, both in individual and group settings. Their ultimate goal was to understand how the predators thought in *all* aspects of life so that they could help them change.

Their patients came from a wide range of backgrounds, physical characteristics, and crimes. They interviewed predators from poor to wealthy, all races, religious preferences, ages, sexual orientations, drug users and nonusers. They interviewed predators who had been previously measured to be of average intelligence and had been tested by the hospital to be physically healthy.

They initially interviewed the patients with no prior knowledge of them, other than what they'd been charged with. When he began his work, Dr. Yochelson initially thought that the criminals would fall into three different crime categories: sex, assault, and property crimes. He assumed that the criminals specialized in one particular category and that one type of crime had nothing to do with other types.

In Yochelson and Samenow's landmark book, *The Criminal Personality*, Dr. Yochelson notes: "Our view was that one kind of crime had little or no relation to another; we saw white-collar crimes as totally different from the crude criminality of mugging or rape."

He found out that he was wrong.

There are no categories.

"What emerged was a great deal of material about crimes in addition to those with which the men were charged. For example, the child molester was also a gunman and the thief a rapist," Yochelson and Samenow report.

A predator is a predator. The crime doesn't matter, but there is a commonality in all crimes.

It's the charge they get out of committing the crime.
The high. The buzz. The adrenaline jolt that the excitement of getting over on someone and doing something forbidden shoots into their brain. One criminal described it:

> *It is just like being in a world all your own. You know that you are doing something that nobody is supposed to do and that you are putting everybody else's life in danger, but you just shrug off these things. It is a sort of feeling of being happy and being scared at the same time, but happiness always comes out on top. After you get finished playing a game like this, you are all ready to want to play it some more. I never get tired of it. It was just exciting, just very exciting.*

The predator mind is also simmering with anger, always on a low boil. He's seething because people constantly don't live up to his expectations. Particularly, that they fail to continually mirror back to him his perception of himself: powerful, unique, superior.

Anything less than full-on worship is unacceptable and assaults their self-image. And even that isn't enough because it's never enough.

Dr. Samenow notes that "anger in a criminal is like a cancer, metastasizing so that anyone or anything in his path can become a target."

This toxic combination of frustration and hunger for excitement is like an explosive just waiting to be lit. The criminal's simmering rage is constantly seeking the flame of excitement to set it off.

In essence, the message that Drs. Yochelson and Samenow convey in their book is: These thinking patterns of the criminal are habitual and result in massive injury to other human beings.

The massive injury to other human beings is what we're concerned with and want to show you how to avoid. We don't want *you* to be that target.

And if you are unfortunate enough to find yourself in a situation with one of them, Chapter 2 provides some information to help you deal with the trauma.

The Violent Psyche

We understand violent psyches as we've been around them for years. Joy understands the psyche of a violent predator from her years in law enforcement. Laura knows them because she was raised with them. Growing up in a violent family gave her insight into the thought process of violence seekers.

People who rely on violence as a solution are like a toolbox that has only one tool. If you only have a hammer, every problem is a nail—there's no other way.

Violent people very often have a predatory mindset. Whether they are violent inside the house and/or outside it, predator thinking is the same: The victim is dehumanized. The victim is an object, a thing, an inanimate item to be used and discarded, like throwing out the milk carton when the milk is gone.

At a conscious level, the predator certainly realizes that the victim is human. But at a subconscious level, they have to reduce their victim to something less than human so that they can do anything they want to, to get what they want. The something that they want may be money. It could be to prop up their damaged ego through a relationship, rape, or murder; it could be any number of things. The point is that they don't regard you as worthy of any consideration beyond what they want to take. So begging, pleading, or appealing to what you consider your shared humanity won't work. How many shows have you seen where the victim is begging for their life and the predator just laughs? In fact, your fearfulness may be exactly what they want because it gives them the feeling of power that they seek. The weakness of your pleading excites them.

In his excellent book *The Killer Across the Table: Unlocking the Secrets of Serial Killers and Predators with the FBI's Original Mindhunter*, retired FBI profiler John Douglas notes that "the one universal among all serial killers and violent predators [is that] other people don't matter, they aren't real, and they don't have any rights." Mr. Douglas is a legendary FBI criminal profiler and spent twenty-five years hunting the worst of the worst violent predators, including Charles Manson, "Son of Sam Killer" David Berkowitz, and "BTK Strangler" Dennis Rader.

The predator *always* preys on people weaker than themselves, and they *always* aim to avoid punishment. They may or may not attempt to conceal their activities, either for further intimidating their victims or for taunting law enforcement.

Predators Sense Weakness

All predators sense weakness. It's *exactly* what they're looking for. They want to extract their prey with the least amount of energy and exposure. And prey, with the exception of humans—especially women—sense predators. Even from a mile away.

Elizabeth and Mark had two disabled golden retrievers, both of whom they'd adopted after each had lost a leg as a result of a prior owner's abuse. Despite their disability, Happy and Sunny enjoyed their daily walks in their neighborhood with Elizabeth and her husband, Mark.

But there was this one thing.

Their neighbor had also adopted a dog, but this dog was actually half wolf. The neighbor and his wolf-dog also enjoyed daily walks. One of the goldens, Happy, was aptly named. Despite being previously abused, he'd regained his demeanor and confidence and was thrilled to experience life on his daily walks. When Elizabeth encountered the neighbor and the wolf-hybrid, Happy continued on his way without giving it a second thought. And so did the wolf-dog.

Sunny, on the other hand, had retained memories of his previous life and was slightly more timid. The first time Elizabeth and Sunny encountered the wolf-dog, it lunged at Sunny. The neighbor's animal had immediately sensed Sunny's weakness and dragged the owner halfway across the street before he was able to regain control. Sunny, of course, was even more terrified after the incident. Elizabeth said that she'd begun walking Sunny before the sun came up, but even in the dark, Sunny could sense the predator a long way off and would immediately turn around to go home.

Human predators have the same ability to detect weakness. As women, our instincts have been hacked by cultural expectations, and many of us lack Sunny's ability to sense danger.

Victim Normalcy Bias

Human beings think in patterns.[3] Our brains gather enough information to identify how we think things will work, or the order in which they'll happen, and we believe that we've identified a pattern. And once we think that we've identified that pattern, we believe that the pattern will pretty much always be consistent. This generally works extremely well and relieves our brain of a lot of administrative detail.

Until something happens.

For example, let's say that you're at a concert and the doors are scheduled to open at 7:30 PM. Of course, you expect them to open right after 7:29 so that you can go in, find your seat, and wait for the performance to begin. Every time you've ever been to a concert or event in the past, the doors have always opened at the scheduled time, so you have no reason to expect them not to. So you don't spend any brain cycles thinking about it. But what happens if there is a broadcast over the loudspeaker at 7:25, announcing that the singer is ill and won't be performing? We were at a concert a few years ago, and that is exactly what happened. Around two thousand people were queued in the lobby of the Broward Center for the Performing Arts in Fort Lauderdale, Florida, waiting for the doors to the concert hall to open in a few minutes. Suddenly, the loudspeaker crackled overhead, and we heard the announcement that the performer had become ill. We expected to see a mad rush for the doors but instead observed a paralysis come over the crowd. Not a soul moved. They were so stunned that they couldn't believe what was happening.

Everyone froze.

This is a very minor example of normalcy bias in everyday life. But our tendency toward pattern thinking can have the same paralyzing effect in a disaster or attack on you. In *The Unthinkable: Who Survives When Disaster Strikes—and Why*, Amanda Ripley points out the detrimental effect that normalcy bias had on the victims of the World Trade Center (WTC) tragedy. She notes that the human brain strategy to seek patterns from the past to identify the future "works elegantly in most situations. But we are slow to recognize exceptions." Ripley describes how some WTC victims waited anywhere from six to forty-five minutes before evacuating the building. "Even though, eventually, almost everyone saw smoke, smelled jet fuel, or heard someone giving the order to leave."

So when something outside our normal pattern does happen, we tend to minimize it and may think that "this isn't really happening to me." It's as though the computer in your brain has been seamlessly running its scheduled programming, but when it runs into an unexpected situation that isn't in its programing, it freezes and grinds to a complete halt. This is also known as analysis paralysis or the ostrich effect: avoiding negative information by putting your head in the sand and pretending that it's not happening.

We mention this because we don't want you to adopt a normalcy bias attitude toward predators. If you haven't had an encounter with a criminal, please don't believe it's because you have somehow been blessed by whatever deity you believe in. And please don't believe that you never will.

We do, of course, hope that you never will, but knowing how they think and about their patterns will go a long way toward helping you overcome normalcy bias in the event that something *does* happen.

Predation Escalation

Like any endeavor, criminals typically start small and build up their skill set as they become more experienced and their appetite for excitement increases. Predators typically begin as petty criminals who prey on crimes of opportunity: a purse in a shopping cart, pickpockets, maybe an unlocked car left running. These economic predators want the quickest buck they can get with the least amount of trouble. They're a nuisance and maybe more if you're in a bad financial situation yourself. But even if you haven't been seriously injured in some way, don't take them lightly.

Some victims may dismiss crimes of "no contact" out of hand. "Why bother? No one was hurt. I can replace the credit cards (or other stolen items)."

If your purse gets stolen, it may be an inconvenience to you because it "just contained credit cards," but it may be the thief's tenth or twentieth crime of the day. If no one reports it, law enforcement not only loses visibility into the crime, but the criminal becomes more confi-

Tips **FROM A COP:**

Report all crimes, no matter how petty they may seem to you. Your report could help law enforcement locate an at-large criminal guilty of bigger crimes.

dent as they begin to believe that they can get away with increasing profits. And their confidence reduces the effects of fear. In this case, fear of being caught.

And as their confidence grows, so does their appetite for bigger crimes to keep that spark of excitement lit.

So what begins with burglary may escalate to robbery. (If you're not sure of the difference, like Laura wasn't, the bulleted list in the next section details the differences between the crimes and why it's important to recognize the variations.) And as the predator becomes bolder and their crimes more sophisticated, they no longer fear contact with their victims nor fear of apprehension. And if they are apprehended, their first couple of jail or prison sentences probably won't be very long until the courts begin to establish a criminal pattern. And keep in mind that violence often means status in their world, so that cycle may take a very short time to spin up.

Another good reason to report *any* crime to law enforcement: tracking, crime maps, and patterns. What seems like a minor incident to you is probably the fiftieth time that week that the predator has committed the crime and the twenty-fifth time that week that it's been reported to the police. You may be able to provide a description or information to law enforcement that no one else has been able to.

There have also been occasions in which the smallest of crimes, when reported, turned out to be the incident that law enforcement needed to apprehend a violent criminal that they've been unable to capture due to lack of probable cause. So prosecution of a "small" shoplifting charge could help in the apprehension of a serial killer.

A set of prints that Joy once took from a car break-in turned out to be the key in apprehending a criminal who was responsible for a long-time crime spree. Had the owner decided not to prosecute, the predator would have gone on to victimize many more people.

By failing to report any crime and giving law enforcement the tools that they need, you could be endangering the life of an innocent person down the road. In fact, that next person could be *you*. If you get robbed or burglarized, the predator knows that you've probably replaced your credit cards, television, or whatever. Do you think that they'll pass you by because you've already been victimized? What better place to grab some more goods?

Levels of Street Predation

As previously mentioned, there are levels and types of predation crimes. These crimes are intentional and premeditated, which is why law enforcement classifies them as felonies, with sentencing time added as the level for potential violence and injury increases:

- **Burglary:** Burglars avoid contact with victims. These are primarily thefts of opportunity, such as an unlocked car or unoccupied home. They're looking for cash or valuables readily converted to cash.

- **Robbery:** As the level of predation increases, robbers are not averse to victim contact or the use of force to get their money or goods. And that's just how they view you: You are bringing them their money. A robbery isn't just a crime of opportunity; the predator may profile their victim or plan to rob them, showing intent.
- **Strong-arm robbery:** The predator uses force or punching to commit the crime. For example, purse snatching. This typically refers to grabbing a woman's purse from her by punching her to the ground. If the victim is over sixty-five, this results in additional charges.
- **Aggravated robbery:** "Aggravated" refers to the fact that the perpetrator used a weapon in the crime. A person threatens someone with a dangerous weapon and/or physical force to steal property from them; the victim may sustain bodily injury.
- **Assault:** This creates fear in another person because of the ability to carry out an attack.
- **Battery:** The harmful contact or touching of someone.
- **Rape:** Forced sexual intercourse involving penetration without the person's consent by body part or object and accomplished either by threats or physical means. In eight out of ten rapes, no weapon is used other than physical force.
- **Murder:** Unlawful killing under conditions specified by law.
- **Serial killer:** Person who murders three or more people in separate events; different authorities can apply different criteria when designating serial killers.

Although this list is by no means comprehensive, it does provide an understanding of crime escalation. And crimes *do* escalate as the predator becomes more experienced, emboldened, and in search of bigger thrills and prizes.

Sexual Predators

Up to this point in this chapter, we've focused on "stranger danger"—the imposing menace that Smokey, the typical women's safety instructor from Chapter 1, focuses on. But also, as mentioned in Chapter 1, women are often in just as much danger from predators we know and love, *inside* our home, where we're supposed to be safe.

Unfortunately, being in our own home, where "being in the wrong place at the wrong time" is taken out of the equation, doesn't ensure women's safety. No matter how much we try to protect ourselves when we're out in the world, being in our home gives a predator three distinct advantages: proximity, vulnerability, and the element of surprise.

How many women in Tony Robbins's audience were referring to feeling unsafe in their own home?

Irrespective of location, the goals of predation never change, no matter what the scenario: manipulation, domination, and control. Manipulation is a given, accomplished by lies and distortion. Sometimes a little, sometimes a lot. And when you start to catch on or pull back, they can hit that "sincere switch," just to keep you guessing. Domination and control are ultimately achieved by violence, always accompanied by threats of escalating violence: "If you don't give me what I want . . . ," "This is *your* fault," or in cases of domestic violence/abuse, "It will be worse the next time."

Charm is *always* the bait whether the predator is on his first date or Ted Bundy is luring his next mark to his car with a fake cast on his arm. And the process is always the same: charm the victim until she lets her guard down.

A key tell in the coercive process is the speed with which the predator wants the "relationship" to progress: It's always fast, even if the criminal seems relaxed and laid-back. The faster they emotionally "hook" the victim, the quicker their payoff.

Chapter 6 will detail scenarios that domestic abusers use to seduce their potential partners, and you'll learn about the process of love bombing, manipulation, and coercion in much more detail. But all persuasive predators have a cover persona and an interview process for selecting potential victims, addressed next. Then, in Chapter 9, Joy's survival rules will detail some suggestions for securing your home to reduce your chances of becoming the victim of a break-in.

The Cover

A key aspect of a defensive living mindset is to recognize that predators are rarely who they present themselves to be. The old adage "You can't judge a book by its cover" is apropos because the majority of them have a very convincing cover.

They need that "cover" exterior to lure their victims, as well as lulling would-be witnesses and the judicial system into believing in that exterior persona. They are well aware of the human tendency to believe that, for the most part, we see people as they choose to present themselves to us and then seem unable to imagine them in any other context.

By default, humans lean heavily toward the belief that what you see is what you get. And once a person has concluded that they like or accept someone (and that impression often forms almost instantaneously), they believe that the person is exactly who they say they are. So if an attractive stranger approaches you in a friendly manner, wearing a big smile, chances are pretty good that you'll drop your guard and smile back. Serial killer/necrophiliac Ted Bundy mastered this art of the smile and found that most women easily responded to that approach.

In *The Stranger Beside Me: The Inside Story of Serial Killer Ted Bundy*, true crime writer Ann Rule wrote that witnesses described Bundy's smile as "something special."

Ms. Rule knew Bundy personally, whom she worked with at a suicide crisis hotline and considered a friend before he became famous as a serial killer. She didn't notice anything unusual about him and observed him to be kind, solicitous, and empathetic.

Chances are also pretty good that if a friend introduces you to one of their friends, you'll more than likely transfer the credibility that you attribute to your friend onto the person that you just met. Affinity fraud takes advantage of this, and Bernie Madoff had it down cold.[4] Many of the victims of his sixty-five-billion-dollar scam knew one another and were members of the same prestigious clubs. They introduced one another to Madoff and automatically trusted him because betrayal from within the Jewish community was unthinkable at the time.

And Madoff worked it for an incredible *forty* years.

Once an impression has taken hold, it is almost impossible to dissuade a person from having second thoughts about their initial impression—despite all concrete evidence that contradicts their illusion.

This default trust that we have in our fellow humans is the currency that predators deal in, count on, and exploit.

They often present themselves to the world as charming, even charismatic. But this engaging exterior is carefully cultivated not only to ensnare victims but also to provide a cover in the event that they're caught. How many times have you seen neighbors of criminals describe them as "such a nice guy" or "I can't believe it; he always waved"?

This is a big issue for victims because they don't find out until it's too late that Dr. Jekyll is in fact Mr. Hyde and that the pleasant exterior is really just a thin veneer for a dark and dangerous character.

That veneer is carefully crafted to conceal their true nature. They are masters of deception.

Our friend Mary called recently, upset because she'd just discovered that her neighbor Bruno, whom she's very fond of, had recently been arrested for a lewd and lascivious act against a child. News reports indicated that he'd attempted to rape his granddaughter's best friend, whom the granddaughter (and presumably Bruno) had known since kindergarten.

Mary insisted that the neighbor was a "nice guy" and wanted to understand how this nice guy could be accused of such a terrible crime. When Joy noted that this is classic predator behavior, Mary became even more distraught—insisting that we just didn't recognize that this was really a good guy. He'd even helped her fix her air conditioner!

"If you met Bruno, you'd see that he's really super," Mary contended.

Joy helped our friend to realize that Bruno the neighbor fits the typical description of a predator, and that is exactly what predators do: hide in plain sight.

She explained that even though Bruno helped Mary with her air conditioning, it didn't mean that he was incapable of being a pervert. Good neighboring and perversion aren't mutually exclusive. But we like to believe that we can recognize a bad guy when we see one.

But as Ted Bundy noted in his interview with Dr. James Dobson just hours before Bundy's execution: "I was a normal person. I had good friends. I led a normal life, except for this one, small but very potent and destructive segment that I kept very secret and close to myself."[5]

What Bruno did wasn't an "accident" or "misunderstanding." His words and actions were very specific. And sadly, it probably wasn't the first time, nor will it be the last that Bruno commits such a crime. Predators typically establish a pattern of escalating violations, as you'll see in the pages that follow.

As an aside, the fourteen-year-old fortunately did everything right to save herself in the situation. She kept her wits about her, knowing that the situation wasn't going to get any better. She managed to keep him at bay and texted her sister to come and get her immediately. Then the two girls called the police.

To be clear, women can be predators as well. Especially when it comes to scamming money. Several famous examples from recent years include Elizabeth Holmes, who raised almost $1 billion from duped investors and was found guilty of investor fraud and conspiracy,[6] and Anna Delvey, who conned big banks and Manhattan's elite. In 2019, Delvey—whose real name is Anna Sorokin—was found guilty of grand larceny, stealing over $275,000 from friends, banks, and hotels.[7]

And, as shown in Figure 3.2 below, FBI data also shows that when it comes to nonviolent crime such as embezzling, women can hold their own.

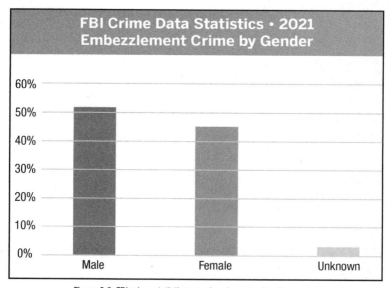

Figure 3.2: FBI crime statistics—embezzlement crime by gender.

We'll cover this more in Chapter 10: "Shams, Scams, and Cons." But know this: violent and sexual predation is almost exclusively the domain of men.

The Interview

Like the serial killer Ted Bundy, some predators conceal their true nature during the "interview process," also known as the con.

When predators are profiling a victim, they appear harmless. They put on their charming outfit, slap a big smile on, and go hunting. The interview is when they determine your physical, emotional, and mental weaknesses. The other purpose of the interview is for you to let down your guard and trust them. Once trust is established, you are more easily manipulated. And this goes for *all* predators, whether serial killers or domestic abusers.

Children are particularly vulnerable to being interviewed because they are so trusting and benevolent. Predators are well aware of this, especially if they know the children's family. The predator isn't always a stranger, he (over 85 percent are male) may be someone whom the victim knows, even a family friend.

In *The Killer Across the Table*, FBI profiler John Douglas describes the MO of child murderer Joseph Kondro, who murdered an eight-year-old girl in 1985 and a twelve-year-old girl in 1996. Douglas notes that the *only* thing that the two girls had in common, other than their preadolescent age, was that Kondro was a close friend of the victims' families.

In fact, he was such good friends with eight-year-old Rima Traxler's stepfather that stepdad Rusty gave him the family code word. The girl was instructed not to enter a car with anyone besides the family until she heard the word "unicorn," which Kondro used.

Douglas also notes that Kondro's MO specifically targeted children of his friends. He didn't have to worry about control as he already had the trust of their family, and the children went willingly.

The predator could be someone who has access to you inside your home in the course of business. BTK (Bind/Torture/Kill) strangler Dennis Rader was a security alarm installer. In many cases, he installed ADT alarms for homeowners concerned about the BTK killings. Rader was a city code enforcement officer, Cub Scout leader, and president of the church council at Christ Lutheran Church in Wichita, Kansas. The boogeyman doesn't always lurk in the dark.

Sometimes, he's an "upstanding citizen," a churchgoing Cub Scout leader.

Fight to the Death

As women, most of us want to extend compassion, empathy, and assistance.

But if you are attacked by a violent predator, you must make the decision ahead of time that you *will* fight back. Hard. This may be in stark contrast to what you consider your value system. To be blunt: If you are, or someone you love is, the victim of an unprovoked act of aggressive violence, all bets are off. We hope that you will make this decision right here and now.

Let us define an attack for you: An attack is designed to hurt, damage, and overwhelm. Not only physically but mentally and emotionally. If you are not in an isolated location, the attack may be the first assault to subdue you until the attacker takes you to an isolated location. Do not go quietly. Do *not* allow yourself to be subdued. Whenever you are attacked, fight back. Keep fighting. Fight to kill.

Even nice girls let the bad guys bleed out.

Laura has been attacked on several occasions. After freezing during the first attack, she decided that she would fight back if it ever happened again. And it did. Twice. The results of both of those instances were completely different. Although one predator held a knife to her throat, she immediately backed a step away from the knife (he was facing her) and smashed his windpipe, driving her fist toward his spine. Another mistook her five-foot-three frame for weakness and also got a smashed windpipe.

And, if you fight back and injure them, even severely injure them, run. Now is *not* the time to see if they're okay or to give them a second chance because, like a mortally wounded animal, they'll be even more aggressive and dangerous. If you've gotten that far, let 'em bleed out.

Even nice girls can let the bad guys bleed out.

Chapter Four
Technology Terror

n 1980, Jessica Hahn, a twenty-one-year-old Pentecostal church secretary, was drugged and raped by her employer, Jim Bakker—a married, powerful multimillionaire who'd made his fortune as a televangelist. Subsequently, she was paid $279,000 from his ministry's coffers to ensure her silence. Bakker's organization, piously named Praise the Lord (PTL), then kept two sets of books to conceal the payoff.

For a while, Hahn kept quiet. She said that "church was her world" and "Jim Bakker was her world." And she knew that revealing what happened would "affect millions of people." But she said that she was "being belittled and being used as a pawn" behind the scenes, so she called into the *Charlotte Observer* in 1984 to encourage them to investigate PTL—financially and otherwise. She noted, "It was like: Hide in the corner and let everyone tell my story or let me tell it." As a result, investigative reporters from the *Charlotte Observer* published a series of Pulitzer Prize–winning articles exposing PTL.

A media maelstrom ignited, due to the prominence of Bakker's television show with his wife, *The PTL Club* (also known as *The Jim and Tammy Show*). Bakker subsequently resigned from PTL and was prosecuted. Bakker's trial was a media circus, with much of the coverage accusing Hahn of exploiting the incident for personal gain. As Hahn comments, "Bakker opened the door for a lot of hate toward me."

Bakker was convicted and sentenced to forty-five years in prison, *not for rape* but twenty-four counts of fraud, primarily for keeping the two sets of PTL books to cover up the payments to Ms. Hahn. Like many abusers, Bakker made himself look pitiful at his sentencing, implying that he was the victim.

His act was pathetic to the point where *Chicago Tribune* columnist Clarence Page protested that Bakker's sentence was too harsh.[1] Again, he was not convicted of sexual assault but for "overbooking" his property of Heritage USA. Ironically, Page noted that "the judge gave Bakker more time than rapists, drug dealers and first-time murderers receive," completely ignoring the fact that the basis of the whole scandal stemmed from the fact that Bakker *is* a rapist.

Bakker's sentence was commuted after five years. But the sudden media glare of the Bakker circus completely overwhelmed Ms. Hahn, who made subsequent career choices that she says turned her into "pretty much a cartoon character."

And although Bakker's sentence was reduced and he faded into obscurity, Ms. Hahn continued to be a media punch line and public punching bag for years to come.

Then, in 1998, at the age of twenty-two, Monica Lewinsky fell in love with her boss and had an affair with him. As a result of the affair, she became the Internet's first victim of cyberbullying two years later.

Unfortunately, as often happens in workplace affairs, her boss was an older married man. And even more unfortunately, he was the president of the United States. The fallout from their affair not only resulted in the impeachment of Bill Clinton by the US House of Representatives but also the impeachment of Monica Lewinsky by the citizens of the Internet.

President Clinton was impeached not for cheating on his wife or for having sex with a naïve young woman while serving as the chief executive but for lying about it under oath and obstructing justice.[2] To quote: "I did not have sexual relations with that woman, Miss Lewinsky." During his impeachment trial, President Clinton pitifully attempted to clarify that because the sexual acts were not performed by him, but *on* him, he did not engage in sex. To be specific, he received oral sex.

Lewinsky, on the other hand, not only had to do the heavy lifting of the "not sexual act" but also became patient zero of the newly discovered online ability of millions to anonymously destroy a woman's reputation. Not because *she* lied but because she was the victim of a sexual predator. In other words, she was eviscerated just because she was a woman who performed a sexual act on a more-than-willing powerful man. In comparison, President Clinton received the lesser of the two sentences.

If Hahn was vilified in the mid-eighties by *thousands* of media outlets, Lewinsky was maligned by *millions* of people online, just a few years later. And this was before social media made it even easier with just a few seconds and a few clicks from each person.

In her 2015 TED Talk on cyberbullying, "The Price of Shame," Lewinsky notes, "Public humiliation as blood sport has got to stop . . . the more shame, the more clicks."

Less than ten years later, that blood sport is hemorrhaging.

Twenty years after President Clinton was impeached, the *Wall Street Journal* reported[3] that another US president, Donald Trump, paid adult film actress Stormy Daniels $130,000 in hush money just before the 2016 election to sign a nondisclosure agreement regarding their consensual affair in 2006 (while he was married). The funds were paid via Trump attorney Michael Cohen from President Trump's election campaign (in direct violation of campaign finance regulations) to stop her from going public. Like Clinton, President Trump also lied and denied the payoff. (Although unlike President Clinton, he was not under oath at the time of the denial.) Mr. Cohen subsequently acknowledged in court on August 21, 2018, that he had, in fact, paid Ms. Daniels as well as another woman, Karen MacDougall, "at the direction of President Trump."

> **"Public humiliation as a blood sport has got to stop . . . the more shame, the more clicks."**
>
> **—Monica Lewinsky**

The media went berserk as expected, but social media had an extended meltdown.

Many of the meltdowns were outraged *not* at President Trump for violating campaign contribution laws but because as an adult film worker, Ms. Daniels is effectively a "slut" whose voice doesn't matter.

To be clear, all the women involved were in vastly different situations: one was raped, one believed that she was in love, and one was a businesswoman. But these cases featuring powerful men illustrate two important points: (1) The court of public opinion is inflamed and amplified by the ability of billions of people to easily and anonymously post online; and (2), just like Jim Bakker's Praise the Lord organization, society keeps two sets of books: one for men, no matter how corrupt they are, and one for women, no matter how young or naïve, or no matter how lopsided the power dynamic is.

Technology and social media have weaponized both sets of those books over the last several years, putting the lives of women at risk in real life.

How Did We Get Here?

To understand any issue, it is worthwhile to take a quick look back to see how things went south.

The Internet is governed (and we use that term loosely) by Section 230 of the Communications Decency Act (CDA). Tucked into a 1996 law overhauling telecommunications, Section 230 prevents an online platform from being held liable from what its users post on the platform. The CDA originally tried to ban online obscenity (hence the name and good intentions) but was struck down almost immediately by the Supreme Court on First Amendment grounds. Of the entire CDA, Section 230 alone survived the chopping block because it enabled free speech.

For all its influence, Section 230 is only twenty-six words long:

> No provider or user of an interactive computer
> service shall be treated as the publisher or speaker
> of any information provided by another information
> content provider.[4]

This means that online media companies are not held responsible for the content posted by users. It also means that users are not held responsible either. In comparison, traditional media, such as newspapers, magazines, and television, are held liable for their content because they themselves produce it.

Social media providers such as Meta (parent company of Facebook and Instagram), Google, and Twitter (none of which existed during the 1990s when Section 230 was legislated) are under no legal obligation to moderate what is published on their platforms.[5]

So, in other words, Section 230 enables online free speech, supported by the First Amendment with no regulation. And many argue that free speech has enabled the Internet to become what it is today: an online marketplace where you can get anything you want with a few clicks.

But it has also created an evil twin: a habitat for a fact-free free-for-all for which no one can be held liable for any published content.

As renowned sex-crime attorney Carrie Goldberg notes in *Nobody's Victim: Fighting Psychos, Stalkers, Pervs and Trolls*:

> I'm convinced Section 230—or, more specifically, the court's broad application of the law—is the enabler of every asshole, troll, psycho, and perv on the internet. From revenge porn websites to rapists using dating apps to hunt for prey, everything bad that happens online is allowed to happen because Section 230 of the CDA exists. The great irony here is that the Communications Decency Act was originally intended to keep the internet safe.

Nobody could have seen this coming when Section 230 was legislated because at that time, users had to use their dial-up phone line to connect to the web, cell phones only made phone calls, and video was out of the question as the network infrastructure could not handle it—because there was no network infrastructure.

Today we take the speed and innovation of technology for granted, waiting for the next phone, tablet, device, or network to make our online experience faster and easier. But in the nineties, the vast majority of lawmakers were just trying to wrap their heads around the fact that the Internet even *existed* and what it all meant.

The rapid tech advances of the last decade have delivered unprecedented, unfiltered content to billions that can be accessed almost instantly (except in sub-Saharan Africa and 30 percent of the rural USA). Which means that kids can see anything that adults can see, including violent sexual content. And even if the little ones don't know how to search yet, or even spell, how easy is it for them to play with an iPad and click on bookmarks that could be set to porn sites?

And it's almost as easy to post videos and pictures as it is to access them.

Section 230 says that anyone can post anything, anywhere with zero liability. So anyone who has a picture of you can post it wherever they want to, whether it's on their social media page or a porn site, and there's nothing you can do about it. And once those images are online, whether placed there with your consent or not, there's no getting them back. Also, since there's no judicial regulation, online platforms have no obligation or interest in removing them if you do find them on their site.

Now, you'd think that since legislation created Section 230 all those years ago and that lawmakers have since recognized the issues surrounding it, they would at least consider doing *something* to rectify the situation. Especially since technology has become so essential to our daily lives over the last decade and even more so since COVID.

But you'd be wrong.

Some legislators *do* recognize that Section 230 has problems that need to be addressed. The problem is that they can't agree on what to do and how to get it done. Some want to make it more difficult to post content; others are determined to make it harder to remove information. Politics aside, it depends on their perceived constituents what view the politicians seem to hold on any given day. Sad to say, others are still clueless, or at least pretend to be.

But there are two things that very few seem to be discussing or even aware of when it comes to what gets shown to you online: algorithms and lobbyists.

Algorithms and Lobbyists

Algorithms are programs that take a lot of data, process the data, and spit out a result. The key word being *process*. The data is processed according to the way that the algorithm is programmed. As a simplistic example, let's say you want to make a cake. You take the data (ingredients), process the data (recipe) by following the instructions of the algorithm, and produce the result (cake). But let's say that you're partial to chocolate, so you put a little extra chocolate in. Now, all ingredients are not processed equally; you've altered the processing and produced a different result from the original program, one that's a little more in favor of chocolate. You're the baker, your prerogative.

Proprietary algorithms determine what you see online and when you see it.

That is what social media companies do: They have their thumb on the scale of whatever data most benefits them, and what you see is designed to keep your attention. Because the longer you pay attention to them, the more advertising they can throw at you, which is why social media is "free."

But as they say in marketing, nothing is free: if you are not paying for the meal, you *are* the meal.

Social media data scientists develop algorithms that process the data that users post and predict which new content will hold their attention. The algorithms not only change on a regular basis; they are proprietary to each platform. In other words, no one outside of a few in the company knows how they're programmed. Meta does not know Google's algorithms, and Amazon does not know Meta's algorithms, etc.

Algorithms are the tech-age version of what was advertised back in the day to create demand for Big Macs: It's their "secret sauce." Nobody knows their recipe.

If you are not paying for the meal, you are the meal.
—Old marketing adage

This is important, because the algorithms determine what you see online and, in the case of search engines such as Google, where in the search results you see a particular company. Let's say your sink leaks, so you do a search for plumbers in your area. Wouldn't you click on the first two or three results on the first page of Google's search engine and start calling them? You would not page down through five pages and write down every plumber. So how valuable would it be for a local plumber to make sure that their business was one of the top two or three listings in your area, every time? Marketers spend a lot of time and money to do just that. So consider another industry besides plumbing that might have a vested interest in a top-ranking website. Pornhub, for example.

Here's a quick example: key *porn* into your favorite search engine. Chances are particularly good that Pornhub ranks first.

Victims' rights attorney Carrie Goldberg calls Pornhub "the Disneyland of online porn." One of the most popular websites in the world, it attracts 10.2 *billion* visits per month as of November 2022[6] (just behind Google, YouTube, and Facebook).

Fun fact: there are approximately 8 billion humans on Earth.[7]

But here's the bottom line for Pornhub and other social media companies hosting Internet content: if the content is posted by a user, then Section 230 rules that social media companies and website owners have *zero* obligation to determine if content is harmful, whether to remove it, who to show it to, and when they see it.

So if a jealous ex decides to post your intimate pictures without your consent, the law shrugs.

Although none of this could have been foreseen back when the Internet was still in diapers, here we are, with the Internet now old enough to vote, and there have been *zero* changes. There is another, more nefarious reason why lawmakers turn a blind eye (or *pretend* that they still do not understand the ramifications): lobbyists.

On January 21, 2022, the *Washington Post* reported that seven of the largest tech companies spent a record $70 million in 2021 lobbying the US government.[8] The companies (Meta, Google, Amazon, Apple, Uber, Twitter, and Microsoft) are spending to limit any legislation that would curtail their power and influence. The *Washington Post* article notes that Meta led the pack, spending just over $20 million, followed closely by Amazon ($19 million), a record lobbying spend for both companies in Washington.[9]

What do these social media giants get for their investment? Exactly what they paid for: zero oversight by lawmakers.

For a short while, it looked as though the habitual inertia of legislators would be overcome by the release of the "Facebook Files" by the *Wall Street Journal* in September 2021.[10] Based on thousands of internal Facebook documents provided to the *Journal* by Frances Haugen, a former Facebook data scientist, the *WSJ* series of articles details how Facebook prioritizes profits over the safety of its more than three billion users.[11]

There were congressional hearings and a lot of pearl clutching aplenty on both sides of the aisle, calling for change. Ms. Haugen testified before Congress in October 2021 in hopes that the bombshell would provoke government oversight of Facebook. But ultimately, Congress could not decide what to do, so they did what they have always done: nothing.

Ms. Haugen's courage in coming forward wasn't in vain, though. We learned that although Facebook publicly claims that it treats all users equally, her testimony revealed that just like PTL, Facebook has two sets of books: one set for those it deems famous or high profile and the other set for everyone else.

As one example, according to the Facebook papers, "In 2019, it [Facebook] allowed international soccer star Neymar to post nude photos of a woman who had accused him of rape, to tens of millions of his fans before the content was finally removed by Facebook." Neymar's content was permitted just because he had been boosted into Facebook's "XCheck" program.

XCheck members are celebrities whom Facebook deems to have enough social cache to post with impunity. As the *WSJ* quotes internal Facebook's documents: "That means, for a few select members of our community, we are not enforcing our policies and standards."

Almost 6 million people can post to a social network of 3.5 billion with no oversight. What could go wrong?

By the way, Neymar's post of the nude woman (who did not consent to her image being posted) was seen by 56 million people before Facebook saw fit to remove it.

Also, by the way, the XCheck club isn't a cozy top 500. In 2020, there were 5.8 million members. One million more than the population of the city of Los Angeles.

Almost 6 million people can post to a social network of 3.5 billion with no oversight.

What could go wrong?

However, these lobbying expenditures are not the only investments that the Big Tech companies are making in influence. Tech industry trade group NetChoice (which includes Amazon, Facebook, and Google among their members) spent over $1 million in the last quarter of 2021 on Facebook ads, a more than fifteen-fold increase in their Facebook ad spending over the previous two and a half years.

Shown at least 24 million times on Facebook in that period,[12] NetChoice baldly states that the increased spending has a single purpose: to educate Americans about the dangers of regulation. "While the techlash is a beast of the Beltway, its resulting impact will be felt nationwide," said NetChoice spokesperson Rob Winterton. "Our campaign aims to educate them about that and what they can do about it."

The tech industry spends on influence because their investments are paying off. As Senator Amy Klobuchar (D-Minn) noted during Ms. Haugen's testimony on Capitol Hill:

> We have not done anything to update our privacy
> laws in this country, our federal privacy laws—
> nothing, zilch—in any major way. We have done
> nothing when it comes to making the algorithms

more transparent. . . . Why? Because there are
lobbyists around every single corner of this building
that have been hired by the tech industry. Because
Facebook and the other tech companies are throwing
a bunch of money around this town, and people are
listening to them.[13]

Lawmakers are ignoring the fact that current laws empower
extremely dangerous content threatening the safety of women and
children.

Porn

We can't discuss the beginnings of the Internet without discussing porn.

The demand for porn has driven technology to develop a lot
of the network infrastructure that we take for granted today. In the
early 2000s, Laura's colleague owned an Orlando Internet company
(before most of the Internet service providers [ISPs] were owned by
conglomerates) and once showed Laura a lengthy list of websites that
his company hosted, commenting, "Look at all the porn sites. Thank
God for those dirty old men; they're making me rich."

Less anecdotally, this was known as far back as 2002 when an
article in *The Guardian* quoted a digital media consultant, "Like it
or not, pornography drives each new, convenient visual technology,
and 3G, which combines powerful new media applications, will be
no different."[14]

Then in 2007, two products, both of which would change the
world on their own, launched independently but almost simultaneously: Apple released the iPhone (the first smartphone that combined
a web browser, camera, and phone in one device), and the website

Pornhub was unleashed on the world. Pornhub billed itself as a hosting platform for amateur content and creators. Users can not only *view* hard-core porn for free but *create* and upload it to the site, also for free.

What are the lottery-odd chances that the first mobile camera with web access was released at almost the same time as the first website to offer free porn created by users? If the gods had conspired, they couldn't have timed the launch of these two any better for each other.

Pornhub has the same cheeky approach to porn that *Playboy* originated: the girl next door. Their social media icon Aria (who is clear that she doesn't herself do porn but knows that everybody wants to talk about it and, more to the point, share it) promotes irreverent, witty content that stays up-to-date on social trends and incorporates Pornhub into them. Including art shows, Pornhub awards ceremonies, and collaboration with Kanye West (Ye), Pornhub's genius marketing has incorporated porn into the mainstream. So much fun!

But on the flip side, despite porn being middle-class, mainstreamed, and bold, there are dark sides to current porn that many women do not understand, and they need to, to keep themselves and their children safe in today's environment.

Our original content for this chapter described the evolution of porn over the last twenty years and how it has gone from third-person perspective where the viewer watches other people having sex, complete with weak storyline (like watching a play), to "gonzo" porn. Gonzo removed the pretense of a storyline, making the entire video a sexual experience, designed to make the viewer feel as though everything being filmed is happening to them.

And to push the boundaries of the first-person experience

further and further, most scenes are extremely violent and degrading to women. Equally as horrific, the women in the videos are depicted as enjoying this vicious treatment.

In *Violence and the Pornographic Imaginary: The Politics of Sex, Gender, and Aggression in Hardcore Pornography,* sociologist Natalie Purcell, PhD, MPA, describes her analysis of over one hundred of the approximately two hundred and fifty most popular "hardcore" heterosexual porn movies from 1970 to 2010. Dr. Purcell observes that since the introduction of gonzo to porn in 1989, scenes of aggressive violence against women became the norm. She notes, "By the end of the 1990s, wall-to-wall sex films with the roughest sexual action were almost synonymous with the word 'gonzo.'" She adds, "In 1989, there was no such thing as 'gonzo porn.' Twenty years later, gonzo is arguably the most dominant and influential genre of pornography."[15]

Gonzo is now mainstream.

This fetishizing of violence against women made us want to, quite literally, throw up.

But how does the evolution of porn translate to real life, and how does it affect the safety of women and girls?

For one thing, many young people come of age believing that the violence portrayed in porn is normal because porn is a leading source of information about sex for young adults.[16] In other words, porn is the new sex tutor. So as porn counselor Maria Ahlin notes in her TEDx Talk,[17] "It's only fair that we ask ourselves: What curriculum is this teacher teaching impressionable young people?" She answers her own rhetorical question: "Porn can produce attitudes which trivialize sexual aggression. Research proves a strong link between porn consumption and acting out sexually aggressive acts like sexual assault."[18] Porn is not just teaching young people about sex. It's also teaching young men that violence and aggression are normal, and it's teaching young women that violent degradation and humiliation are part of pleasing your partner.

For another, the strangulation that is often depicted in porn movies is leading not only to an alarming rise in women's homicides but also an increasing reliance on the consensual strangulation games defense on the part of the perpetrator. Studies show that this defense was rarely used before 2010. However, some studies have shown that since then, there's been a 90 percent increase in the use of that defense in criminal cases.[19]

And finally, a report from the US National Institutes of Health (NIH) gets to the heart of the issue:

> Violence against women and girls continues to be a widespread problem. One of the main causes of this violence is the structural sexism present in societies that continues to be perpetuated through pornography, especially among young people. . . . A recent study concludes that the age at which users start consuming pornography is currently *eight years old (authors' emphasis)*. Aside from this finding, it is also worth highlighting the results related to gender, as these observed that men start watching porn earlier than women, with 70%–80% of men starting before the age of 16 and 48% of women at older ages, between 16 and 18. As a result, many minors—especially men—are currently accessing pornographic content without sufficient maturity and knowledge on affectivity and sexuality.[20]

As mentioned earlier, the surprise wedding in 2007 of camera smartphones and Pornhub could not have benefitted either one any

more. The result was the simplified ability to upload hard-core porn to a free
website with just a few clicks.

Not surprisingly, much of it contained violence and privacy violations

**Porn is a leading
source of sex
information for
young adults.**

against women and children. According to the *New York Times* in
2020, Pornhub was infested with rape videos. It monetized child
rapes, revenge pornography, spy cam videos of women showering,
racist and misogynist content, and footage of women being asphyxi-
ated in plastic bags.[21]

As most of the media put it, in polite terms, most of Pornhub's
content contained nonconsensual material obtained from anonymous users. As a result, Visa, Mastercard, and Discover suspended
the use of their credit cards on the site. Ensuing public outrage didn't
budge Mindgeek, the parent company of Pornhub, but strangling the
money flow certainly did.

Pornhub demonstrated that they can actually respond quickly
when they want to, removing non-verified videos. The number of
videos hosted on Pornhub decreased by a whopping 79 percent. Ten
million videos were dropped from the site *overnight*, bringing the
number of hosted videos from 13.5 million to 2.9 million.[22]

However, many of the other porn sites still retain the same type
of content that was dropped from Pornhub, if not the exact same
content because anyone can still upload anything to many of them.

If you're wondering about teen porn viewing habits, consider the
following stats from a recent survey of 1,358 teens,[23] ages thirteen to
seventeen:

- Seventy-three percent have consumed pornography (41 percent during the school day);

- Seventy-one percent have viewed it in the last week; and
- Fifty-four percent first saw it when they were thirteen or younger.

Finally, consider the impact that seeing this content has on children who happen upon a freely available gonzo porn website on a phone or iPad. Not surprisingly, children have described feeling "grossed out" and "confused," particularly those who had seen porn when they were under the age of ten.

With no age verification on most porn sites, this isn't a stretch. Parents may not even be aware that their children have seen it, and there is often a gap between what parents think their children have seen and what the children have actually viewed. For example, a study in the UK[24] showed that 75 percent of parents in the study didn't believe that their children had seen porn online. But over half their children (53 percent) reported that they had, in fact, seen it.

But, as bad as this content is, and it is *bad*, there is a worse hellscape: the dark web.

What You Need to Know About the Dark Web

Unless you know what you're doing, it's a good idea not to venture into the dark web. But the good news is that you can't get there by accident.

Some people confuse the dark web with the deep web and use the terms interchangeably, but as shown in Figure 4.1 on the next page, they're vastly different.

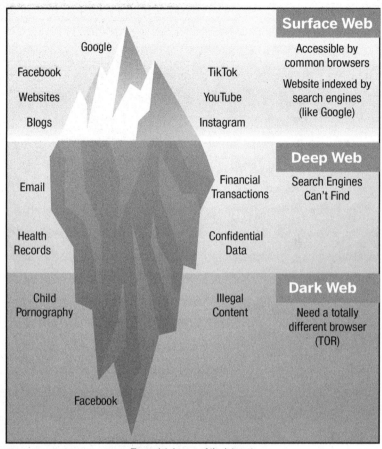

Figure 4.1: Layers of the Internet.

The surface web is the layer of the Internet that we're familiar with. It's the area that you use every day with browsers such as Firefox, Edge, and Chrome. It's indexed by web crawlers and accessible to search engines such as Google. The deep web can't be accessed by search engines, so it's used to store important information such as confidential data that can't easily be located. If you don't know where it is, you can't get to it. However, to access most of deep web content, you have to verify your identity, usually with an ID and password.

On the other hand, information on the dark web is not only anonymous, but you can only get to it with a special web browser, known as The Onion Router (TOR). TOR isn't particularly complicated, but it does require some configuration.

You can't just download TOR and start treasure hunting for content on the dark web.

TOR not only hides the identities and location of the user *and* websites but also encrypts network traffic as it crosses the Internet so that it can't be traced.

In other words, *everything* is anonymous on the dark web. No inconvenient verification processes to hassle you. Which makes it the ideal network environment to host websites and content that make the 10 million videos that Pornhub dumped look harmless.

Everything is anonymous on the dark web.

To find content on the dark web, you have to know the website address. You're not going to just stumble upon it. In other words, you can't do a Google search for a plumber. There *are* limited search engines on the dark web, but you won't find much in them. Doing a search on the dark web would be like going to a small town and asking the locals a bunch of foolish questions. Pretty quickly you'll be noticed—and not in a good way: "You're not from 'round here, are ya?" And bad things could happen.

So those who frequent the dark web have to know what they're doing and exactly where to find what they want to access. And those who host content on the dark web don't want to be found by Google, or any other means of casual searching.

It's important to point out that the dark web is not illegal. There are some legitimate businesses on the dark web, such as Facebook.

But the dark web is used primarily for criminal activity. As an aside, Facebook says that it provides its services on the dark web for users who want to remain anonymous, which seems like an odd mix for a company focused on being social. How would you find your friends? But the threats to women and children's safety on the dark web don't come from legitimate businesses (although that could be debatable regarding Facebook). The primary dark web customers and services that we're concerned with are far more nefarious. As an example, let's use a celebrity from a well-known family as the poster child of a dark web consumer: Josh Duggar of the television show *19 Kids and Counting*.

On April 29, 2021, Duggar was arrested for "receiving and possessing material depicting the sexual abuse of children"[25] via the Internet. During the subsequent trial, James Fottrell, director of the Department of Justice (DOJ) High Technology Investigative Unit, described what he found on Duggar's work computer. He testified that the laptop was partitioned into two parts: one public facing that contained business software and records. The other was a far more technical partition with a separate password. This was no accidental configuration. Nor trivial.

The secret partition contained the TOR browser. More than one hundred images of child sexual abuse material and several videos had been downloaded onto the computer.

Some of the material was so abusive that Joy cried all night when she read about it because she knows what it looks like. She's seen similar material in the homes of predators who she's busted.

A twenty-eight-year law enforcement veteran cried just reading about it.

And one of the Duggar videos was so disturbing that the law enforcement agent described it as "one of the most offensive" that he had seen in his career.

We looked Agent Fottrell up on LinkedIn. He's been a computer forensic investigator for the DOJ since 2002, so almost twenty years at the time of Duggar's arrest. And he found the content that Duggar had downloaded as one of the most offensive that he'd ever seen. That's a heavy statement. It's also a statement that was struck from the record as opinion, not fact.

Josh Duggar. Wholesome-looking, always-smiling, Christian-Baptist-espousing Josh Duggar was aroused by a video featuring child pornography.

Think you know what predators look like and act like in public? Take a good look. Mr. Wholesome is the face of a predator.

The Manosphere

The anonymity provided by the Internet is not isolated to the dark web. It also facilitates hate and calls for violence against women by the "manosphere." Loosely defined as a collection of web-based communities aligned by their common interest in men's issues, the manosphere is often associated with online harassment of women and real-world violence.[26] It is a decentralized network of websites, blogs, gaming platforms, and chat rooms filled with misogyny and satire (it is all just a joke!), overlapping other violent ideologies such as white supremacy.

Members of the toxic manosphere are intensely threatened by feminism and believe that society is rigged against men, particularly regarding what they believe men are entitled to or feel that they richly deserve but cannot have. There are recurring themes, primarily consisting of rage that they cannot have sexual access to any woman they want at any time they want and that women should return to the subservience and domestic home activities of the 1950s. Some of these attitudes are not new, but what *is* new is the ability that technology provides for them to gather in an online community, weaponize their hate against women, and radicalize others to join them as male supremacists.

To be clear, they are not wistfully longing for an earlier era. They demand total domination and control over every aspect of women's lives.

The Internet provides a platform for their misogynistic extremism, enabling online mobs howling for violence against women.

Online anonymity is paramount in these communities, enabling the participants to espouse extreme levels of violence, misogyny, and their own feelings of oppression and victimization.

The manosphere is composed of four categories:

- **Men's rights activists (MRAs)**, who advocate political changes that will benefit men. However, much of their activism consists of harassment and abuse toward feminists and other female public figures.
- **Men Going Their Own Way (MGTOW)** is a community that argues that women are so toxic that men should avoid them altogether. Some MGTOW will date women but avoid anything serious, such as getting married, while others won't even be friends with women.
- **Pickup artists (PUAs)** is a group that claims to teach men "seduction strategies" so that they can be more successful in sexual conquests. Many of these "techniques" are dangerous to women, exhorting to consider women solely as sexual

objects, encouraging insults, and disregarding consent. There are many expensive online classes for teaching PUAs how to pick up women (and don't take no for an answer). The important recommendation for you is: If you notice that your date is disrespecting or is subtly (or not so subtly) insulting you, leave immediately. Appendix 1 offers more dating tips that include some of the techniques encouraged by PUAs. Although PUAs don't seem to be as widespread as they were a few years ago, many young men looking for dating advice still can be assisted onto PUA websites by the predictive algorithms of social media.

- **Misogynistic involuntary celibates (incels)** include men who believe they are entitled to a relationship with a high-status woman but are incapable of finding a partner due to their self-perceived lack of attractiveness and social status. Misogynistic incels are one of the most extreme MRA communities, committing extreme acts of violence to demonstrate their frustration with lack of sexual access to women they deem desirable.

Effects of the Manosphere and Other Violent Online Communities on Women's Safety

How do these online and misogynistic communities affect violence against women in the real world? The following is a summary of shootings and attacks by self-identified MRAs, particularly incels. But keep in mind that the total number of attacks is much larger as many MRAs also identify as white supremacists.

- In 2014, a self-identifying misogynist incel murdered six

people in Isla Vista, California, and injured fourteen others. This incident was the inspiration for many others.

- The largest mass shooting in Oregon history occurred in 2015 by a man who likened himself to the Isla Vista shooter, and who shot and killed nine people at the Umpqua Community College in Roseburg, Oregon.[27]
- The shooter at Aztec High School in Aztec, New Mexico, in 2017 cited incel inspiration online. The shooter used the pseudonym of the Isla Vista shooter on several online forums.[28]
- The mass shooting at Marjory Stoneman Douglas High School in Parkland, Florida, resulted in the tragic death of seventeen people and injured seventeen others. The shooter also mentioned the Isla Vista shooter in online forums, noting that the Isla Vista shooter "would not be forgotten."[29]
- In 2018, a self-identified incel drove his van into pedestrians in Toronto, killing ten and wounding thirteen. Before the attack, he posted, "the Incel Rebellion has already begun" along with several references to misogynist incel terminology and the Isla Vista shooter.[30]
- Also, in November 2018, another misogynistic terrorist in Tallahassee, Florida, who also worshipped the Isla Vista shooter killed two women and injured four people in a yoga studio. The Secret Service subsequently posted a case study on this shooter: "Hot Yoga Tallahassee: A Case Study of Misogynistic Extremism."[31]
- In 2019, an Ohio incel wrote a manifesto claiming he would "slaughter women out of hatred, jealousy and revenge."[32] He claimed that the slaughter would take place in May 2020. Soon after writing his manifesto, he attended US Army basic

training but was discharged. He was subsequently arrested in March 2020 after his mother called the authorities.

- In 2021, the only mass shooting in the UK since 2010 occurred when an incel shot five people dead in Plymouth, England. He had previously posted misogynistic rants on YouTube, which were subsequently removed.[33]

- In March 2022, authorities in Costa Mesa, California, reported a self-described incel who approaches, harasses, and attacks women with pepper spray. He then posts videos of the confrontations online.[34]

MRA activists have also used violence to target women and their families. In July 2020, an MRA lawyer murdered the son and wounded the husband of US District Judge Esther Salas. Judge Salas was overseeing a case in which the shooter argued that the men-only military draft was discriminatory. Other adherents to MRA activism have also attacked divorce court judges and their wives and even killed themselves.

Technology-Facilitated Violence and Abuse

Actress Ashley Judd begins her 2017 TED Talk, "How Online Abuse of Women Has Spun Out of Control,"[35] by quoting some of the ongoing abuse that she has received online:

"Ashley Judd, stupid fucking slut."

"You can't sue someone for calling them a cunt."

"If you can't handle the Internet—fuck off, whore."

Judd notes that although she's been the target of gendered hate speech and misogyny since she joined social media in 2011, she became the victim of a targeted campaign of cyberbullying and hate in the most unlikely way: because she's an avid fan of University of Kentucky Wildcats basketball.

It all started with an innocuous tweet regarding a game between her favorite team and the Arkansas Razorbacks. Judd was unhappy with the way the Razorbacks were playing, and like many fans, tweeted her opinion: "*@ArkRazorback dirty play can kiss my team's free throw making a -- @KySportsRadio @marchmadness @espn Bloodied 3 players so far.*"

Ms. Judd describes the ensuing chaos:

> The response to that was a huge sexist pile-on, where it really started with, you know, the outrageousness of my thinking that as a female basketball fan I was entitled to have an opinion about officiating, to just a generalized, you should die; I want to rape you; I want to ejaculate on your face; you shouldn't be taking up oxygen; there was a picture of you, I wish it was a picture of your deathbed. You know, all of this stuff that I got.[36]

According to the online abusers, Ashley Judd is not entitled to the good-natured ribbing that rival sports fans exchange during a game, simply because she's a woman. Instead, she's immediately subjected to millions of graphic threats of rape and murder. Have we mentioned that misogyny has weaponized technology?

And the abuse was not a one-and-done incident. Two years later, she noted, "It is routine for me to be treated in the ways I've already described to you. It happens to me every single day on social media platforms, such as Twitter and Facebook."

Ms. Judd was subjected to the type of terror enabled by technology-facilitated violence and abuse (TFVA).

TFVA is a broad term used to describe the use of digital technologies to inflict harassment, abuse, and violence.

Although there is no internationally agreed-upon definition of TFVA, the UN describes it as the following:

> Online violence which takes place in the digital world e.g., on social media platforms, virtual reality platforms, workplace platforms, gaming, dating, chat rooms and other digital platforms and technology-facilitated Violence Against Women and Girls (VAWG) which is facilitated through different digital tools e.g., GPS/location-based technologies, AI, transportation apps, communication tools such as mobile phones, etc. Online and technology facilitated VAWG takes many forms—sexual harassment, stalking, zoom bombing, intimate image abuse, trolling, doxing, misogynistic or gendered hate speech amongst others. Some forms of VAWG such as intimate partner or domestic violence and trafficking are also facilitated through different digital tools including mobile phones, GPS, and tracking devices amongst others. For instance, abusive partners or ex-partners use tracking devices or other digital tools to monitor, track, threaten and perpetrate violence.[37]

And following societal norms, this violence primarily targets women and girls. The International Center for Research on Women (ICRW) notes a UN global estimate that "almost three-quarters of women and girls *have experienced or been exposed to online violence.*"[38]

Read that again: three-quarters of women and girls have experienced or been exposed to online violence.

Misogyny has weaponized technology, making this type of victimization more common than any in-person form. TFVA challenges what has been traditionally defined as violence: a physical attack. So what does online violence, which is a contradiction by definition, really mean? Not surprisingly in a world where the line between virtual and physical is increasingly blurred, it's complicated. First of all, as the UN points out:

> **Misogyny has weaponized technology, making this type of victimization more common than any in-person form.**

Evidence shows that the impacts of online and technology facilitated VAWG can be as serious as "offline" violence. Survivors can experience significant harm to their health and well-being including self-harm, depression, and suicide as well as symptoms of post-traumatic stress disorder, particularly when the abuse is frequent. Young women and girls also experience serious psychological impacts in response to online violence, including feeling physically unsafe, lower self-esteem or loss of confidence, mental or emotional stress and problems at school.[39]

However, as a relatively new concept in society, many, especially those not familiar with technology, don't understand it. And as law professor Suzie Dunn notes: "Scholars, legislators, advocates, and the general public are still grappling with what new behaviors such as online stalking, image-based sexual abuse, and harmful digital misrepresentations are and how they should be condemned or regulated, if at all."[40]

Secondly, TFVA facilitates online stalking, which has real-world consequences. In the summer of 2021, an armed stalker fired into the front door of TikTok star Ava Majury's house with a shotgun. At the time, Ms. Majury was a fifteen-year-old social media star with more than 1.2 million followers on TikTok and more than 300,000 Instagram followers (netting thousands of dollars in sponsorship deals).[41] A teen who had harassed Ms. Majury online for months through various social media accounts blasted into her home, but his weapon jammed. Her father, a retired police lieutenant, chased him off, but he returned. The attacker was subsequently shot and killed by Mr. Majury.

Subsequently, Ms. Majury had to withdraw from school, citing threats from another stalker who attended the same school as she did.

But the stalker wasn't forced to leave school; she was. The message that was sent to both stalker and victim is unmistakable: the victim is the problem.

Weaponization of Technology Gadgets

Chantel closed the front door, then leaned her head against it and slowly exhaled. Home free. She'd just unloaded the last box from the car into her new apartment. Now she and little Terrell Jr. were finally safe from her former partner. Now she could unwind, and they could start their new life without the threat of constant terror.

She poured herself some coffee, then sat down to distract herself with social media for a minute before unpacking the few things that she'd managed to salvage. Fortunately, Jr. was happily playing with Legos, unaware of the drama that they'd just escaped.

Suddenly, there was a sharp knock at the door. She heard a familiar laugh. "Hey, hey! Surprise! Bet you didn't think I could find you so soon."

How did Terrell Sr. know where she was? Who could have given her up?

Little did she know that a common tracking device had shown Terrell exactly where she and Jr. were at all times. It would take Chantel's sharp-eyed cousin to find the source hidden in Jr.'s school backpack: an AirTag. It took her cousin longer to dig it out of the bag than it took to find the AirTag's location with the iPhone app.

Although handy to locate missing luggage and pets, tracking devices such as AirTags have made the lives of victims a living hell. Apple AirTags are Bluetooth tracking devices that are a little bigger than a quarter. Although there are others, the ubiquity of Apple devices has made it far easier for perps to track victims.

Apple provides instructions[42] for locating such unwanted devices if you think you may be a target. If you can't locate it on your own, seek the services of a professional. Your local tech store may be able to help.

Miniaturization of video cameras enables you to set up doorbells and equipment throughout your home to monitor for intruders, but it has also enabled predators to record videos of women and children in their most private moments without their knowledge. Complete with infrared and night vision, hidden spy cams can be disguised in deodorant cans, plants, alarm clocks—just about anywhere. Whether it is children taking a shower, women having sex, or even just undressing in a vacation rental, perps have been known to use these images to blackmail women, post on porn websites, and sell the images on the dark web.

Airbnb and other short-term vacation rentals (STVR) allow security cameras in "public" or "common" spaces on properties; they
are not permitted in bathrooms, bedrooms, or other sleeping areas.
Most STVR hosts will note the location of security equipment and
they'll be readily visible, but it's a good idea to look around after you
check in.

If you suspect that there may be hidden cameras in your location, you aren't powerless. There are downloadable apps on your
phone or hardware devices available online that can help you detect
these hidden devices. Be sure to report this electronic Peeping Tom
to law enforcement.

Gaming

Research indicates that more than half the US population (54
percent) are digital gamers.[43] And a poll of parents indicates that
two-thirds of young people in the United States under eighteen play
games online, putting it only behind watching YouTube videos as an
activity.[44] The explosive success and growth of the gaming market
equates to massive online opportunity for predators.

We're both (very casual) gamers and have noticed a massive increase in aggressive predation, just in the last couple of years. And
if *we* have been hit up on a lot online recently, the level of targeting
toward vulnerable children has to be almost unimaginable.

Catfishing, Grooming, and Sextortion

This isn't new content, but it bears reminding to keep children
safe online. Children are trusting and benevolent; most of them trust
adults, and many trust everyone. The key word is *trust*. They believe

what they're told and love to play. Set loose in online games, a more ideal target for predators can't even be imagined. And more so since online games are often the entertainment of choice since COVID. Multiplayer games such as Fortnite, Minecraft, or Call of Duty provide easy access points. Catfishing (creating a fake persona) allows the predator to pretend to be in the child's gender and age group, mimicking their language and phrasing. They become friends with the child, manipulating them, gradually and subtly exposing them to the sexual aspect (grooming) of the relationship. Some preteens have even left home to meet the predator.

If they can't meet with them physically, the perp can scam the child into sending them sexually explicit pictures of themselves, which can then be sold online.

And it gets worse.

Predator Jonathan Kassi was arrested in connection with the suicide of seventeen-year-old Ryan Last, a victim of sextortion.[45] The online predator assumed the persona of a young woman and sent Last a revealing picture of a female and asked for one back. When he did, the cyber scammer demanded $5,000, or he would release Last's intimate picture online and send it to his parents. Last panicked and took his own life.

If your children are online gamers, check on them frequently. Have honest, direct conversations with them so that they know that they can come to you and rely on you for support when (not if) they're approached by online groomers.

If you are approached by predators online, block them from your profile and report them to the administrators of whatever platform you're on. Take screenshots. You do not need to be polite. No warning, no request: Block them. Report them. Delete them.

Virtual Reality

Virtual reality (VR) and augmented reality (AR) take gaming to an amazing level. It is total immersion in the game experience. Your brain knows that you're not really "in" the game, but you could forget that in about five seconds because it's designed to be a first-person experience.

Gamers choose an avatar, or persona, to represent them in the game, and the avatar is what other players see. The avatar can be controlled with electronically enhanced equipment, such as guns or boxing gloves, that gives the user the impression of the actual physical experience. But you are the one having the experience, not your avatar. As a result, if you're interested in skiing, boxing, or some other sport, the enhanced equipment enables you to get into "character," enhancing the experience of the games to provide a great workout.

Unfortunately, the virtual experience is so real that being sexually attacked online can cause emotional trauma.

Virtual and augmented reality technology is still in its infancy, and there are already reports of online sexual assault. A researcher reported that her avatar was sexually attacked on virtual reality platform Horizon Worlds. In the incident, "Two male avatars are in the room, one of whom is observing while the other appears very close to her. The pair make lewd comments and share a virtual bottle of vodka."[46]

Corporate accountability group SumOfUs notes that Meta, the hosting platform, needs more comprehensive plans to combat harm in the "Metaverse." The group also notes that "virtual assaults can be intensely traumatic. It still counts, it still has a real impact on users." Meta's response: Meh.

Laws and Law Enforcement Online

Aside from Section 230, which essentially gives the tech platforms free reign to do whatever they want, there is zero legislation regarding online platforms in the United States.

Part of the reason is that tech moves at lightning speed while the pace of the judicial system and legislators is gradual. As in, gradually the Ice Age ended. In other words, the judicial system was never designed for such rapid change and can't keep up. The other reason is that the virtual world is borderless. Who defines the law, who has the power to legislate it, and who can enforce it? Not to mention the fact that there is a total lack of political will to do so.

We can't solve these issues unless we acknowledge them and force our leaders to address them.

The #MeToo online movement was an effort to not only obtain justice against sexual abusers but also to harness that momentum to address historic systemic issues faced by women. Although there was a "flurry of legislation related to gender equity"[47] at state levels, aside from a single piece of legislation, the federal government was unfazed. Unsurprisingly to us, women who have been around awhile, the pushback from society against #MeToo was fierce, and the movement has languished in the years since it took off.

The other part of the equation is that this is indeed a technical revolution. A revolution unlike any other in history, and one that the current authorities don't know how to deal with, so they ignore it.

Women's lives are being lost and ruined as a result of society sticking its head in the sand. Our leaders typically wait for a crisis before acting.

The crisis has arrived.

Chapter Five
Persuasion-Proof

A large part of our "nice girl" social conditioning surrounds being agreeable. In essence, women are not only expected to give *to* but to give *in* to others—no matter who the others may be. This value construct is a powerful form of regulation over not just the behavior of women but where it all starts: in our minds.

In other words, thought control.

Many women have been trained since childhood to alter our thinking, attitude, or behavior just because we're told to—even if the resulting thoughts or actions are not in our own best interest.

Our conditioning is not unlike the training of an elephant calf. Elephants are among the largest and strongest land animals on earth, so the only way that humans can control them is to start when they're young. The baby elephant is tied to a tree with a rope around its ankle so it can't escape. The little elephant eventually outgrows the rope and could easily snap it when it grows into adulthood. But because it is conditioned to being tethered as a calf, it gives up seeking freedom for the rest of its life.

The same type of mind highjacking has been used on women, effectively kneecapping our self-confidence. It turns out that self-confidence has a direct correlation on whether or not we feel strong enough to push back when someone wants us to comply. In *The Psychology of Fraud, Persuasion and Scam Techniques*, Dr. Martina Dove notes: "Perhaps the most worrying thing about compliance is that it has been linked to low self-esteem and inferiority, as well as a negative view of self."

If we don't have faith in ourselves, and if we look to others for validation, it's an easy sell for someone to position *their* perspective as a provider of that validation, especially if you've been traumatized. So it's important to realize that nothing short of a brain injury can *force* you to think the way that someone else wants you to. *You* are the only one in charge of your mind and your attitude. Even if you are threatened or coerced, you may choose to physically comply, but your thoughts remain your own.

> **The same type of mind highjacking has been used on women, effectively kneecapping our self-confidence.**

The rope can no longer hold you.

Dr. Viktor Frankl, a Jewish psychiatrist who survived three years in four concentration camps during World War II, wrote in *A Man's Search for Meaning*, "Everything can be taken from a person but one thing: the last of the human freedoms—to choose one's attitude in any given circumstances, to choose one's own way."

The guards took everything from Dr. Frankl, including his hair and his freedom. But they could not penetrate his mind, no matter what they did. The conditions in the concentration camps were so horrific that many prisoners succumbed to corruption, bullying, or despair, exactly as the Third Reich intended. But Dr. Frankl did not. He consciously refused to turn his mind over to the Germans. So if a Holocaust victim in a concentration camp could refuse to give the Nazis control over his thoughts and attitudes, any of us could stand firm when someone attempts to play a mind game on us. Frankl was persuasion-proof, even coercion-proof.

Keep Dr. Frankl in mind when you feel that someone is trying to influence you, to change your mind to do something that may be against your long-term self-interest. You are the only one who ultimately knows what's best for you; no one else possibly can, no matter *how* they frame themselves. Choose your own way.

And, as we've mentioned before, criminals are well aware of the social conditioning of women and will try to use it to their advantage. Every day, at least a few of them tried to get over on Joy, seeing her first as female, then as cop. Imagine what would have happened to her if she'd allowed herself to be influenced by every suspect that she encountered.

So being persuasion-proof is not only in your best interest overall, it could very well save your life.

Because women's thought processes have been affected so subtly and thoroughly, we might not even notice that a lot of the time, we give away our personal autonomy to fulfill a societal form of restriction. As we'll talk about, this can happen in a number of ways, but it follows a continuum of pressure; from a rather mild experience to those becoming more deceptive, dangerous, and threatening, the tension increases: influence, persuasion, manipulation, and in too many instances regarding women, coercion. Keep in mind that these categories aren't strictly divided because more often than not, they overlap.

Figure 5.1 shows how much pressure each phase progressively applies on you, especially because as a woman, you're expected to acquiesce right away.

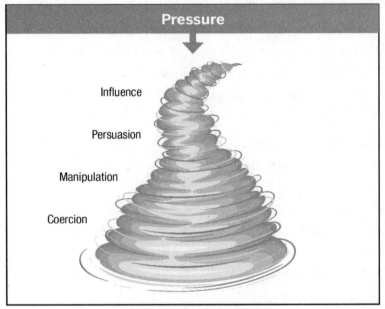

Figure 5.1: Persuasive pressure whirlwind.

The upside-down tornado illustrates the whirlwind that can mentally and emotionally surround you when you're being pressured to change your mind or someone wants something from you. And the farther you get into the funnel, the greater the stress on you to give in. We'll discuss all these phases in turn.

It all starts with influence, with more bulldozing applied during the persuasion process, then more deceit and pressure piling on during manipulation, and finally, coercion, which is a direct threat. And the more you resist, the more you'll be squeezed to comply. Know right now that if you continue to stand your ground and re-main persuasion-proof, you're going to make the people who want to manipulate you very unhappy. You may even be called names, like cold, mean, or the old standby: bitchy. Perhaps they'll even threaten you. Unfortunately, that's what a lot of people resort to when they don't get what they want from women.

Interestingly, very few pull this name-calling or threatening act on men. Men certainly have their own hierarchy of domination and control, but nothing like the expectations people place on women.

Remember what Gavin DeBecker observes in *The Gift of Fear*: "When men say no, it's the end of the discussion. When women say no, it's the beginning of the negotiation."

But even having the awareness that some will ratchet up the pressure on you to comply, and knowing the techniques they might resort to, can aid you in remaining persuasion-proof. We've had many people tell us that even having the realization about what's really going on has helped them to stand their ground and resist being manipulated. You can do it too.

Age of the Influencer

Just what is "influence"? It is the mechanism, sometimes very subtle, of trying to change someone's thoughts, attitudes, or behavior. It could be just an approving or disapproving glance, which speaks volumes to women who've been raised to please others or those in an abusive relationship.

The persuasive pressure whirlwind begins with influence, which is low touch/low stress. It may be focused or implied, directed specifically at you or not, true or exaggerated, but you can pretty much choose to take it or leave it. The person trying to influence you may have not even have any idea whether or not their efforts have had an impact, such as in the case of a television commercial or YouTube video. So at this stage, your choices are fairly easy: you can turn off the video, say no to the bartender, and unfollow that person on Instagram.

Influence may or may not be personal, although it feels personal to the person who is doing the changing. It may involve, but doesn't *require* involvement between, the influencer and the person being influenced. If you brush your teeth, wear a seat belt, or hold the door open for a stranger, someone had a positive influence on you at some point. If you grab a beer during a Super Bowl commercial, wear the brand of eyeliner brand your friend wears, or find yourself watching TikTok while waiting in the checkout line, you've also been influenced.

Either way, your thinking could be changed, and you may or may not decide to take some action. But there could be some things going on behind the scenes that you may not be aware of.

On April 1, 1929, the front page of the *New York Times* read: "Group of Girls Puff at Cigarettes as a 'Gesture of Freedom.'"

The article referred to the scandalous behavior of the day before, when a young woman named Bertha Hunt stepped into the New York City Easter Parade and lit up a cigarette.

In public. The horror.

Hunt was soon joined by nine other young women, and they chain-smoked their way up and down Fifth Avenue. The behavior of the women was outrageous because smoking in public was unacceptable for women at the time, associated (as usual) with prostitution and loose morals. She reported that she'd gotten the idea to march when a man on the street asked her to extinguish her cigarette because it embarrassed him. Hunt told a reporter that "I talked it over with my friends, and we decided it was high time something was done about the situation." Dozens of newspapers reported the story of the fashionable young women smoking their "torches of freedom." And just like that, Hunt and those courageous young women broke a taboo and struck a blow against social barriers.

But was it really "just like that"?

It turned out that when she wasn't marching in Easter parades protesting gender inequality, Hunt had a day job as an admin for a man named Edward Bernays. Bernays was a nephew of Sigmund Freud, but he's better known as the father of public relations and propaganda. When Bernays saw how effectively the US government used propaganda and viewpoint positioning to sell the First World War to the American public, he came up with the idea to use similar techniques to sell products. His methods soon racked up an impressive collection of corporate customers, including General Electric, Procter and Gamble, and the American Tobacco Company.

In reality, Hunt hadn't "talked it over with her friends" at all—the whole thing was a setup—by Bernays. He came up with the concept of staging events to generate publicity, which in turn would generate sales. So convincing women to associate cigarettes with "Torches of Freedom" changed the world in more ways than one and went down in history as the world's first PR stunt.

So imagine Bernays as he glanced around his office while conjuring up his scheme. As Hunt comes into view over at the next desk, he realizes he doesn't have to go far for the face of his new PR campaign. He doesn't even have to leave his office; she's sitting right there. He actually doesn't have to do much at all, leaving the heavy lifting to Hunt. But he does have to at least make a few calls: The scores of newspaper reporters who "just happened" to be nearby at the parade were there because Bernays had notified them in advance. Then, for good measure, Bernays had Hunt wire well-known young women, giving them notice of her "campaign."

And the world's first influencer was launched.

But here's where it gets good: Bernays initiated the stunt not because of his staunch support for women's suffrage but because the American Tobacco Company had engaged him to boost cigarette sales. And at the time, women were an untapped market. As a result, young women jumped at the chance to showcase their newfound symbol of liberation, cheerfully lighting up in public and flipping a symbolic finger to the man with every puff. Cigarette sales soared.

And we've been persuaded (and exploited) by mass media ever since.

Now in case you think that Bernay's success in manufacturing demand for the tobacco market was a fluke, consider the most important meal of your day. Are you convinced that a healthy breakfast consisting of something like bacon and eggs could be your gateway to a productive morning? If so, you can thank Bernays for that as well.

In the 1920s, most people ate a light breakfast, consisting of maybe coffee and a roll. But then the Beech-Nut Packing Company approached Bernays to help them increase bacon sales. So Bernays had his staff doctor send out a letter to 5,000 experts, asking them if a big meal in the morning could be better for people's health. Over 91 percent of them wrote back and agreed, giving Bernays the perfect pitch: "Forty-five hundred physicians agree that a hearty breakfast improves health." Not coincidentally, most of the newspaper articles he planted also referenced bacon and eggs.

Today, a century later, 70 percent of bacon is eaten at breakfast. Bernays was on to something.

Thanks to the rapid acceleration in technology and social media, we live in the age of the influencer. And as opposed to a century ago when Bernays hired a doctor to write to five thousand other physicians, anyone today can be an expert and an influencer and reach out to five thousand—or five million—people.

Bernays's marketing formula was so simple and so profitable that although the media has changed dramatically since then, his methodology has essentially remained the same for a hundred years: *Manufacture a problem and then engage an "expert" to pitch the solution to the problem.* As a result of the process, your perspective on the problem itself is reframed. They are, after all, experts.

And once you adopt the expert's view of the "problem," there is only one logical next step: adopt their "solution."

This is true whether the influence is personal, online, or mass media, such as television, radio, or podcast. Keep in mind that most of the time, the influencer doesn't want you to know that you're being worked because if you catch on, you'll more than likely opt out.

Bernays's evil genius lies in the fact that he was the man behind the curtain in his campaigns. He himself was nowhere near the Easter Parade, and he had a doctor send out letters on behalf of Beech-Nut Packing Company. In the age of the influencer, there are many evil geniuses out there wanting something from you, especially because your life may have been upended as a result of COVID.

Women's wallets took a massive hit during COVID, especially if they had limited childcare options and had to leave the workforce to care for their kids. As a result, many flocked online, desperate for at-home options to make money. Influencers with screens full of scams were there waiting.

In *Get Rich or Lie Trying: Ambition and Deceit in the New Influencer Economy*, Simeon Brown details how companies like It Works! and LuLaRoe have targeted desperate young women. Lurking behind faux-feminist empowerment messages, they faux-promise the opportunity to earn a good living selling products as an influencer online . . . *for hidden fees.* Brown notes:

> It Works! had long been accused of "preying on directionless millennials and single moms." It had incentivized young women to auto-enroll into large monthly payments with the promise of earning a higher commission earlier. In reality, the only way they could make anything was to recruit their friends and family or enlist other young women facing precarity in the workplace. The model of affiliate marketing the company uses is part of an old tradition to which the internet has given a new life and a million different masks. There are more businesses like It Works! than can be counted, and they are exploiting millions under the guise of offering young women empowerment in the age of get-rich feminism.

Shades of Bernays. We'll discuss scams like this more in the next chapter. But for now, we just want to raise your awareness and encourage you to make sure that you look behind any influencer curtain, in person and online. So crush that cigarette, push that plate of bacon and eggs away, and make sure that you're aware of all the ramifications before saying yes to anything or anyone.

The influence stage is where you practice declining, saying it often and early. Because it's easier to get out without penalty at this point. The predator will go off in search of easier and more compliant prey. But once you start saying yes, it's a long road back to no for women. Now there's nothing wrong in saying yes, if you're *certain* that it benefits you or is somehow in your long-term best interest (and tell yourself the truth).

If not, be persuasion-proof and get out as soon as you can.

How the Effects of Persuasion Can Affect Your Safety

In *The Dynamics of Persuasion: Communication and Attitudes in the Twenty-First Century*, Dr. Richard M. Perloff notes that "persuasion represents a conscious attempt to influence the other party, along with an accompanying awareness that the persuadee has a mental state that is susceptible to change."

In other words, since it's a deliberate attempt to change your mind, the persuader is going to be aware of where you stand regarding their request or demand. It's often a personal exchange, not a broadcast or event for whoever is watching or listening. As a result, the persuader can observe whether or not your mind has changed and if not, to continue to apply more pressure.

This is the second phase of the persuasive process whirlwind. The influencer has become the persuader. They want something from you, which you may or may not be inclined to give them or do for them, but they're on a mission, so the stakes are higher.

Persuasion can be positive or negative, but it is rarely neutral because it is *designed* to effect change. Like influence, persuasion can also be used for good purposes: therapists try to persuade their clients to change, parents persuade their children to eat spinach, recovering people persuade newcomers to stop drinking or doing drugs.

On a more personal note, be aware of persuasion attempts while dating. We'll discuss this more in Chapter 6, "Dating the Wolf." But it's worth mentioning that if you're aware, the early stages of dating tell you a lot about someone. Consider the following exchange at the end of the night:

You: What a great time! Thanks for coming out; maybe we can do it again soon!

Date: What?! Already? The night has just started, let's go around the corner for a nightcap!

You: No. I really have to get to work early tomorrow.

Date: Aw, c'mon. Just one more. I have to go in early tomorrow too, but I want to spend time with you more. Come on. What do you say?

You: All right. Just one more.

End scene. You've just let your date know that you can be persuaded and thereby controlled. For too many, this may be the first step on the path to being a domestic abuse victim because domestic abuse and violence are all about control and domination. We'll discuss this in the following chapters.

But for now, be aware that although you initially made your wishes known, they were disregarded, and then you were pressured. And, as a result, someone successfully changed your mind. How much do you think that they'll respect your boundaries or decisions in the future? Pro tip: they won't.

If someone attempts to persuade you to do something against your best interest, or that you just don't feel like doing, remember Dr. Frankl. No amount of persuasion or even coercion could convince him to adopt the Nazis' perspective, to turn against his fellow prisoners, or to give in to despair. If he could maintain his mental state in those dire circumstances, so can you.

To that end, Dr. Perloff makes an interesting observation. He maintains that because being persuaded involves choice, all persuasion is actually self-persuasion. He notes:

> One of the great myths of persuasion is that persuaders convince us to do things we really don't want to do. They supposedly overwhelm us with so many arguments or such verbal ammunition that we acquiesce. They force us to give in. This overlooks an important point: People persuade themselves to change attitudes or behavior. Communicators provide the arguments. They set up the bait. We make the change or refuse to yield.

People persuade themselves. One of the great myths of persuasion is that persuaders convince us to do things we really don't want to do.

While on duty at the Fort Lauderdale–Hollywood International Airport, Joy was once called by a Transportation Security Administration (TSA) agent to check out a suspected drug mule. A mule is a person who transports drugs, usually for a cartel. This suspected mule had scanned positive by the TSA metal detector for an item in her private parts. To be clear, TSA is first and foremost concerned with passengers transporting bombs and weapons, so any metal object on a passenger requires an investigation by law enforcement. Suspects are placed in a closed room where they can be questioned in privacy.

Joy: "Ma'am, what is the item that you're hiding?"

Suspect: "I don't have anything. I'm not a criminal. Let me go, I'm going to miss my flight."

Joy: "Ma'am. Please. We know you have an object under your clothes. Tell me what it is. The bomb squad is on the way, and we're going to find out."

Suspect: "I don't have anything. I told you!"

Joy: "What is the square object concealed under your clothes in your crotch area? The bomb squad is on the way, if they remove an object, it won't be good."

Suspect: "Oh, that. Somebody gave it to me. It's just a book." Then she casually reached into her pants and retrieved a tinfoil-wrapped brick from her intimate area.

Joy: "A book, huh? How were you going to turn the pages?"

The brick turned out to be black-tar heroin, and the suspect was jailed without the benefit of her "reading material."

In this exchange, Joy and the suspect had opposing agendas, so each tried to persuade the other to change their mind. They both wanted something from the other person: The suspect wanted Joy to release her, and Joy wanted the woman to admit that she was holding contraband. Obviously, Joy held the advantage of power in this particular instance because she was detaining the suspect.

Notice how the suspect still held her ground despite the fact that she knew that Joy was aware that she was lying. But when the suspect realized that she was busted and couldn't go any further, she then flipped her script and adopted the technique of minimizing the entire situation. This is very common, so don't be surprised if someone pulls it on you.

Mocking, laughing, and minimizing or degrading. All these might be used against you during the whirlwind of persuasive pressure. Shrug them off. They're all just methods to get you to doubt yourself and give in.

Many suspects tried to convince Joy to doubt herself, and she notes that persuasion is a key skill for criminals. In fact, you basically can't be a predator or con unless you can sell someone on your version of reality. Serial killer Donald Harvey once noted to the FBI: "You've got to be able to talk a junkyard dog out of a garbage can."

As a cop, Joy had many suspects go to great lengths to try to persuade her not to arrest them, even to the point of insisting that she didn't see what she knew she had seen. Their motto seemed to be: "Who are you going to believe? Me or your own lying eyes?"

Some insisted that the stolen car that they were driving belonged to them, despite no registration or insurance. Others claimed that they were on their way to the police station to turn in the drugs they'd found, and the best one: "Oh my God! These aren't my pants (and neither are the drugs in my pocket)."

She recalls that some lie so arrogantly that it would be easy for someone who didn't have faith in themselves to start to believe a suspect's reality-bending claims of their innocence.

Have faith in yourself.

Manipulation

Manipulation is the third phase of the whirlwind of persuasive pressure. Although influencers and persuaders may or may not be truthful and may or may not have your best interest at heart, manipulators flat-out lie.

They don't tell the truth for a couple of reasons: First, because if you knew their real agenda, you wouldn't comply. Second, because what they really want may not be in your best interest.

The Dynamics of Persuasion defines *manipulation* as "a persuasion technique that occurs when a communicator hides their true persuasive goals . . . misleading the recipient by delivering an overt message that disguises its true intent. Flattery, sweet talk, and false promises are manipulative techniques."

But Dr. Perloff also points out that although manipulation involves deception, you still have free choice. So, though you're being had, you're still at the stage where you can decide whether or not to comply. And although deceit and high-pressure tactics are a given if you're being manipulated, if you keep your wits about you and use your safety intuition to see through it, you can still get out, hopefully unscathed.

Let's use a car transaction as an example. Say you're sitting in the car dealer's office, negotiating for a car. With a big smile, the dealer's business manager assures you that this is the best deal in town for this model and then pushes the pen and a pile of legal documents across the desk toward you. What do you do?

Diane was in this situation when she went to buy a car for the first time by herself. She knew she was being manipulated but felt so pressured and overwhelmed that she just shut up and signed to get it over with. Then she spent the next three years kicking herself for giving in.

But she learned from this and knows that the next time she buys a car, she'll face the same manipulative tactics. But Diane is now aware that she has several options: She can do her homework ahead of time and know whether the sales manager is telling the truth, she can whip out her phone and go online to compare prices in real time—or she can just walk out.

The important thing to remember about manipulators is that they are experts in detecting and preying on your emotions. They know what you want and how to appeal to you. The manager at the dealership knew that Diane really wanted that make and model *at that moment* and made it easy for her to get what she thought she wanted. In retrospect, she didn't need or want a car or payments that large. But there's a reason why the motto of sales is "Don't let the customer cool down."

Before Joy worked in law enforcement, she worked in retail security for large department stores. These huge retail stores suffer multimillion-dollar losses every year from theft, and store security's number one mission is to curtail shoplifters.

Although she started in security as a teen, she quickly realized that despite her young age, she was up against manipulative pros. She realized that the job didn't just consist of detecting the shoplifters, it was also ensuring that the swindlers didn't deceive Joy by pretending innocence. It was a mental game as well.

The thieves were quick, conniving, and brazen. Joy saw large blouses folded so small that they could fit into a three-inch box. And when she would nab one, they'd pull a five-dollar item out of their bag and throw it down like a gauntlet and scream at her.

"There. You caught me! You have it; now let me go!"

In the meanwhile, they were wearing hundreds of dollars' worth of unpaid merchandise and thousands of dollars more stashed in bags or their purse.

Almost all the apprehended thieves vehemently denied stealing. Some threatened Joy with her job, shrieked at the general manager, and swore that they would sue the store for defamation. They were so adamant in their denial that they sometimes had Joy rethinking what she saw on the security cameras. Some of them discerned that a teen like Joy might be frightened about losing her job and thus manipulated with threats, so they piled them on.

In the beginning of her career, sometimes she'd pause and think: *Did I really see that?* It turned out that, yes, she did see that.

Because when she trusted her burgeoning safety intuition, she was spot-on, 100 percent of the time.

So if a criminal is good enough to manipulate a security professional into doubting their "own lyin' eyes," think how effective they could be in convincing you. The most important thing for you to ask yourself in any situation is: Am I allowing someone to bend reality to get me to retract faith in myself, or am I standing strong?

We hope that by this point in the book, you know the answer to that.

Coercion

Coercion is the final and sometimes fatal phase of the persuasive pressure whirlwind. If you're being coerced, you're being seriously threatened in some way. In the first three phases, you had a choice in whether or not you complied with requests or demands that someone made. With coercion, your choice is stark: Comply or something terrible will occur to you or something/someone that you value. And if it's gotten to this point, the horrible thing may occur anyway, no matter what you do. You're dealing with someone who is violent and completely unpredictable. So if you believe that you're being coerced or the situation is headed in that direction, do not wait to make your getaway.

If someone is threatening you, don't dismiss the situation, hope they'll go away, or try to pretend that it isn't happening. It is. This is an emergency, and you're in danger, maybe in mortal danger.

Women are usually coerced in one of two ways: threatened by a violent stranger during the commission of a crime—such as assault, robbery, or rape—or by someone they know and love, usually an intimate partner. Being threatened in this way by someone you know is considered coercive control. It's interesting that although some countries such as Australia and the UK consider coercive control punishable by law, the judicial system in the United States does not.

You may not be familiar with the concept of coercive control. It's possible that you've been or are a victim and are not even aware of it—it's *that* insidious.

But as we mentioned earlier, the control patterns are typically established early in relationships. When you let someone know early in the relationship that you are open to being persuaded or controlled after you've already said no, you're opening the door to a dangerous dynamic. Persuasion quickly becomes insistence, which then can rapidly become coercive. Comply or else.

Domestic violence, domestic abuse, and coercive control aren't just about violence, they're about domination and control. Those with a pattern of domestic abuse (and it *is* a pattern) profile their potential victims the same way that law enforcement profiles criminals: They look for a specific behavior pattern. So if you let someone know early in the relationship that you can be controlled or manipulated, then it's game on.

Find out early on if your date can take no for an answer, and if they can't, then you say no and go.

How to Be Persuasion-Proof

Research has shown that our ability to be influenced or persuaded rests almost entirely on our frame of mind. Remember Diane who couldn't say no to the sales manager at the car dealership? It was a momentary weakness for which she financially paid dearly. The payments for the upsold car that the dealer persuaded her to buy were $350 more a month than she'd budgeted for. Over the life of a four-year loan, that's almost $17,000.

There are a lot of other things she could have done with that $17,000 that she just handed over to a stranger.

But if you find yourself repeatedly saying yes when you don't want to, then you may have a little more work to do. If you're not sure, remember what Dr. Frankl taught us: you determine your own way.

It may be that your childhood conditioning to acquiesce is still a large part of your belief system. If that's the case, you can change your beliefs whenever you want to. You've been saying yes to everyone else for all this time. Start saying yes to you first.

And if you're like Laura, you may have to take it in small steps. As a recovering people-pleaser, it took Laura a good while to start making decisions on her own behalf. Although she is still a kind person, she isn't necessarily considered nice by as many people as she used to be.

A large part of the reason that it took so long is that a lot of people who'd benefitted from her generosity became angry when she started pushing back on the expectations that they had. She was initially puzzled because she thought that they'd be happy that she was finally setting some healthy boundaries. There were many responses, but "happy" wasn't among them. Leeches don't like losing a host.

If that happens to you, be aware that those people who have a negative reaction to your assertiveness are the ones who've been using you for their own purposes. Those parasites are aware that you're waking up, and their favorite tools are shaming and mocking. But keep going.

Start small. Say no to small requests from strangers and build up. If you can stand strong against the manipulation of people you don't know, you'll soon be able to do so against colleagues, friends, and family as well.

This doesn't mean that you have to be nasty; you can still be polite but firm. Sometimes, it's all in the language. As it turns out, employees at the Apple Store were banned from using the word "unfortunately" when delivering bad news.[1] "Unfortunately, your hard drive crashed." Instead, they were encouraged to take a more positive approach: "As it turns out, your hard drive crashed."

As it turns out, some people won't take to the subtle or positive approach, so you'll have to dial up the message: "That won't work for me" is also effective and sends a stronger message. But if they persist, you're just going to have to be blunt and say no. Men say it all the time. Some even repeat themselves: "I said no!"

And if you're afraid to start saying no, do it anyway. Do it afraid.

There are so many ways that people want to use you to their own ends, but you can cut a lot of these off early on if you're aware of it and use your safety intuition.

Society has had to control women like this, not only to take advantage of them in so many ways, but also because it is terrified of their passion. And especially what women could do with that passion for themselves if they realized that they own it.

Which is why we want you to develop your own power of being persuasion-proof.

Chapter Six

Dating the Wolf

R
emember Sunny, the three-legged golden retriever from Chapter 3 that could recognize his nemesis, the wolf-hybrid from a half mile away, even in the dark? But when it comes to dating, too many women seem to be eternally caught in *entre chien et loup*, a French phrase that refers to twilight: that uncertain time between day and night when it becomes difficult to distinguish between dog and wolf, love and hate, the known and unknown.

The "wolf" is a metaphor for a predator who views women as a conquest. A wolf is a deceitful, unscrupulous person who uses pretense to conceal their masquerade of reality. In dating, the wolf, regardless of gender, is a dating con of the most dangerous variety. Because in addition to charisma, they bring two nuclear-grade weapons to the dating game that can render most women virtually defenseless: love and sex. We have all wanted both at some point in our lives. And *if a con knows what you want, they can manipulate you.*

For example, you may relate to this sentiment from a scene in the series *Schitt's Creek*. The character of Jocelyn Schitt describes her reaction to her husband: "It's just that I know what it's like to be in bed with a naked Roland Schitt, and I am powerless against that!" The whole point of that tongue-in-cheek scene was that few of us would find Roland's disheveled and eccentric character as alluring as his wife did. We've all been Jocelyn at some time or other. On a more innocuous level, who wouldn't want to cozy up to a harmless, fuzzy animal, like a lamb? As opposed to Roland, they are adorable! You just want to cuddle up with that soft, soft fleece. They seem so sweet and snuggly that you just can't help *falling in love with them*. And therein lies the strategy of the wolf: lead with velvety fleece and charm to soften you up for the real fleecing, which is headed your way.

As masters of the con, wolves are very aware of the importance of managing first impressions, which is why they put so much stock into their bespoke lamb outfit. They know that every scam is just a little different; the variations depend on your specific weak spot, where the swindler perceives that you can be exploited. So one size definitely does not fit all.

And since appearances can be variable, your job is to use your safety intuition to recognize the wolf by their patterns of behavior, irrespective of appearances.

Because you can never be sure of the lighting.

What's Past Is Prologue

A common interpretation of the line "What's past is prologue" from Shakespeare's *The Tempest* is that (without intervention) our history sets the stage for our future.

We believe this is certainly true for women, even on a global basis. Every culture has such internalized expectations of girls and women that have been passed on from generation to generation that those presumptions are inescapable. These views are pervasive, demand perfection, and rain down shame when we, quite naturally, fall short. Because although no one can meet those standards, men are somehow exempted. No matter the culture or geography, women are expected to have the perfect body, hair, home, partner, children, and job. And when it comes to these standards of perfection for women, the only difference between cultures are the respective exterior decorations.

But these demanding ideals of women affect the choices we make in every area of our lives, particularly when it comes to dating.

The expectations whisper to us, even when we aren't aware of it: If you don't lose weight, you'll never find someone. If you never find someone, you'll be nothing. You'll always be nothing. Fix your hair. Would it kill you to wear a little lipstick? You're so pretty when you smile. Why did you get that tat? If you don't see yourself reflected in someone's eyes, you're nothing. If you don't blah, blah . . . you're nothing. If you do blah, blah . . . you'll never. . . . You. Are. Nothing.

These societal views are so pervasive, they become ingrained in the subconscious of many women. They become the things that we tell ourselves, often to our own detriment.

Take Jackie, for instance. Jackie had gone to Vegas with her boyfriend, Seth, and they planned to get married the next day. It had been Seth's romantic getaway idea. He'd managed to get time away from his busy job and had planned and paid for everything. Leave it all up to me, he'd said. Just the two of us, he'd said. All to myself, he'd said.

But outside the Las Vegas airport, he'd just said something else: "I lied. I don't have any money. I'm being evicted from my apartment. I don't have a job. I can't even afford to pay for this trip; you'll have to. Will you still marry me?"

Jackie gaped at Seth's crooked smile as his lies crumbled her dreams, and she almost collapsed on the blistering sidewalk on a day that she'd fantasized about for years. The love of her life had just taken a sledgehammer to her dreams.

It wasn't the money that worried her, she did well enough. It was those expectations she'd heard since childhood and so often in growing up that were still screaming at her, only now they were in her own voice.

On the outside, Jackie was trim and petite. After innumerable diets, makeovers, and therapists, she couldn't have been further from who'd she'd been growing up. She was seventy pounds and forty years away from the chubby, frizzy-haired girl at school that everyone, including her parents, made fun of. But on the inside, she was trapped in time; nothing had changed. Her internal, eternal seven-year-old self, her parents, and society still ruled her with an iron fist. "If you never find anyone, you'll be nothing."

She said yes.

Seth was a nice-enough-looking man. Although he was balding and appeared to find the seventy pounds that Jackie had lost, he didn't look to be malicious. He looked fluffy, like a lamb. His eyes even appeared to be kindly, the type you'd bring home to meet your family and friends. But that is the thing. There was no mark of Cain to distinguish him, and she couldn't see his fangs. He looked normal. Because as mentioned, we're so often caught in entre chien et loup that we can't distinguish the features of the wolf.

After the wedding, Jackie paid for Seth, a man in his fifties, to go to information technology (IT) school to learn the latest technology so that he could find a job. In return, he assumed her identity and drained her bank accounts. She finally paid him enough to go away, but with his newly acquired hacking skills, she may never really be rid of him. Just as she may never be free of her seven-year-old self that knew the truth but still said, "I do."

Let's debrief Jackie's situation: What could she have done differently? Where in the process could she have broken it off? First of all, she could have given the relationship time to mature. Due to the societal messages that women receive, we are often quick to jump into a relationship, even marriage. Jackie was in her forties and hadn't been married. The pressure from society was intense, and she was desperate. It was a good probability that the desperation vibes she gave off were intense. Predators like Seth sense those vibes a mile away. It was also a good bet that Seth didn't feel the same societal pressure.

Also, by giving the relationship time, she could have gotten proof that Seth really was who and what he said he was. It doesn't mean that she had to get his tax returns and pay stubs on the first date. But in time, if she'd kept her eyes open and her safety intuition engaged, she would have uncovered the truth about his finances and whatever else he had lied about. That time would have also given her the opportunity to ask probing questions and to verify his answers. Many women hold back from asking too many questions, fearing that they'll be too personal. The truth will come out anyway, and it's a lot easier to get out before you become too involved. Or too pregnant.

Can we remind you that the purpose of dating is to not only build a relationship but also to find out more about that person, including discovering and uncovering the entire truth? To begin with, if you're just looking to hook up, continue to follow this safety advice as people aren't always who and what they say they are. And if you're considering a long-term relationship, really dig deeper into what they tell you and don't hesitate to look for the truth.

Also, Jackie didn't call anyone she knew for support when she found out the truth. No one. She could have excused herself for a minute and called a friend or family member who she knew had her best interest in mind and asked for their feedback. Hopefully, the person on the other end would have advised her that she should turn around and get her ass the hell out of there.

That's what real friends do. Hopefully, you have some real friends in your life who will tell you the real deal. And the real deal doesn't involve falling victim to society's expectations. And if you don't have those kinds of friends, you can join our online community. We welcome you, and we will give you respectful and thoughtful feedback.

And finally, she had to be prepared to walk away at the first sign of lying. Chances are pretty good that there were some red flags in that relationship long before the airport scene. But because Jackie chose not to see them and then to move ahead even when she knew by Seth's own admission that he was a deadbeat liar, she chose to stay.

No one had a gun to her head. She made the choice to move forward and will literally pay for that decision for the rest of her life.

But Jackie didn't just make one single choice, she made a series of choices.

We all do. And they all start long before the first date.

Before the First Date

In Appendix 2, we provide you with a chart of specific dating red flags. But before you get into or even think about a relationship, it's important to take a realistic look at yourself.

Because, by far, the most important tool that you'll have to make the necessary choices to avoid an airport drama like Jackie's is your mindset—as ultimately, regardless of any dos or don'ts that we contribute—your way of thinking determines what you want and what you'll refuse to settle for.

Before Laura met Joy, she had a long history of bad relationship choices. In retrospect, 99 percent of it had nothing to do with anyone else and everything to do with Laura. She had issues stemming from being raised in a family riddled with domestic violence, alcoholism, and trauma. After a long time of blaming other people for her problems, she took responsibility, quit dating for several years, and focused on doing the necessary work to heal from those problems. As a result of that undertaking, she now sets appropriate boundaries, is much calmer, and makes much healthier choices.

If you're noticing that you are only attracted to and are attracting a certain type of person, and that all your relationships are showing a pattern, it may be time to look at yourself. Because when you think about it, there's only one thing that all those relationships have in common: you.

If there are things about yourself that you've been intending to work on, the time to do it is *before* you get into a relationship, not after. Not for anyone else but for you. Doing the necessary work, whatever that means to you, will give you more confidence and a different type of energy. Also, you wouldn't want to get into a relationship with someone and *then* tell them that you're going to change the person that they were initially attracted to.

We met up with our friend Erika, and she looked totally different than we'd ever seen her before. She'd lost a few pounds, grew her hair a little, and carried herself a lot differently. She was confident and owned her space. The conversation turned to dating. Erika told us, "I haven't been seeing anyone for a while. I'm taking a time-out, going to the gym, walking my dog more, and eating better. I've been intending to do it for years, and now I'm holding myself to it. I initially started all this to attract a different type than I've been seeing, but I've kept going for me. It turns out that I'm actually okay with being by myself for a while, and I feel a lot better."

Although they'd worked on themselves in different areas of their lives, both Erika and Laura felt more confident in themselves. As a result, they both ultimately attracted people who showed up differently from the people that they'd been with before. For Laura, if a little was good, more has always been better, so personal upgrading turned into a lifelong pursuit and has paid huge dividends in all areas of her life.

We all have old patterns that could use a little updating. Yours may not involve therapy or going to the gym; maybe you've been meaning to go to school or pay off some bills. Whatever it is, maybe it's time to take a break and focus on you. Chances are good that you'll not only feel better about yourself but that the people you'll attract when you're ready to start dating again will match your new and improved confidence and energy.

And until the right person comes along, by focusing on yourself you'll be far less inclined to put up with the same old stuff that you may have found yourself dealing with in the past. Because your newly acquired confidence will enable you to get out when you see and feel a predator's hustle coming three blocks away.

The First Date

Whether you're already friends or have just met, there comes a first date: officially, a time with a potential romantic partner. Whether this is a hookup or you're looking for more (we'll assume more for this conversation), this is a key opportunity for you to gather a ton of intelligence on your potential mate, spoken and unspoken. It's also where you'll convey just as much information back to your date. Whether this person realizes it or not, everything on the date is a signal that you should be aware of: location, attire, mannerisms, the works.

Christopher Goffard provides a good example of some first date red flags in the *LA Times* "Dirty John" series:

- **Red flag:** Date doesn't dress for occasion. Their first date was in a nice restaurant, but one dressed for the moment, and one didn't. "Candles flickered along the polished-mahogany bar; jazz drifted from speakers. Debra Newell had taken pains to look good. Her cornsilk-blond hair fell in waves over her shoulders. High black Gucci heels, designer jeans, Chanel bag. Her date, John Meehan, looked a little weathered, and he dressed lazily—shorts and an ill-matching preppy shirt."
- **Red flag:** Inappropriate touching too soon. "John began caressing her back. She thought this was moving a little fast, but she decided to allow it."
- **Red flag:** He wouldn't leave. "She became uncomfortable. It turned into a fight. He just didn't want to leave, and she had to insist."
- **Red flag:** Pushing quickly. "The intensity of his attention was flattering. The next day he called to say he was sorry. He knew

he'd overstepped. He just wanted to spend every minute with her."

And that was just the first time they'd met. By the second or third date, he was telling her he loved her, that he wanted to marry her. By her own admission, Debra had a "bad picker" when it came to relationships. "Where other people saw red flags, she saw a parade."

So attention to details matters. And you should take the opportunity on the critical first date to register every element, not only for a potential partner, but for your personal safety. If even the slightest detail is off or if your safety intuition blinks red, bail. This sounds harsh, but you don't have to settle and you also can't afford mistakes at this point that may become dangerous further into your relationship—especially when it comes to your security, and this includes your long-term safety.

Here are the top twenty things to keep in mind:

1. Location is key. Pick a place that you're familiar with and make sure you know where every exit is, including the back. If your date picks somewhere that you're not familiar with, go to the area ahead of time and check it out. We've both done this ourselves. Go to the same place the first several dates so you get to know the staff.

2. Have confidence and have fun. Dating is a skill, and the only way to develop it is to be self-assured and get out and do it. Having faith in yourself also makes you more fun to be around.

3. Meet them there. We can't stress this enough. No one needs to know where you live right away. Take Uber or Lyft if possible so a potential stalker can't see your license plate.

4. Let a friend know where you are and who you're out with. Send a picture. One guy we know sent bogus pictures to potential dates, then sat in his car to see if the person who showed matched the picture they sent him! If this happens to you, leave immediately. It's not only a mind-game move, it can be really bad if something happens and no one knows what this person looks like.

5. How is your date dressed? Are their clothes appropriate for the location? Are they clean, and does it look like they've at least made an effort to look good for you? We've observed many people out on dates where one person (usually the woman) looks like she spent all day getting ready for the evening, and the other person (almost inevitably a man) appears as though he's just finished doing the yard. That's cool if someone wants to be casual, but they can pull off casual and still look like they spent a minute getting themselves together. To us, the lawn-mower man (or woman) approach indicates a marked lack of respect for the occasion—and for you. Take a page from the "Dirty John" series: If your date can't make the effort to clean themselves up for you, don't go any further. Because it won't get any better.

6. Are they checking out other women in the location for a better opportunity?

7. Notice how they treat the waitstaff. Are they rude, sarcastic, or verbally abusive to them? Or are they polite without flirting with them?

8. Do not leave your drink unattended, even for a minute. If you have to go to the restroom, order a fresh drink when you return.

9. How do they talk to you? Do they talk over you? Is the conversation one-sided?

10. Are they respectful? As we'll discuss in the next section, some people, particularly men, are being coached to dominate the dynamics of the date to show that they themselves can't be dominated. An indication of this can be conversational digs, such as pointing out that you have lipstick on your teeth or complimenting your nails and then asking if they're real. Known as "negs," these backhanded compliments are designed to lower your self-esteem to better manipulate you. This is verbal abuse, and any indication of it should propel you out the door. Immediately. You're being played. No explanation needed. No apologies or excuses accepted.

11. No matter what, do not tolerate disrespect. Whether it's labeled "teasing" or "joke" or "humor," if they disrespect you on the first date, it's just the beginning because they know that you'll put up with it.

12. Do they overshare or interrogate you on your past relationships? This isn't a therapy session on either side, and you really don't care about their hard-knock life, nor do they care about yours at this point. We all have issues and problems, and if someone is leading with all their woes, you're getting a mess, not a date. It's also none of their business what happened in your past relationships, nor any of yours what happened in theirs. If they complain about their "crazy exes," dismiss yourself. Because you can take it to the bank that you are a future crazy ex. They are the one making their exes crazy.

13. Keep the conversation light. You're just checking them out and vice versa. Developing a relationship is a marathon, not a sprint. You're just looking for chemistry and common interests here. Talk about current events, something funny that happened at work or school, or something just as innocuous.

14. Ideally, you should pay for your own meal/event on the first date, and so should they. Not only to eliminate any expectation of quid pro quo (I paid for your dinner or event, so you owe me sex), but to also remove it as a reason for a second date—"You can pay next time"—setting you up for a next time when you may not want to see them again.

15. If you do expect your date to pay, tactfully let them know that ahead of time. Some women do have that expectation, and you don't want it to become awkward if your date didn't anticipate paying. To eliminate this issue altogether, you could go meet in a public place such as a park or just initially go for coffee.

16. Are they a fair tipper? Because the way that they treat money with the waiter is the way that they'll treat it with you later in the relationship.

17. Can they take no for an answer without mocking or demeaning you? If they want to go home with you and you aren't into it, how do they respond?

18. Ensure your ride home ahead of time. You don't want to be stuck in a potentially bad situation waiting for public transportation and leaving yourself exposed to a wolf who has made you uncomfortable.

19. Be clear about your next steps. If the date didn't go as you'd hoped, don't lead them on. Alternately, if you had a good

time, say so and follow it up with a casual comment, such as "Maybe we could do it again sometime."

20. Ultimately, how the date winds up will depend on you. If you want to hook up, hook up, but only if you feel like it. Don't allow yourself to be pressured or think that it's an expectation.

And, finally, if the person seems to be too good to be true, they probably are. Because you may be the potential victim of love bombing.

Love Bombing

Love bombing is a manipulation technique that wolves use to get people to fall in love with them. It's characterized by over-the-top attention, gestures, and gifts early in the relationship to hook you into thinking that "this is the one."

This type of control is insidious enough in and of itself, but the biggest danger of love bombing is that it's the gateway to hell because it is the first step in a pattern of domestic abuse. It's the part that no one understands when they ask, "Why does she stay?"

But no one except people who've been in this situation understands the answer: She stays because she's been love bombed. She fell in love with a wolf and didn't know that it was the bait for the abuse to follow.

Nobody would ever stay in a relationship that is abusive all the time. So the hook that victimizers use to get women to fall in love with them is to sweep them off their feet right from the start. It is the back-and-forth swings of tenderness and abuse that hook and re-hook the victims, like an addiction.

Love bombing is the crack cocaine of domestic violence

relationships. People who have been addicted to crack describe the first rush as the closest to bliss they've ever felt. Crack hits the brain within eight seconds, but the high only lasts for fifteen minutes or so, followed by an intense low. And after the first time, the rush never feels quite the same, so they're trapped chasing that elusive first high as their life spirals out of control. Love bombing is like that first hit of crack.

Initially, they shower you with attention, affection, and gifts. You feel special and validated. This is especially intoxicating if you grew up in an abusive or dysfunctional family or are at a low point in your life. It feels as though someone finally understands you and loves you the way that you've always wanted and deserved.

We'll delve into this vicious cycle more in Chapter 7, but for now, know that the domestic abuse cycle starts right here.

Let that sink in.

All this attention is solely designed for one purpose: to set the hook that will emotionally bind you to the wolf. It's bait to set you up so that you'll tolerate the emotional, mental, and perhaps physical abuse that will follow.

Of course, we all want to be wanted and loved. It feels good! But there is a difference between infatuation and love bombing, and the difference is respect. Respect means that the other person also takes your boundaries into consider-

Love bombing is the gateway to hell, the first step in a pattern of domestic abuse.

ation; disrespect indicates that they are pushing for their own needs before yours. A key indicator of a healthy relationship is consideration for the other person, and that goes both ways. For example, a love bomber will get upset when you try to set limits on them or the relationship in any way. As an illustration, suppose they want to stay with you for the weekend, but you have to study; they'll try to manipulate or mock you or give you the silent treatment.

Within five weeks, Debra and "Dirty John" moved in together in a $6,500/month rental house in Newport Beach, California. She paid for a year in advance and the lease was only in her name. He claimed he had tax problems.

If Debra had used her safety intuition and not rushed into the relationship right away, she may have asked herself the same questions that her daughters did: Why was his wardrobe a mess, with constant baggy shorts and sweatshirts? What kind of doctor (as he claimed to be) had dirty fingernails and didn't have a car? Why weren't they living in the house he claimed to own in Newport Beach, and why had she not seen his other house in Palm Springs?

They were married in less than two months. Debra had been love bombed by a wolf. John claimed to be a doctor, an anesthesiologist who'd just returned from Iraq after a year of volunteering with Doctors Without Borders. He also claimed to have two houses, one in Palm Springs and the other in Newport Beach, California. But the truth was that he wasn't a doctor, he hadn't been in Iraq, hadn't done humanitarian work, nor did he have any houses. Instead, he was released from prison just two days before meeting Debra online.

But like all love bombers, he was charming. "He'd tell me how beautiful I was, ask me about my day, and rub my back," Debra says. "I was infatuated with him."[1]

As we'll discuss in Chapter 7, a lot of seemingly innocuous dating behaviors, like those displayed by Dirty John, are actually points of a web of abuse that is being spun around you. We want you to be able to recognize these patterns so you can escape being ensnared. Figure

6.1 below gives you some examples of love bombing versus a healthy relationship.

Love Bombing	Healthy Relationship
Expensive gifts soon after meeting	Brings flowers to date
Introduces you to kids/family right away	Gets to know you before introducing family
Demands all your time	Understands that you have a life
Pushes for a commitment	Allows relationship to develop
Immature, needs to be saved in some way	Responsible, doesn't require you to save them

Figure 6.1: Love bombing vs. healthy relationship.

And once you're hooked, you'll put up with it because, like crack, you'll always be seeking to get that first rush back—the way that the wolf made you feel in the beginning.

Which is why you need to get out *the instant* you recognize that you're being love bombed. Because the longer you stay, the more difficult it will be to leave.

Dating Sites

Dating sites and apps are a great way to meet people that you'd never meet otherwise. Whether you're looking for true love or just a hookup, someone who meets your criteria is also online looking for the same thing. And two things are on your side online: statistics and artificial intelligence.

But although the gods of odds and algorithms are in your favor, you still need a game plan to sort out the pervs, predators, and wolves. That's all. Just like "all" you have to do to avoid drowning is hold your breath long enough. But don't despair, we can help you with your dating strategy. And you can keep breathing.

The quality and focus of different dating sites vary, and no matter

> **The quality and focus of different dating sites vary, and no matter what your age, faith, sexual orientation, or identity, there's something for you.**

what your age, faith, sexual orientation, or identity, there's something for you. So research the different sites, and see which audience they serve before you give them your credit card. Also, we suggest paying them because, as we've mentioned before, if you're not paying for dinner in the digital world, you're on the menu.

Some sites allow you to run background checks that will help you uncover a potential wolf, scammer, or catfish (impersonator). However, keep in mind that although useful, the checks aren't foolproof, and you should still be wary and follow the advice in this chapter when meeting in real life.

Here are five tools to help you keep yourself safe as you throw your line into the online shark pool.

1. Be honest. Don't put up a picture that doesn't represent you, especially as you are right now. If you've changed your hairstyle or gained/lost a significant amount of weight, don't use the outdated image. Every photo tells a story. Show scenarios of yourself in your everyday life doing the things you like to do. Obviously, the more provocative the picture, the more pervs you'll attract.

2. Be clear about your goals. If you don't like long walks on the beach, don't say so. When Laura had a dating profile, she was

up front about drinking: "If you enjoy drinking on a daily basis, you'll be happier elsewhere." No judgment, no apologies. No confusion about the definition of social drinking.

3. Talk ahead of time. Chatting on the phone, not just texting. Have a real conversation for at least a half hour. Consider it like a job interview. Very few jobs invite you to a real interview without a phone interview first because you can pick up a lot from actually speaking to someone: inflection, age appropriateness, etc. You may not be comfortable on the phone, but this is good practice. Be friendly, but don't be afraid to ask questions: Are you married? Kids? Pets? Throw some friendly banter in among the questions so it doesn't sound like an interrogation.

4. During your conversation, determine if they're H.O.T. Whether or not you find them attractive is up to you, of course. But in this case, H.O.T. means do they have housing, occupation (their own cash flow), and transportation? Because whatever they lack in any of those areas, they're looking for someone else to provide it. And you are looking for a date, not a project. Of course, you should also be H.O.T. yourself.

5. Look your potential date up online, and check their social media before you go out with them. We can't tell you how many violent situations could have been avoided with a simple search. If you can't find them on social, consider it a red flag. The name they gave you may not be their real name or they may be a predator with a record who's changed their name so their past doesn't catch up with them.

But no matter which platform you use, if you experience any type of harassment or violence as a result of using a dating site, report it not only to law enforcement but also to the dating site. Popular applications claim that they have a commitment to user's safety; hold them to it.

Sexual Assault

The issue of sexual assault can be a minefield in dating. For one thing, the definition may be poorly understood and actually varies from state to state (which means that prosecution differs as well, depending on what state you're in).

For another, most girls and women are trained to believe that if they're assaulted, it's somehow their fault. The resulting shame traumatizes and silences them. We're told that that there is *something* in our power that, if it were changed, would magically protect us. If we "dressed differently" or "hadn't had so much to drink" or hadn't been so "sexually active," we wouldn't have been the victim of sexual violence.

This is Monday morning quarterbacking to flip a script: that somehow the victim *caused* her own attack. It's as if the perp isn't a human being with a thought process and a moral code so is therefore absolved of consequences. The victim is perceived as being just *that* powerful—but somehow not powerful enough to prevent the attack that she "brought on herself."

And, as a result of that conditioning, many of us may not even realize that we've been assaulted.

The terms *sexual assault* and *rape* are generally used interchangeably. But sexual assault includes more than rape and is defined by the US Department of Justice as any "nonconsensual sexual act proscribed by law." This could include:

- Attempted rape;

- Fondling or unwanted sexual touching (including groping, kissing, etc.);
- Forcing a victim to perform sexual acts (including oral sex);
- Unwanted sexual penetration (which could include non-body parts or objects);
- Sodomy without consent; and
- Sexual contact with minors, consensual or not.

Keeping those descriptions in mind, consider the following scenarios:

Scenario one: You and your partner are involved in a hot make-out session. You're into it, so it's consensual. Then they push your head downward, indicating that they want oral sex. You say no, but he continues to force you. Although you haven't been attacked by a stranger, you didn't consent. So according to the previous definition, you've been assaulted.

Scenario two: You're at a party and have had a few drinks. You came to the party with some friends. You've always thought that a particular friend is cute, so you flirt a little. Then when you're alone in a secluded spot, your flirty friend finds and surprises you with a kiss. You're buzzed and he's drunk, but you say no, not happening. Then, he forces his hand into your pants. Again, you haven't been attacked by a stranger, but you *have* been assaulted.

Scenario three: You just broke up, and your ex comes over to pick up a few things. You let them in, expecting that they'll grab their toothbrush and whatever and then leave. You turn around to grab a drink from the fridge and suddenly find yourself pinned against the stove. Your ex demands breakup sex. Even though you've had sex with this person before, if they continue *without* your consent this time, it's rape.

Scenario four: You're having sex that you both consented to. But suddenly, things take a bad turn, and now you're getting hurt. Some people who have gotten all their sexual information from violent porn may think this is how it is. When does it go from sex to assault? This happened to a woman in central Florida. They were engaged in consensual sex when he changed gears and assaulted her. Fortunately, she pressed charges, and he was actually tried and convicted of rape.[2] A forensic medical exam showed that she suffered a "violent physical attack."

The key to all these scenarios is your consent. Every time. Every. Single. Time.

You are not obligated, under any situation, to have sexual contact with anyone.

But, as women, we are socialized to feel obligated, sometimes even after the first kiss. Which is why it is so important that you recognize your sexual agency and report sexual assault, which is a felony. Although women tend to be pressured for sex while on a date, it is always your consent or it's rape. The Rape, Abuse and Incest National Network (RAINN) website (https://www.rainn.org/under -standing-consent) provides an excellent resource on understanding consent.

Rape

Although reported cases of sexual assault aren't tracked by the FBI, the violent crime of rape is. Figure 6.2 illustrates a ten-year representative sample of FBI rape statistics.[3]

Rape Victim Demographics

Location Type		Victim's Relationship to the Offender	
Sort By Category		**Sort By Category**	
Residence Home	71%	Acquaintance	25%
Unknown	6%	Relationship Unknown	16%
Highway/Alley/ Street/Sidewalk	4%	Otherwise Known	9%
Hotel/Motel	4%	Boyfriend/Girlfriend	8%
Parking Garage/Lot	2%	Stranger	8%
Total	562,767	Total	581,045

Figure 6.2: FBI rape statistics.

Irrespective of the fact that most rape crimes are not reported to law enforcement, two things become readily apparent with the data that is available:

- The majority of rapes occur in a residence (not in a dark alley);
- Of the known relationship status between victim and offender, the victim is somehow acquainted with the perp, i.e., not a stranger.

Of course, this doesn't mean that "stranger danger" doesn't exist because it certainly does. But it also means that you're not safe just because you are acquainted with someone, or you think that you know them.

Which means that date rape *is* a crime. And as a crime, it should be reported to law enforcement. For more than 12 percent of completed rapes, the victim is on a date with the perpetrator. This is also true of 35 percent of attempted rapes.[4]

Don't let yourself be shamed into silence or tell yourself that it was nothing. In her compelling book *Is Rape a Crime? A Memoir, an Investigation and a Manifesto,* Michelle Bowdler reminds us that it is the least reported criminal offense and that less than 1 percent of rapes are likely to result in conviction. These statistics are abysmal and need to change. Women need to speak up and speak out when they've been victimized. And, obviously, the judicial system desperately requires updating.

If you have been raped, know that it is *not* your fault. Nothing you have done or not done puts this responsibility on you. We implore you not to be one of the silent victims—report it and *press charges.*

Joy has assisted many rape victims and tells us from the other side of the badge what it's like to take such a call:

> *In all the years of working the road as a deputy, I observed that the one call that all men and most women shied away from was a rape call.*
>
> *When I started in law enforcement, I was always interested in catching the bad person, more so if a victim was injured. So my reports were meticulously detailed to assist the detectives with as much information as possible. Deputies gather the initial reports, then the case goes to the detective unit to follow up, gather evidence, and interview potential witnesses. Ultimately, it's up to the district attorney to decide if there's enough evidence to prosecute. I always wanted to ensure that no detail was left out, because you never knew what technicality could make or break a case.*
>
> *But rape calls call for far more than just writing the report. They need to be about ensuring that the victim isn't further traumatized after all they've already endured, because these women have been broken. I have friends and family members who are rape survivors, so I know the toll that it takes.*

Usually, the woman didn't want to speak to a male officer and requested a female. This was not always as easy as it sounds, especially depending on the size of the department and the number of women on the force. And even if women were on the shift, were they working that day? If so, could they break free to rush to the call? Unfortunately, that wasn't always the case, and we had to make do.

Most guys didn't want the call anyway because it was excruciatingly uncomfortable for them to hear such an intimate, horrific story told painstakingly in explicit detail. So, unfortunately, they wanted to get it over with as soon as possible. While I understand their discomfort, in their haste, they were doing the victim a grave disservice by rushing through the interview process. And, sadly, who knows how much evidence could have been overlooked because they just wanted to get it over with?

If a male officer had to handle the incident, they tried to do the best they could, but it was difficult if they weren't able to extract enough information to write a report. Even the few female officers were tired of always being the "go-to" for having to handle these calls. They would look for a volunteer.

I almost always stepped up. I worked in Pompano Beach, Florida, at the time, the third largest city in Broward County. Pompano was busy with crime around the clock, from sunup to sundown, so, sadly, there was no shortage of violent crime victims. It may sound hokey, but chasing down the predators that did such things to these victims kept me going when I wanted to drop.

If I were assigned to the call, I was well aware that it could take hours, if not all of my day because I dedicated whatever time was needed to help the victim begin to process the horrific violence that she'd just endured. This is not to make myself stand out from my colleagues, nor to disparage them. Most of them did the best they could.

In addition to officers going to the crime scenes of assault victims, some victims came into the police department reporting their crime story days or months after it occurred. It may have taken all that time for them to process the violence or to be able to just begin to talk about what had happened.

A lot of times, the victims didn't want the police cars showing up in droves to their house, where the neighbors would ask questions, or they would feel embarrassed. When the victim came into the lobby of the department, there was a small private room where the report would take place. If they wanted to leave, they could just walk out without going through a sea of people.

When I met with the victim, they would usually start their story with "You're probably not going to believe me, but this really happened."

I am a firm believer in prosecuting criminals. I made sure to get that point across to the citizens I served for my entire career. It is a tough sell with most people, but rape victims were the leeriest. They never believed the police would follow up.

I would tell them, "I know it took a lot of courage for you to come in here; I'm here to listen." And however long it took,

I listened. Then I explained the next steps. And the victims always jumped to the key question of whether they should press charges.

This was an entirely different conversation because the judicial system retraumatizes victims of rape. The victim's attire, alcohol level, and sexual history are considered relevant in the courtroom, while the accused perp often sits there and smirks. One of the reasons that the rape conviction rate is so low is that many women can't cope with the thought of being attacked again—this time by the court system.

But it is ultimately up to the victim to decide whether to press charges. And if the victim refuses, the DA drops the charges. Another reason for the abysmal conviction rate for rape.

"One step at a time," I would tell them.

What I heard all the time was that the victim wanted to blame themselves. Hard.

It's difficult to assure them otherwise when sitting across the table at a one-time meeting, but it's worth trying. They need convincing. More like a mantra: You didn't do anything wrong; you didn't do anything wrong; you didn't do anything wrong. It sounds like it should be easy to understand, but a traumatized brain has difficulty processing what just happened. It's something that not everyone can relate to.

What a lot of people don't understand is that victims of sexual assault have had their life upended in one encounter. Choices and decisions were denied. Safety and security trashed. Their trust in people was crushed.

Being aware of this, I tried to be very, very delicate when driving the victim to the sexual assault treatment center.

First, the ride to the facility. It was always important to let the victim of an assault sit in the front seat of the police car. It sounds like no big deal, but no one sat in the front of my car unless they were another cop or a ride-along guest. These victims deserved to be the exception.

Then, I would clear out the front seat and let them know they could unlock the door and open the window whenever they felt like it. The back seat of a squad car doesn't provide such luxuries; the doors and windows are secured for a reason. But these victims weren't criminals who needed to be secured. They needed to know they had their control back. It was important for them to begin to feel in control again, starting right now.

I have taken far, far too many trips like that. And I have seen far, far too many predators walk free because they weren't reported when they began offending, the statute of limitations had run out, or their victims were too terrified to testify.

All the rape statistics you see represent victims who have taken a trip like this. I don't want you to have to ride in the front of a cop car.

Alcohol/Drugs

First of all, we aren't the anti-alcohol/drug brigade. Laura is a recovering alcoholic/addict who quit drinking only because she went through more booze than a Times Square bar on New Year's Eve—in a single night.

So we get it. No judgment.

On the other hand, there's something that we think you should know about alcohol when you're on a date: It turns off your internal burglar alarm. Here's how.

Malcolm Gladwell has an insightful chapter regarding alcohol in *Talking to Strangers: What We Should Know About the People We Don't Know.* He discusses the path of alcohol through our brain without getting into a lot of geekdom. It's pretty interesting, but we'll spare you the details and get right to it. Gladwell writes, "Then it finds its way into the amygdala; your internal alarm system. The amygdala's job is to tell us how to react to the world around us. Are we being threatened? Should we be afraid? Alcohol turns the amygdala down a notch. It turns off your internal burglar alarm."

So, in essence, it disables your safety intuition. One college health service director actually calls alcohol "the most common date-rape drug."[5]

If you're sitting around having a few drinks in your apartment with your friends, who cares? You're safe. But if you've had too many in a bar, even with your friends, you're prey for the wolf.

A friend once pointed out an attractive lesbian wolf in action at a bar. "See that blonde? I've seen her here before. Watch her. She'll approach a group of drunk women and single one out. Then she'll cut her away from the pack with a dance and a drink. Ten to one that she goes home with her."

The friend was right. And once we became aware of it, we've seen it happen countless times.

And if you're on a date with a wolf and your safety intuition is

Alcohol turns off your internal burglar alarm.

disabled, to quote a Whoopi Goldberg line in the old movie *Ghost*, "Molly, you in danger, girl."

Don't Confuse Attraction with Rescuing

Our culture dangerously tells us that women need a good reason to not date someone. It tells us that if we turn down *any* date, we're being "too picky" or our standards are "too high." Worst of all, we can even tell that lie to ourselves.

This message is treacherous for everyone. It indicates that others *have a right* to us, that we are "owned" in some way and that we lack autonomy. As a result, many men (and others) become angry and violent when they hear the word "no" from a woman. They seem to have the attitude that they've gone to the pound to rescue a dog on death row and the animal chooses euthanasia instead.

Also, there are many who believe that it's a woman's job to "rescue" others in some way, whether that rescue mission is in the woman's own best interest or not.

So women are sold two conflicting fallacies: not being in a relationship is such a terrible situation for women that we should be desperate to date anyone in order to "save" us from being alone, and conversely, we also need to save the world, one broken person at a time.

As women, we don't want to leave anyone in peril. We think that we can save everyone and may confuse rescuing with attraction.

Wolves look for sympathetic women who want to take care of them or save them. But the truth of the matter is that no adult can be saved by anyone else. We've all made mistakes, we're all broken in some way. But you aren't the cavalry. Broken people will always be broken in some way until they learn how to repair themselves. No one can "fix" anyone else. We all have to save ourselves.

Let's call those old rules for women "legacy" and retire them. The new rules say: You don't need an excuse *not* to go out with someone. The fact that you just don't want to is reason enough.

Daylight Dawns on the Wolf

It's the lighting that makes it difficult to perceive the wolf, and they take full advantage of that. But in addition to your own safety intuition, there's another way to help you clarify your night vision and see the wolf from a few angles: Ask for feedback from those who care about you and listen to them.

As we mentioned before, real friends could have helped Jackie determine whether or not she should marry a guy who just confessed that he lied, was broke, and homeless. Debra Newell's daughters knew that Dirty John was a wolf. When Debra finally broke up with him, John tried to kill her daughter, who wound up killing him while defending herself.

If your friends and family have warnings for you about someone that you're involved with, start paying attention to their observations. Where you may see a little lost lamb, they may have a different vantage point with better lighting and be able to identify the long, pointed snout of a wolf.

Chapter Seven
Just a Domestic

inda relaxed in the large tiki hut, dreamily listening to the beautiful Papuan woman describe the geography and rich culture of New Guinea. It seemed like paradise.

As she concluded her talk, the woman smiled and asked the small group of vacationers if there were any questions. Linda jokingly responded, "Do you have any questions for us?"

To Linda's surprise, the woman replied, "I do. I have a question for you, since you have traveled the world and have seen many things."

Her smile evaporated as she continued, "My husband is a good man. But he drinks the wine far too much. And on those nights, he beats me until I can no longer feel the beatings. I must ask you, have you ever heard of such a thing anywhere else in the world?"

Paradise lost.

Shocked, Linda wondered to herself why, in a world so interconnected—even in New Guinea—a vulnerable woman could feel so isolated and desperate that she would ask visiting tourists if they'd heard of "such a thing."

But no matter how connected we are by technology, our world ensures that regardless of where they live, every victim of domestic abuse and violence feels exactly the same: that they are the only ones.

Domestic violence, also called intimate partner violence (IPV), involves the physical, sexual, financial, and emotional abuse of one person by another in order to intimidate or frighten. Although, in our experience, the majority of perpetrators are men and most of the victims are women, the dynamic is not isolated to this scenario. It occurs within people of any sexual orientation, gender, class, economic stratum, and even between blood relatives.

Of all the situations threatening women's safety, a relationship of this nature is one of the most dangerous. The reason that it's dangerous (in addition to the physical threat) is that it is deeply misunderstood, even by the victims themselves. Because it isn't "just" violence, it isn't just physical, and it isn't isolated to poor, uneducated people or those in far-off places that some may consider too "foolish" or "weak" to extract themselves from their horrific situations.

The statistics alone are staggering: Before COVID, the United Nations (UN) estimated that 736 million women[1] (30 percent of women ages fifteen or older) have been subjected to physical and/or (IPV), non-partner sexual violence, or both at least once in their life.

However, since the stay-at-home lockdown of the pandemic, the UN reports[2] that violence against women (VAW) is a shadow pandemic. IPV has intensified dramatically.

- Forty-five percent of women reported that they or a woman they know has experienced a form of violence since COVID;
- Sixty-five percent of women reported experiencing it in their lifetime;

- Seven in ten think that verbal or physical abuse by a partner has become more common.

In addition, the *American Journal of Emergency Medicine* said that domestic violence cases increased by 25 to 33 percent during COVID.[3] Domestic violence professionals that we've spoken with indicate that those numbers have not come back down, even as the worst of the pandemic has abated in public life.

The UN states that the global epidemic of VAW is a human rights violation. And, as the UN report[4] indicates, it has devastating immediate and long-term consequences. These horrific stats represent women from all walks of life, all colors, faiths, economic levels, sexual orientation, and every demographic that can be categorized. We believe that these numbers greatly underrepresent the facts because we know of many, many women who have never reported the violence perpetrated against them by a partner.

The global epidemic of violence against women is a human rights violation.

Yet there is little sense of national urgency, let alone global. The US Violence Against Women Act (VAWA) was finally reauthorized in March 2022 after languishing in the Senate while *under control of both parties* since 2019. In addition, the judicial system tends to treat cases of IPV as isolated situations instead of the systemic catastrophe that it is. Law enforcement can only enforce existing laws, no matter how many times they are called, so the issue lies with our existing judicial system. If you'd like to help, please consider contributing to/ or getting involved with your local domestic violence shelter.

But our legislative, judicial, and law enforcement officials may find it challenging to grasp the urgency of VAW because, until quite recently (when considered in the context of human history), it was considered a *family matter*. For years, domestic violence had been considered a "personal" matter handled behind closed doors rather than a criminal justice violation.

The abuser wasn't considered a criminal who would be apt to threaten society at large, and the violence, no matter how severe, was "just a domestic."

Turning Point—The Trial of the Century

Ironically, it took the "trial of the century" late in the 1990s to shine a needed spotlight on the role of the abusive characteristics of IPV and to bring domestic violence out of the shadows. The trial of Orenthal James (O.J.) Simpson unveiled the role of Simpson's abuse and pathological jealousy in the brutal murder of his ex-wife, Nicole Brown Simpson. In fact, prosecutor Marcia Clark's determination to successfully prosecute Simpson was largely driven by her belief that, aside from one arrest, O.J. Simpson's history of domestic abuse allegations had not been adequately investigated by celebrity-struck police officers.

To provide context, in 1994, former pro football player and actor O.J. Simpson was on trial for the stabbing and murder of Nicole and her friend, Ron Goldman. Police records revealed that Simpson beat his wife so badly on January 1, 1989, that she required hospitalization. Brown also reminded police that they'd been called to the residence *eight* times *before* the 1989 incident. As Simpson told responding officers, "The police have been out here eight times before, and now you're going to arrest me for this? This is a family matter. Why do you want to make a big deal out of it when we can handle it?"

However, as Clark notes in her compelling book *Without a Doubt*, prosecutors were originally inclined to put "domestic violence on the back burner for the time being." She said: "I'd handled DV cases before and they were very tricky. Husbands usually do not batter their wives in front of others. If a wife is killed, there is rarely an eyewitness to the murder. Or to the years of abuse that preceded it."

Then, a former boyfriend of Nicole's testified to the grand jury that he witnessed O.J. jealously stalking and harassing his ex-wife. Keith Zlomsowitch briefly dated Nicole after her divorce from O.J. He testified of several incidents where he spotted Simpson stalking Brown and that Simpson had even hidden in the bushes and viewed Brown and Zlomsowitch having sex.

According to Clark, "Zlomsowitch had given us valuable new evidence—including the information about the stalking episodes—of Simpson's behavior as a jealous husband."

Then Brian (Kato) Kaelin testified to the grand jury that he'd witnessed a scuffle between Simpson and Nicole in the fall of 1993. Simpson had smashed "French doors-wood frame splintered, door broken on hinges," the police report noted. Simpson, back out in the guesthouse with Kaelin, was railing angrily, "She's been seeing other guys." Like all abusers, Simpson wanted complete domination and control over his partner. He felt that he, and only he, was entitled to her. And when she was interested in men other than himself, he became as unhinged as the French doors that he splintered.

Although interesting, it still wasn't enough for the DA's office to focus on O.J.'s jealousy and abuse as a factor in the trial.

Until they unexpectedly got a call from Nicole's bank to inform them that Nicole had rented a safe-deposit box. Clark's office sent a couple of investigators down to drill the box and obtain the contents.

Marcia Clark notes, "The contents were more disturbing to me than anything I'd seen to date." She saw what the *Chicago Tribune* described as "a trail leading to the dark and violent side of their marriage." It contained Brown's will, letters of apology from Simpson, and photographs of Nicole's bruised and swollen face.

Clark asks, "Why would a woman keep those things in a lockbox? There was only one explanation. Even as she was trying to break free of O.J., part of Nicole accepted that she would never really escape, that O.J. Simpson might murder her. The message in the box was clear: *In the event of my death, look for this guy.*

Interestingly, it took Brown's safe-deposit box with years of evidence for the prosecution to even begin to consider domestic violence as the motive for her own death. Clark was close, but she still wasn't convinced. "As usual, I hung back. I knew the risks. We were dealing with ambiguous and volatile testimony. It's difficult to convince jurors of either sex, of any race, that spousal abuse is a crime."

Less than three decades ago, the Los Angeles District Attorney's office remarked that it is *difficult to convince a jury that spousal abuse is a crime.* But the evidence provided by the contents of Nicole's safe-deposit box was *finally* compelling enough to convince Clark to feature Simpson's compulsive jealousy as the motive for her murder.

The *Washington Post* reported the opening of the Simpson trial on January 25, 1995: "Prosecutor Christopher Darden offered the motive: the jealousy of an abusive and obsessive ex-husband. 'He killed Nicole for a single reason,' Darden told the court. '. . .He killed because he couldn't have her, and if he couldn't have her, he didn't want anyone else to.'"

Unfortunately, neither evidence of years of abuse nor overwhelming physical evidence was enough to obtain Simpson's conviction.

But, as Rachel Louise Snyder mentions in *No More Bruises*, the tragic fate of Nicole Brown initiated the marked change in attitude regarding how Americans viewed battered women. "For many, Nicole Brown Simpson became the face of a new kind of victim. She was beautiful, wealthy, famous. If it could happen to her, it could happen to anyone."

Many years later, Clark notes in an article in *Vogue* magazine: "To me, one of the big silver linings of the Simpson trial is the advances that we've made in understanding domestic violence as a lethal problem. Before the trial, I think there was a widespread sense that it was a family affair, a normal part of a relationship, not really a crime. The reality is that it's very much a crime, a very serious one. I wanted to mention that: Something good did come from the trial at the end of the day."[5]

But even those who have lived through domestic violence may have become so accustomed to it that they consider it the norm. The mind hack is so insidious that it could even take them over fifty years to recognize it.

Domestic Violence and Domestic Abuse

As we noted in Chapter 6, victims are captivated into domestic abuse relationships by love bombing. They quickly fall in love because their would-be abusers shower them with attention. They're overwhelmed by their partner's intensity and passion, overlooking any red flags they may observe. They believe that the honeymoon will last forever, and then they stay in the relationship despite the abuse, because now they're emotionally hooked and are positive that if they only wait long enough, the romance will resume.

Many who judge the victims for staying don't understand how this can happen. They can't imagine themselves in that situation. Well, neither did the victims.

> **Simply put, in terms of the law, domestic violence often refers to a specific physically violent episode.**

In order to understand, let's first take a look at the difference between domestic violence and domestic abuse.

Simply put, in terms of the law, domestic violence often refers to a specific physically violent episode. One person strikes, assaults, or shoves another. At such an incident, the police are called, the fight is broken up, and somebody goes to jail. At least that's how it's supposed to work.

The point is the violence is physical. There are laws against it, so it can ostensibly be prosecuted. Sometimes, the judicial system will even do something about it.

But it's actually just the tip of the iceberg.

The focus on physical violence is too narrow because it doesn't fully explain the entire dynamic of domestic violence, domestic abuse, and coercive control. Certainly, the violence is horrific, so why do the victims stay? Why didn't Laura's mother, Gert, leave her violent husband, Bill, the moment that he laid a hand on her? Why didn't she ever leave the house? She certainly had opportunity. Bill worked two jobs and was often gone for twelve to fifteen hours at a time. She could have walked out the door at any time.

But she didn't. For many years, she didn't even try.

Imagine how hard it would be to explain her behavior if you were unable to reveal that the woman is confined in a jail cell.

Professor Evan Stark, emeritus professor at Rutgers University and author of *Coercive Control: How Men Entrap Women in Personal Life (Interpersonal Violence)*, further asserts that "the domestic violence field faces a similar predicament when it tries to account for how battered women behave without identifying their 'cage.' . . . Start with the cage and everything changes."

Start with the cage and the puzzle pieces click into place.

Domestic abuse, aka coercive control, is the cage. Coercive control is a pattern of oppressive behavior intended to control someone and strip away their sense of self. It is the emotional and mental control of the abuser over the victim that surrounds the relationship. But the cage and sense of oppressing control is designed to only be seen and felt by the victim. Which is what makes it so insidious and why the outside world doesn't understand what's really going on.

Because only the tip of the iceberg is visible.

Shown in Figure 7.1, coercive control is the huge, dark underbelly of the beast that can't be seen. As opposed to violence, which is visible, physical, and a crime that could be prosecuted, coercive control is invisible emotional and mental control, and unregulated by law in the United States.

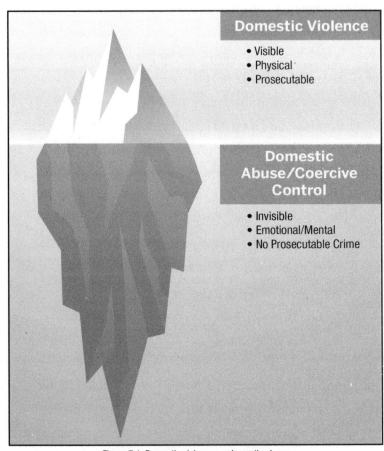

Figure 7.1: Domestic violence vs. domestic abuse.

To be clear, there are many cases of coercive control without vio-lence. Domestic violence adds the component of physical violence to emotional abuse. And although emotional abuse can exist in almost any type of relationship, domestic violence/abuse is almost exclu-sively between intimate partners and/or family members (including parents, siblings, and children).

Domestic violence is often episodic. In other words, something seems to set the abuser off, and often that something may seem inconsequential to the casual observer. But once the abuser is triggered, the victim can guarantee that violent action is imminent. Strangulation, beating, kicking, stabbing, etc., all constitute domestic violence. And once domestic violence has begun, it will never, ever stop. The abuser knows that if they can get away with it once, they'll be able to again. And again, and again.

Remember the escalation of the criminal in Chapter 3? The same applies to domestic abusers. The violence escalates, thinking that they'll never get caught and can treat their partner as property with impunity. That is why once a violent incident occurs, it is so imperative for the victim to leave the relationship permanently and immediately *if they're able to.*

Ironically, crimes perpetuated against family members are harder to punish than if they were committed against total strangers. If someone randomly just walked up to you and attempted to strangle, kill, or rape you, it would be a fairly straightforward process to press charges. Not so the case if the perpetrator and victim have a relationship or are related to each other.

Domestic violence often goes hand in hand with coercive control, layering yet another level of terror. Coercive control is the total and systematic psychological and physical domination and control of the victim. We'll discuss coercive control at length, but for now, consider domestic violence as the battle and domestic abuse as the war.

Joy was often called for domestic violence incidents, but the courts rarely recognize, let alone punish, systematized coercive control. This is akin to focusing on a bike thief in your area when there's an arsonist on the loose. In fact, it's even worse because although there are laws against arson, the American judicial system and even American society barely recognize coercive control. There are currently no laws against it. And if there are no laws, there are no charges and no punishment.

But before getting into that, let's take a look at how coercive control systemically creates women who don't leave, why they aren't weak, and how their behavior mimics that of a surprising group— American soldiers who were held as prisoners of war (POWs) in North Korea during the Korean War.

The Puzzle

In a world that seems to grow more accustomed to violent movies, cartoons, video games, porn, and news every day, domestic violence still causes most people to close their eyes or look away. Some of the actual victims are unable to consider it, even to themselves.

In her TED Talk, Leslie Morgan Steiner, a former *Washington Post* executive with two degrees from Ivy League colleges, noted that when she was married to her abusive ex-husband, she didn't see herself as being abused. Instead, she viewed herself as a strong woman in love with a troubled man and that she was the only one who could help him.[6]

Ironically, the world stigmatizes abuse victims far worse than their abusers. And because of that stigma, many victims ignore their instincts or safety intuition about the true danger of the situation. They may believe that they are crazy for thinking that what is being done to them is abusive. Or they often adjust to the situation—which can be deadly. Abuse is a rapid corrosive, and by the time they come to the realization or admit it, their self-worth may be so deteriorated and depleted that they don't have the energy to escape.

The trap rusts shut.

It took Laura's mother, Gert, almost twenty years to leave her violent husband. Laura's dad, Bill, was a product of generational domestic abuse, who then became a victimizer himself. Gert kept the family violence so secret that when she showed up at her sister Kay's house to announce that she was "leaving the bastard," Kay was stunned. So shocked that she involuntarily blurted, "You're leaving *who*?"

To the outside world, the family was perfect for many years. Bill was clean-cut and usually had two jobs, but money was always tight. The kids always had new Easter outfits, shoes, and the fresh home-made haircut that Gert specialized in to save money. But they seemed happy enough. There was Bill's continual sarcasm and "playful" put-downs of his wife, but she didn't seem to mind, so neither did anyone else. Everyone knew they loved each other.

They'd had a whirlwind romance, and Bill had swept her off her feet. She'd do anything for him.

Laura's Aunt Kay often told the story of an incident that occurred when Gert and Bill were dating, and Bill needed a pillow. He had just gotten out of the Army and had nowhere to go, so he was sleeping on his sister's couch. Bill called Gert at 1:00 AM one night and told her that he couldn't sleep without a pillow. So she walked nine miles that bitterly cold winter night to bring him one from her parents' house.

But whenever Kay told the pillow story, she inevitably ended with, "She had such a good heart then."

As time went on, Aunt Kay retold the story quite often. She seemed to enjoy the telling as though it brought her back to a time when her sister seemed "normal." To a time when Gert was a "nice" girl. A time when she was so kind that she was unable to sleep herself if someone she loved couldn't rest and she could find a way to allevi-ate their discomfort.

But that nice girl wasn't the mother that Laura knew. The mom that Laura grew up with appeared to be mentally ill. It wasn't an official diagnosis, but Gert's violence and cruelty simply could not be explained in any other way. What could have happened to change someone from a kind young woman with a good heart to someone that was so cruel and violent that her children dreamed of murdering her?

Laura could accept her dad's rampages. After all, his whole family was like that. Just like his father and brothers, he was barbarically violent. And also like them, his violence was primarily directed at his wife, although the kids certainly didn't get off scot-free. As his alcoholism progressed, so did the frequency and intensity of his violence. What may have been a slap early in the relationship became a blow to the head a few years later. But never, never in the face—which actually demonstrated that he wasn't out of control; he knew exactly what he was doing. Initially, Laura and her siblings only heard the horrific onslaughts on Saturday nights when Bill got paid and the beer flowed freely. But as time went on, the incidents happened more and more frequently.

But her mother's cruelty went a step further, bordering on sadism. Inventing cruel "pranks" on her children and pets for no other seeming reason than a source of amusement. Her kids could be walking down the street on their way home from school to see their favorite stuffed animals swinging from homemade gallows on the outside of the house. Gert had plenty of time on her hands to concoct ways to terrify her kids as she rarely left the house.

The cruel family jokes that Gert played on her children seemed, in an odd way, to cheer her up. So much so that it could be difficult to characterize her demeanor as that of a battered woman. She could be social in her way, enjoying long hours on the phone with high school friends and family. She would pace back and forth in the dining room for entire afternoons with phone and cigarettes in hand, stretching the long phone cord as far it would go before turning around to retrace her steps. There were also occasional family dinners at the homes of a few relatives but never venturing outside the doors of her house without her husband, not even to the grocery store. Laura and her siblings were tasked with family shopping, a list, and cash fastened to their pocket with a paper clip.

It would be a long time before Laura realized how isolating her mother's situation actually was.

Gert had other odd habits as well. Her choice of clothing, for example. She seemed to have a daily uniform, consisting of sweatshirts and baggy jeans, even in the summer. Laura and her sisters often made fun of her apparent lack of interest in her appearance. They wondered to each other, "Would it kill her to wear a little lipstick?"

Laura would come to understand why her mother chose that particular look.

Over the years, Gert's behavior grew increasingly bizarre, even after she'd left her alcoholic and violent husband. She'd have seven or eight beers and then call family friends late at night, railing about perceived injustices done to her by her parents and sister. None of it was true, and none of it made any sense.

As an adult, when Laura related her childhood experiences of her mother's violent episodes to her aunt and grandmother, who were clueless about them till that point, their inevitable response was, "She wasn't always like this." Aunt Kay would then recite the pillow story, always ending with the "She had such a good heart then" comment. The two statements were bookends. A reminder to all who heard it that Laura's mother had mysteriously changed in some way, and they'd be damned if they knew how.

It was a puzzle. But some of the pieces were missing, and no one knew where to even begin looking.

The mystery endured for decades, long after the main characters had passed away, for over half a century to be specific. Then just a few years ago, as Laura idly sat drinking coffee one day, her aunt's "good heart" statement seemed to surface out of nowhere. And, for perhaps the millionth time, Laura once again considered the long-unanswered question of her mother's behavior.

"What could have happened?"

But this time, she was struck by a strange thought.

"Could it have been the violence?" Then, almost reflexively, she countered her own thinking: "Well, that's stupid. Who in the hell can't take a beating?"

Who in the hell can't take a beating?

Decades later, her mother's puzzle pieces *clicked* into place. Laura sat frozen in the chair as full understanding of her family rushed in after all that time.

It would take more months for Laura to realize that her mother's increasingly bizarre behavior may not have been the result of some mysterious mental illness. More probably, it was connected with traumatic brain injury (TBI), brought about by the frequent head trauma of her father's violence. Recent research by the US National Institutes of Health (NIH) demonstrates that "TBI and domestic violence function as risk factors for each other. Those who receive TBI from domestic abuse and do not receive treatment often suffer from cognitive dysfunction, memory loss, and mood irregularities."[7] Now Gert's odd clothing choices also finally made sense: the long sleeves and baggy pants could cover any bruising.

But let's also look at her behavior in a different context; in a scenario described by Evan Stark in *Coercive Control: How Men Entrap Women in Personal Life (Interpersonal Violence):* "A woman wears the same outfit every day, rarely goes out, and continually paces back and forth in a small space. *Imagine how hard it would be to explain her behavior if you were unable to reveal that the woman is confined in a jail cell.*"

It took Laura *fifty* years to recognize the homemade jail cell and the role of domestic violence and abuse as the cause of her mother's bizarre behavior and mental illness. The answer was hiding in plain sight.

When Laura did finally make the connection, she was stunned at the realization. Abuse was so pervasive in her family that she had taken it for granted.

The violence was just so *ordinary*.

Domestic Violence Calls and the Police

A domestic violence call is one of the most dangerous that police encounter. It is one of the few that require more than one officer on-scene, and it is always a priority, not only because the situation can be so volatile, but also because there may be weapons involved.

It is also the type of call that they receive the most.

Joy encountered numerous domestic violence victims who called the police during an incident. They were so angry at the offender that they screamed at Joy, "Take him to jail!" Some women were injured more or less than others. But for the most part, they yelled, "Get out and stay away!" Then they happily signed the prosecution affidavit for their partner to be prosecuted.

But there were too many times to count when those victims then jumped into their car and raced Joy down to the jail, sometimes arriving before the squad car. What would possibly impel the victim to rush to the jail after their abuser had just been arrested? To watch them get booked?

No. To pay the bond, releasing their abuser.

They would loudly insist to Joy that they changed their mind and were no longer pressing charges, ensuring that their conversation could be heard by the person in handcuffs. This seemingly puzzling situation has a simple explanation: Once the immediate danger was over, the victim knew what would happen when the perp was released from jail. And the next time, it could be worse.

As a result of these situations, the laws in many states have changed. Sixteen states and the District of Columbia have mandatory arrest laws for domestic violence: Alaska, Arizona, Colorado, Connecticut, Kansas, Louisiana, Maine, Mississippi, Nevada, New Jersey, Ohio, Oregon, Rhode Island, South Dakota, Utah, and Washington.[8] This means that law enforcement is required to remove one of the partners in a domestic dispute and take them to jail.

Some state laws also read that the defendant now must first see a judge before they're released, a process that may take anywhere from twenty-four to seventy-two hours, depending on when the incident occurs—it could be longer over a weekend.

In other words, the abuser can't just bond out and leave; there's a mandatory cooling-off period. Having to see a judge helps to keep violent offenders confined longer. And in many cases, it enables the victim the breathing room they need, hopefully to make plans to leave.

In other states, law enforcement officials may make an arrest if there is probable cause that domestic violence occurred. Officers will evaluate each party's accusations separately and are discouraged from arresting more than one party—only the primary aggressor.

Domestic Abuse Victims and Korean War POWs

During the Korean War, almost *75 percent* of the 7,200 American prisoners of war (POWs) who were shot down over North Korea falsely confessed to using germ warfare against the Koreans, and they also broadcast propaganda over Korean radio. And after the war, twenty-one of those POWs immediately defected to Communist China *instead of coming home.* Now, most of these were elite pilots. They were men of intelligence and strong character. What type of torture could the communists have developed to break our best warriors? This seemingly traitorous behavior had never been seen before in the US military, which was what made it so surprising and alarming.

After the Korean War ended, during the 1957 Symposium on Communist Brainwashing to explain the bizarre behavior change of the POWs, Dr. Harold Wolf noted that the "communists are skilled in the extraction of information from prisoners and in making prisoners do their bidding. It does appear as though *they can force men to confess to crimes which they have not committed, then apparently to believe in the truth of their confessions and to express sympathy and gratitude toward those who have imprisoned them.*"[9]

As anyone would expect, this phenomenon alarmed US military and intelligence experts and was the subject of much speculation for years after the war. It was *so* puzzling that the analysists and psychologists concluded that the communists must have developed a method of mind control, so they coined a new term: *brainwashing.*

Defined by *Encyclopedia Britannica*, brainwashing is "any technique designed to manipulate human thought or action against the desire, will, or knowledge of the individual. By controlling the physical and social environment, an attempt is made to destroy loyalties to any unfavorable groups or individuals, to demonstrate to the individual that his attitudes and patterns of thinking are incorrect and must be changed, and to develop loyalty and unquestioning obedience to the ruling party."[10]

The Chinese communists running the POW camps in North Korea weren't like the Germans or Japanese in WWII or the Germans in WWI who basically held American soldiers in work camps (albeit still in horrific conditions). The Chinese wanted total control over prisoners' hearts and minds, similar to the reeducation camps being implemented by Mao in China.

After listening to experts who interviewed the returned pilots about their experiences in the POW camps, the symposium panel concluded that POW brainwashing was accomplished not by brute force as in prior wars, or by hypnosis, exotic drugs, or any other mysterious brain damaging procedures as they had expected to find. Instead, the prisoners had been persuaded. And this persuasion was accomplished in large effect by a surprising method: isolation.

The Effects of Isolation in Breaking American POWs

It is worth noting how powerful the effects of isolation were on the American POWs. In the symposium, Air Force psychologist Albert Biderman, who interviewed the returned soldiers, described the process.

> He would typically be isolated, isolated in a small cell where he has no furniture except perhaps a cot and a slop jar, no view

outside, and absolutely nothing to do. Quite alone, no contacts with the guards allowed, no outside contact of any sort, in fact, nothing told what will happen to him, but knowing very well that anything can happen to him, and that he has no real recourse from it. He can be deprived of sleep by being forced to sleep in a rigid position, being awakened whenever he goes to sleep. The temperature of his cell can be changed. His food can be cut down. He can be required to stand or sit in a regular position. All this acting over a period of time is extremely uncomfortable and produces gradually increasing states of fatigue, loss of discrimination, and indeed, if all of these physiological disturbances are continued [inaudible] with the deprivation of sleep, the unusual position, and the disorganizing in most of the reactions going on steadily, one finds often that in a period of somewhere between three to six weeks the prisoner has approached a point that is very near to a delirious state. That is to say he is dull, he lacks discrimination, he may lose orientation for time and place, his recent memory is impaired.

If this goes along far enough, he may hallucinate. He reaches a stage in which he will confabulate sometimes. All of this in an effect of fear and above all an intense feeling of loneliness and despair, an intense wondering about what will happen to me, and an intense need for someone to talk to.

Now, into this, steps the interrogator.

Now the first thing the interrogator does is exploit the need of the prisoner to talk because here is a man that has come near to the end of his rope.

And the prisoner, regardless of how he may dread the interrogation, is usually glad to talk to his interrogator and since the first interrogations are usually concerned with gathering further background or biographical material about the prisoner, he usually finds this talk going rather freely. As the talk continues, and if the interrogation is going on at night and at unusual times, the prisoner further deprived of sleep, the tales, the sharing between these two, and the life experiences of the prisoner, and the needs of the prisoner for someone to relate to, builds up often quite a close relationship between the two.[11]

Biderman was so painstaking in detailing the POW experience because he wanted his audience, medical doctors, to be able to feel how the captured soldier felt. He wanted them to emotionally feel a soldier's isolated confusion because their medical training hadn't prepared them in an intellectual sense for what was, at that time, a national scandal: the scandal of American POWs who seemed to have lost their minds. The doctors were at the symposium specifically because they found it hard to understand how the North Koreans were able to get the American soldiers to do their bidding, confess to crimes they didn't commit, and express gratitude toward the sworn enemies of America. All within a very short window of time.

It seems straightforward to look back from the vantage point of history and to see how the North Koreans used coercive control on the Americans. But it is clear now precisely because Biderman, based on his interviews with the returned POWs, was able to see how they had been coerced. In other words, he reverse engineered the coercion process.

Isolation and the CIA's Secret
Mind Control Program

As a result of the speed that POWs' brainwashing occurred, the US Central Intelligence Agency (CIA) was convinced that the communists had developed a secret mind control drug.[12] So the CIA began researching their own mind control methods, obsessed with developing their own methodology of erasing a person's personality and inserting one that allowed the CIA to control their beliefs. Dr. Sidney Gottlieb, head of the CIA's technical services, was convinced that the drug LSD was the magic potion that would enable them to do so. The CIA gave his secret project, MK-ULTRA, basically a blank check, enabling him to secretly buy up the entire world's supply of LSD in 1953 and experiment with it on unknowing victims.[13] But after spending unsupervised millions of dollars and destroying thousands of lives of unwitting and often unwilling victims, the CIA concluded in the early 1960s that they could not achieve the mind control state with their nefarious experiments with LSD.

Instead, CIA psychologist John Gittinger later concluded, "By 1962, it was at least proven to my satisfaction that 'brainwashing,' so-called—as some kind of esoteric device where drugs or mind-altering conditions and so forth were used—did not exist. . . . By then, the general idea that we were able to come up with is that 'brainwashing' was largely the process of *isolating a human being*, keeping him out of contact, putting him under long stress in relationship to interrogating and interviewing—that they could produce any change that way, without having to resort to any kind of esoteric means."[14]

The massive amount of expense and effort that the CIA put into victim influencing and the resulting conclusion of isolation on a human being has a direct effect on understanding victims of domestic abuse.

Power and Control Wheel

As a result of his interviews with the POWs and study of the isolation methodology that coerced them to confess to crimes they couldn't possibly have committed, Dr. Biderman developed a methodology that described the brainwashing technique used by the communists. In his testimony to the symposium, Biderman surprisingly stated that inflicting physical pain was not necessary to "induce compliance"; they only had to make the victims believe that the captors were capable of it, and psychological manipulations were extremely effective for that purpose.[15]

Remember, not all instances of coercive control involve domestic violence.

Biderman established that three primary elements were at the heart of coercive control: dependency, debility, and dread. To achieve these effects, the Koreans used a number of techniques.

His conclusions resulted in what has come to be known as "Biderman's Chart of Coercion."[16] In his chart, Biderman summarized eight mechanisms that the communists implemented for brainwashing the American POWs.

The eight mechanisms are:

- Isolation;
- Monopolization of perception;
- Induced debilitation and exhaustion;
- Threats;
- Occasional indulgences;
- Demonstrating omnipotence;

- Degradation; and
- Enforcing trivial demands.

These same techniques are used by domestic abusers to control their victims.

As investigative journalist Jess Hill notes in *See What You Made Me Do*, the only difference between abusers is that the North Koreans deployed these techniques tactically while abusive husbands and partners seem to replicate the system unconsciously.

In other words, the methods and techniques that are used on the abused women who are hardwired to love their partners are the *same techniques that broke trained soldiers.* The National Network to End Domestic Violence provides a chart that compares Biderman's Chart of Coercion to the methods of power and control used in domestic abuse.[17] It's important to emphasize that, at its core, domestic abuse is all about domination, power, and control. Biderman pointed out that not all eight elements need to be present for brainwashing to occur.[18] Each element in and of itself has some power to distort the victim's reality, interfere with perception, reduce a person's self-confidence, and extract compliance. These are the same techniques that broke America's best warriors in a matter of six to twelve weeks, made them confess to crimes they didn't commit, and caused twenty-one of those soldiers to immediately defect to the enemy after the war.

These are also the same methods that were passed down from generation to generation in Laura's father's family. The same methods that broke Laura's mother.

These same principles of power and control in intimate relationships were independently reflected in the Power and Control Wheel (Duluth Model) shown in Figure 7.2 on the next page.[19]

Figure 7.2: Duluth Model, or Power and Control Wheel.

The Duluth Model of Power and Control (aka Power and Control Wheel) was conceived and implemented in a small working-class city in 1980–81.[20] It was developed out of the experiences of over two hundred battered women who attended support and educational groups in Duluth, Minnesota.

The Duluth Model not only describes tactics used by abusers, it also engages legal systems and human service agencies to create a distinctive form of organized public responses to domestic violence. It is characterized by:

- Clearly identifiable and largely shared assumptions and

theories about the source of battering and the effective means to deter it;

- Empirically tested intervention strategies that build safety and accountability into all elements of the infrastructure of processing cases of violence; and
- Well-defined methods of inter-agency cooperation guided by advocacy programs.

In other words, separate studies of two very different populations concluded that similar tactics are used to dominate and control.

Yet we *dare* to call the victims, these domestic POWs, weak and castigate them because they don't leave.

But although the Koreans POWs were captured against their will and held in the camps in North Korea, domestic POWs are lured with their full consent, and when they finally realize what is happening, they are in love with their captor and the leaving isn't quite that easy.

The captured POWs weren't in love; they knew they were at war.

Are You in Love at War?

Are you like Laura and her mother, not recognizing the signs of an abuse victim?

If you are or have been in an abusive situation, we are hopeful that you are beginning to see that you are *not* weak. You are brave, strong, and independent. But you were captured. Like the soldiers were captured.

But like Laura's mother, you may not know that you are a POW. If you are in this situation, you aren't weak. Love doesn't make us weak; it makes us vulnerable. And vulnerability isn't a fault, it actually takes someone with extraordinary courage to be vulnerable.

But your vulnerability, your superpower, has been used against you.

We hope that this is the first step in a journey of compassion for yourself. That you can begin to love yourself enough to know that you don't deserve this.

Love yourself enough to know that you don't deserve this.

No one deserves this.

The first step in recovery is admission that you are in a situation. To admit, even just to yourself at first: I have been abused. The reason that you have to admit this to yourself is to break through the denial. No one can make you do it, and no one can do it for you. But nothing further can happen to help you heal until those walls of denial begin to crack. Even if it's a hairline crack. Even a dam cannot withstand the power of a hairline crack. Neither can the dam of denial.

Can you dare to say it out loud? Can you confront the demon with your own voice? Even if you say it quietly in the shower?

But also know that the journey out, *if* you decide to get out, is also fraught with danger. The decision to stay or to go is yours, and yours alone. If you decide to leave, please enlist help. You must make the decision alone, but that is the only "alone" part. None of us could flee or recover on our own. It takes a community.

Find *your* community.

But if you believe that the odds are against you, we can tell you from experience that *the odds only matter if you're playing the odds.*

Since leaving an abusive situation is so difficult, mired in mental, emotional, physical, economic, legal, and even political entanglements, what are the solutions before it even begins? We believe that awareness and education are key and that the best defense in this situation is an enlightened offense.

We also feel that the attitudes of women, particularly younger women, are slowly changing. Some women are no longer willing to sacrifice themselves on the altar of society's judgment and accept that they are somehow flawed if they are without a partner to complete them at all times. This attitude is a powerful defense against the chronic shaming of women in this regard.

Biderman also noted in the symposium that informing the soldiers of the practices that were used on them "made them considerably more anxious. However, if you can accept the statements of the returnees that had they only known what it was that they were to encounter at the start, they would have been more than able to cope with what occurred. Accepting these statements, *we feel a considerable confidence that to be forewarned is to be forearmed* in this instance."

The military POWs indicated to Dr. Biderman that they could have changed the outcome of brainwashing if they had known what they were up against early in the game.[21] We believe the same holds true of domestic POWs.

We believe that women who are armed with the knowledge of early warning signs of a domestic abuser can recognize these patterns of domination, power, and control.

We also feel a *considerable confidence that to be forewarned is to be forearmed in this instance.*

Chapter Eight

Financial Security Is Key to Your Safety

L aura sadly gazed down at her grandmother, Mimi, in the casket, finally at peace. Laura's aunt came up beside her and said sarcastically, "She didn't die, she escaped."

Aunt Carol's comment was spot-on. Laura glanced over at her aunt and said, "I never quite thought of it that way, but you're right."

Aunt Carol was referring to Mimi's husband, Laura's grandfather.

Mimi was one of the few people in the family whom Laura could count on during her turbulent childhood. And it turned out that Mimi had her own turmoil to deal with as there were family whispers of domestic violence and rape at the hands of Laura's grandfather. Laura struggled to reconcile the rumors with the idyllic image she held of the grandfather who had been so kind to her. But looking back, she recognized the flashes of violence in him. In those days, she didn't realize that one person could harbor both Jekyll and Hyde personalities and that one could cover for the other.

Mimi claimed that she couldn't leave him because if she divorced, the church would no longer allow her to receive Holy Communion. But the truth was that Mimi couldn't afford to flee because, although she'd worked for the last half century and still managed a fabric store into her seventies, her tightfisted husband controlled the checkbook. As a result, Mimi was often in poor health throughout her life but was rarely able to seek medical care due to the "cost." By the time her cancer was diagnosed, it was too late for treatment.

Of the same generation, but on the other side of the financial spectrum, Joy's grandparent's had equal access to their financial resources. If she had needed to, Joy's grandmother could have afforded to escape because she'd ensured access to her own funds. In a different time and place, Joy leaned forward on her Gram's comfortable sofa. Joy had approached her grandmother for a car loan and awaited the verdict. Gram left the room and returned with an armful of tubes. She carefully lined the cylinders up in the dining room and extracted flip charts full of numbers, which she carefully laid out on the table. In the days before spreadsheets, Joy's grandparents had devised their own system of keeping track of their investments, but her grandmother didn't require her husband's permission to give Joy a loan. Gram scrutinized the detailed graphs with the focus of a mariner analyzing a nautical chart before a hurricane. "All right. I can lend you the money at the end of next month. And because you've paid me back on time before, I won't charge you interest."

Financial security is literally a matter of life or death.

Money = Choices and Control

Money is important not only to buy what we need to live but also because it provides us with the ability to have choices.

Money also equals control. You've heard the golden rule of finances: They who have the gold, make the rules. Most importantly for women, it equals dominion over our own lives, which we've lacked since the dawn of time. Lack of economic resources meant that, like Mimi, many women have had very limited ability to control their most basic living factors: choice of housing, partner, if/when we'll have children, and whether we can leave a dangerous partner. And if we have no control over those important components of life, the limited choices we do have can put us in desperate situations.

So financial security is key to long-term safety. Although that's always been the case, it wasn't actually possible until more recently than you may think. Mimi and the generations of women before her lacked the ability to control their own lives because society literally blocked access to the most important fundamentals that enable independence: money and family planning. Women couldn't even open bank accounts until the 1960s,[1] single women were denied birth control prescriptions until 1972,[2] and men had to cosign for women's credit cards until 1974 because financial institutions considered women to be "financially risky."[3]

As a woman of her age, Mimi wasn't used to having access to funds, whereas as Gram was more financially astute and ensured that she wasn't cut out of what was rightfully hers. Women and money have long had a complicated relationship, primarily because we'd been separated for so long.

Don't You Worry Your Pretty Little Head

Up until the early part of the twentieth century, women were doomed to low-paying jobs if they could manage to get paid at all, confined to domestic servitude or textile mills, making pittance wages. This meant that aside from a few famous cosmetic and hair care business icons, such as Helena Rubenstein, Madam C. J. Walker, and Elizabeth Arden, there were few opportunities for women to move ahead economically unless they "married well." And for the Black, indigenous, and other minority communities, oppressive racism limited even that option and doomed entire families and generations to abject poverty.

Women were discouraged from even considering their own finances. Instead, like domesticated animals, they were to rely on their husbands and fathers to care for (and control) them. The prevailing and condescending attitude was that money matters were just too much for the female brain: "Don't worry your pretty little head" about financial matters; a man will take care of it for you. This perspective gave women little ability to determine the course of their lives, not unlike the family dog.

All that changed on a global basis with World War I. While men fought in the war, women on both sides were recruited into the war machine on the back end, making munitions, serving as nurses for the war wounded, and filling the jobs that the men had left back home.

And at the end of the Great War, after that taste of freedom, women refused to be re-harnessed back into their domestic subjugation.

Then when World War II broke out, men were drafted back to the killing fields—and women to the factories. During the war, six million women took wartime jobs in factories, three million volunteered with the Red Cross, and over 200,000 served in the military.[4] The federal government even provided funding for childcare so that more women could work outside the home to support the war effort. Although women were paid at lower wages than men for the same jobs, a factor that still exists in some places today, women finally got our own paychecks and began to determine our own lives.

So up until that era, women literally *had* to be in a hurry to get married. There were few other employment options, leading to desperation to grab the first eligible bachelor to come along. Lest women drag their feet into marital servitude, society had a few choice monikers to shame them along—"old maid" or "spinster"—as being an unmarried woman was considered a fate worse than death.

And as Laura learned from Mimi, if getting paid can be the first step to financial security, it isn't the last. Because not only do many women not consider the long-term safety ramifications of wealth and debt, but society still tries to control where and how we spend our hard-earned cash.

Consider the toll that being female exacts on our wallet.

Invisible Taxes of Being Female

In addition to, in some instances, being paid on a different scale than men, society also taxes women in a lot of different ways that we're so accustomed to that we never stop to think about them. Called the "pink tax,"[5] it usually refers to similar products marketed toward women that are more expensive than those geared toward men. However, we note that it should also include the additional cost of goods and services that society demands only from women, particularly mothers, which we'll call the million dollar pink tax.

For example, although the following items and services may be optional for men, most are expected of women. And, of course, a lower income doesn't mean that you're exempt from these expectations (and associated expenses).

And these don't include additional import tax or tariffs on women's clothing,[6] triple the price for women's dry cleaning (three times the cost for same type of garment),[7] etc. Although some of these items may not appear to be expensive or a big deal at first glance (looking at you, period products and housework), like a daily cup of take-out coffee, it adds up over a lifetime. There's also the "grooming gap" for women, which means that if you don't conform to societal expectations, you'll get paid less, not including the loss of free time daily to do hair/makeup/etc., the equivalent of two full weeks per year.[8]

Housework in particular is massively devalued. It needs to be done, and even if one partner pitches in, the job of planning, organizing, and ensuring that it's all done usually falls on the other partner. Housework is so undervalued that it should be considered within the national gross domestic product (GDP). The US Bureau of Economic Analysis makes a weak attempt at explaining why it only started surveying household time tracking in 2003: because there are no "transactions to track."[9]

However, an academic assessment of these transactions has been available since the 1930s when the statistics for the GDP were first formulated by Simon Kuznets of the National Bureau of Economic Research (NBER). When reporting to Congress, Kuznets noted that he specifically omitted domestic labor because "no reliable basis is available for estimating their value."[10]

But Claudia Goldin, Henry Lee Professor of Economics at Harvard University, in *Career and Family: Women's Century-Long Journey toward Equity*, notes a 1934 PhD study that attempted to quantify the value of unpaid work in the household. It was available to Kuznets, but he ultimately chose to omit it from his calculations.

Goldin notes that "the effect is staggering, a full 20% of the GNP." The GNP is the total market value of the final goods and services produced by a nation's economy during a specific period of time (usually a year).[11] The US GNP at the end of 2022 was almost $27 trillion.[12] Twenty percent of that is over $5 trillion—a year.

We mention all this so that you can have an awareness and start to take hold of your financial health and to manage these expenses in time and in money where you can. This is also some recent research over the past several years that may have an impact on you: children and clothes.

Economic Equivalent of Being Hit by a Meteorite

When many people acknowledge the gender wage gap (if they think of it at all), they only consider the aspect that women, on average, tend to be paid less than men. This is reflected by 2020 US Department of Labor statistics: "All women were paid, on average, 83% of what men were paid. But many women of color were paid even less. Black women were paid 64% and Hispanic women were paid 57% of what white, non-Hispanic men were paid."[13]

The Department of Labor notes that efforts to close the wage gap must address multiple factors that drive down women's pay: discrimination, occupational and industrial segregation, and more. But not addressed within those statistics is the cost of children.

In *Of Boys and Men: Why the Modern Male Is Struggling, Why It Matters and What to Do About It*, Richard Reeves (senior fellow of Economic Studies at the Brookings Institution) gets straight to the point: "For most women, having a child is the economic equivalent of being hit by a meteorite. For most men, it barely makes a dent."

This is despite unprecedented increases in women's education levels and the desire for the current generation to have both career and family. The good news is that for women who want both career and family, for the first time in history it is more possible than ever before. For those who do, their education and family planning are key.

> **The good news is that for women who want both career and family, for the first time in history it is more possible than ever before.**

Goldin's *Career and Family* gets to the core of the issue for this generation of women: "If a woman's career has a chance to flourish and she manages to have children, the ultimate time conflict emerges. Children require time; careers require time."

The only thing we can't create is more time.

An economic historian and labor economist, Goldin goes on to detail how many couples negotiate this puzzle, a negotiation that, because of still-existing ancient work and family care structures, can still leave women at the short end of the financial stick. And although many domestic and childcare tasks can be outsourced and who knows what artificial intelligence will someday bring to the equation, only so much of that can be done without impacting your relationship with your children. Otherwise, why have them?

Goldin also notes the timing of pregnancy in a woman's life: "When women become pregnant soon after college, they are less likely to continue with their schooling. Careers may be put on hold. The opposite occurs when a pregnancy can be delayed. Goldin also notes that employment has increased almost steadily over time for women as a whole."

Melinda French Gates adds to the urgency of this conversation by noting how lack of family planning contributes to women's poverty. Cofounder of the Bill and Melinda Gates Foundation, one of the world's largest private charitable foundations, she provides details in *The Moment of Lift: How Empowering Women Changes the World*: "It took us [the foundation] years to learn that contraceptives are the greatest life-saving, poverty-ending, women-empowering innovation ever created. When women can decide whether and when to have children, it saves lives, promotes health, expands education, and creates prosperity—no matter what country you're talking about."

But although deciding if/when to get married and if/when to have children aren't solely economic decisions, neither are those life choices just the romance, flowers, and happily-ever-after stories we've been sold for so long. And though we're not suggesting that you run a spreadsheet on your children, here's the bottom line: According to a Brookings Institution analysis of the US Department of Agriculture data, a family will spend over $300,000 to raise a child from birth to age eighteen.[14] It turns out that day care can cost more than college!

To the point, a woman will primarily pay that amount, hopefully with a partner to share the cost. But these estimates also assume that the youngster will begin to be self-supporting when they're eighteen, which may or may not happen. Due to the explosive cost of housing, economic circumstances, or other reasons, particularly since COVID, many young people are either choosing or are forced to remain at home well into their twenties and even early thirties.

If you are still/again living with your parents, hopefully you have a real economic need, such as going to school or some type of job training. As we'll discuss shortly, we know that COVID may have knocked the air out of your schooling and career plans, but we have faith in you and know that you can rebound. And as upsetting as it is, it's a good introduction to being flexible and adapting to the inevitable ups and downs of economic cycles.

Adults who live with their parents reached historic highs in 2020, according to a recent census.[15] Twenty-two percent of men and 13 percent of women ages twenty-five to thirty-four lived in their family's home. The data also shows that more than half of women and men ages eighteen through twenty-four have lived consistently with their parents since 2011. Of course, we don't know what the circumstances are surrounding these numbers, and it's none of our business.

But it *is* our business to point out that you might not only expect to bear the expenses of raising a child but now maybe even well into adulthood. If you are the parent in a situation like this, know that the funds that you're paying for your offspring's room, board, and cell phone plan could be going into your retirement fund. You may want to take another look at your financial arrangement with your young roommate, especially if you're supporting them and they're heavily contributing to the video console or designer handbag industries.

If you find yourself in this situation, for your own sake, we encourage you to make some sort of equitable economic arrangement out of it. Your future self will thank you, and it will lessen your chances of being a burden on the future self of your kids.

How Education Impacts Your Bottom Line

Sitting at the dinner table one evening, teenage Laura took a deep breath.

She had an announcement for her family. "I'm going to college." She waited for the response. It was instantaneous. Her father hurled his dinner plate past her head. Mashed potatoes stuck to the wallpaper as the gravy looked like molten lava dripping down the wall.

"The hell you are. Girls don't go to college."

Laura sat stock-still, trained from long experience to freeze at her father's outbursts. Her mind, however, was calm and unfazed. *Just watch*, she thought to herself.

Growing up, she saw the effect of alcoholism, violence, and poverty on her parents and family and vowed to herself that she would be divergent. As an avid reader, Laura recognized through books from an early age that education would be a mitigating weapon in her personal war against poverty.

She had to learn through reading. No one in her family for generations had gone to college, nor did they have any interest in it, which was why she knew what her father's reaction would be when she announced it. Knowing nothing about student loans or grants, she joined the Army to finance her education through the GI Bill. And she kept going to night school while she worked full-time at IBM until she got her bachelor of science degree—fifteen years after she started.

Her parents yawned at the news of her graduation. Laura just smiled to herself at their reaction. At least no plates went flying. Their response wasn't unexpected. They had no idea because they had no point of reference in their lives. They weren't given the gift of reading.

Joining the military also provided Laura with another, unexpected benefit: entry into technology. Working on Pershing nuclear missiles, which used computers in their guidance and control systems to deliver the warhead, gave her a background in technology that she used to forge a career unlike anything her family could have dreamed of. And as the tech industry exploded, she grew alongside it as a technologist with a front-row seat as it expanded into every area of our lives.

Laura was right about getting that college education; it was a massive factor in her success. Many doors were opened due to that degree, and just as importantly, others were not closed as they would have been without that diploma.

And more women than ever are also signing up for success by means of a degree. According to a *Harvard Crimson* report: as of 2022, 60 percent of college students are female, and in a recent admissions cycle, they outnumbered male applicants by 35 percent.[16]

But getting a formal education just to get a degree won't accomplish anything except to ensure that you'll have a mountain of student debt without the return on investment (ROI) of making that investment pay off. It will need to have a practical application that you either can utilize to join a company or become an entrepreneur. The big advantage of an education is that you don't have to learn things the hard way—at the school of hard knocks.

You may be in a position right now like Laura was: no money, no family support, and no idea of how to get an education or what to study. If that's the case, there is one plus that can ace almost all the crap hands life may have dealt you: determination.

> **The only thing that overcomes hard luck is hard work.**
> —Harry Golden

As publisher Harry Golden said, the only thing that overcomes hard luck is hard work. Laura can confirm. It will take a lot of work on your part, but so what? If you're in a hole, what else do you have to do besides change your life? Laura can also attest that personal growth is the best tool to keep despair from eating you up if it seems like the world is against you. Know that if you do decide to put yourself on such a path, you may not get a lot of support from the people around you, especially if they have a vested interest or are getting something from your being stuck. Dismiss them from your life. They'll be back when you start to become successful, and in that case, remind them that you already dismissed them.

When she took charge of upgrading her thinking, Laura changed her mental programming by listening to a lot of self-improvement talks. She was destitute, so she got them from the library. Today, you can find them online, and they're still at the library. That kind of thing really works, so give it a try if you've been brought up by people who didn't know any better or have never recovered from broken lives themselves.

She also recommends developing a dark sense of humor to keep yourself amused in the process. That also helps. A lot.

But what are some practical strategies that you can utilize besides reprogramming your subconscious, developing an iron will, and having the ability to laugh at lousy situations?

If you're interested in joining the technology world but don't have a degree, tech career site Dice recommends some companies that don't require a degree for entry-level positions and may be a good start.[17] Most of those companies such as Microsoft, Apple, and Google also pay for continuing education, so they can finance your schooling. A lot of other companies also provide tuition financing, so consider working for some of them.

You may also want to consider massive open online courses (MOOCs), which are free courses available online for anyone. You can use them to build new skills, change careers, and some colleges even offer degrees.

Although Laura got a BS, she didn't pursue a post-graduate degree because it didn't provide an ROI in her field. Instead, she got technical certifications because that's what tech companies were looking for. She passed more than one hundred tests in various areas of technology, such as Microsoft, networking, security, and more. Even while employed, she scoured job site postings to see which direction the industry was headed and would then get certified in that area. Once she even went to Bangkok for a month of network schooling because the course provided the same information at 20 percent of the cost of classes in the States, including a vacation for Joy and travel expenses. Every time she changed companies armed with another certification, she negotiated a raise over her current salary to make the education investment pay off.

You can do the same thing. Look up technical certifications and see if you can self-study or qualify for government-subsidized funding to get certified. It may give you the opportunity to break into the industry. The tests don't require a degree because they measure your ability to actually do the job. Testing also isn't free, but it's nowhere near the cost of a college semester.

Joy also recommends a similar strategy to those looking to get into a law enforcement career. Some deputies she knows started as safety aides or dispatchers until they could apply to the police academy. There are also always openings for corrections officers. If there is a career path that you're interested in, find a way to apply in a similar capacity and work to attain the qualifications you need for the job you're looking for. Even if you're facing stiff competition in a field, with determination, you can outwork anyone.

Finally, in today's world, you're never going to be done getting an education. It's lifelong. Back in the day, a person could become an accountant, cop, or whatever and coast through the rest of their life. That isn't true in any occupation today. Everything changes every day, and to be successful, you'll have to be adaptable as well. But as women, we're masters at that already, aren't we?

Look to the future in the way the sports greats play their game. Laura has always taken Wayne Gretzky's philosophy to heart: "I skate to where the puck is going, not where it's been." See if you can discern where your field is going and be one of the first to get there. We believe that once you start flexing your mind and looking to the future, you'll never want to stop. So it becomes fun *and* profitable!

Debt

Laura sat by herself in the back of the church annex at a recovery meeting, sobbing quietly so that no one could hear.

How had it come to this in just a short year?

It seemed like a lifetime ago that she'd lived in a middle-class suburb and held a well-paying technical position at IBM, a company similar to Apple. Friends and family never really knew what she did for the last ten years and didn't care. All they knew, and ever needed to know, was that she was an IBMer.

The large corporation was not just her job but the foundation of her identity. It had given her so much: financial security, college funding, and ultimately what she'd never had growing up, respectability. Emerging from that hardscrabble, alcoholic family where she observed her parents' seemingly bottomless ability to make terrible choices, it made her realize how money could transform disasters into mere inconveniences.

And having a comfortable bank account enabled her to tell herself that she wasn't like them.

But alcoholism is a great equalizer.

Because after making fun of her parents' drinking for all that time, she discovered for herself that a few cocktails can really smudge the lines between good and horrible decisions. And after a number of years of "a few drinks" on a daily basis, that line evaporated completely. Somewhere in that blur, she crossed the one-way borderline into what her Irish ancestors called *the failing*, a polite term for chronic alcoholism. Then, just like her parents, she leapt from one bad decision to the next, including quitting her tech job to open a retail casket store. It turns out that you can do a lot of drinking when you're sitting alone in a store filled with coffins. And Laura's terrible decision-making ability achieved the seemingly impossible: it got worse.

So now, here she sat in the back of the church room; no permanent address, almost $100,000 in debt, and living on credit cards. And judging from the resounding silence to 300 resume submissions, also unemployable.

She'd come to the recovery meeting in her best IBM suit, thinking that maybe one of the church people would notice how well she was dressed in comparison to the rest of the shorts and flip-flops crowd. They'd probably wonder who she was and want to offer a job on the spot.

It worked.

She stayed afterward to help take the trash out, the only member of the cleanup crew in a red skirt and matching heels. Her friend Jan approached her as she picked up the last empty coffee cup.

"Hey, Laura. I heard that you're looking for a job," Jan said. "The bakery that I go to every morning is hiring. I can put in a good word for you."

Laura drove up to the bakery and broke down again. She turned off the ignition and looked in the rearview mirror at her reflection. She looked terrible. Dabbing at the smeared mascara and touching up her lipstick, she was ready for her interview.

As ready as she'd ever be for a bakery job, anyway.

She strode past the "Help Wanted" sign in the window and opened the glass door.

"Hi, my friend said you'd be expecting me. I'm here about the job." She pointed toward the sign in the window.

The woman appraised Laura, who was decked out in her black silk suit. "Do you have any front counter experience?"

Laura gaped at her. "Experience? They give me money and I give them rolls. How hard can it be?"

"Thanks. I'll call you."

As Laura opened the car door, she realized that the manager hadn't asked for her name, let alone her number. And burst into tears again.

Fifteen years of college, and she couldn't even get a bakery job.

Almost $100,000 of debt. It was dizzying.

But what was really overwhelming was the amount of interest that type of red ink rapidly accumulates. Laura used a friend's address and kept getting more credit cards, using the new one to pay off the minimum payments of the others.

Debt isn't inherently bad. In some ways, borrowing money from a bank can actually be a long-term wealth building strategy: You get a loan to buy a reliable car to get you to and from your job to generate income, a mortgage provides you with a stable place to live, and you can write the interest off on your taxes. But consumer debt and credit card fees can be financial instruments from hell if you aren't careful.

It took almost ten years of moving up in the tech industry, but Laura ultimately paid off all her credit cards without declaring bankruptcy and became debt free. Now it didn't matter if she was laid off, and she didn't have to worry about not being able to leave a violent relationship. Mimi would have been proud.

Here were some of the steps she used:

- Got a job;
- Lived with others for seven years until debt was paid off;
- Only bought needs, not wants; didn't accumulate new debt;
- Tracked credit cards on spreadsheet, paying them off one at a time;
- Acquired tech certifications and upped income every time with better jobs;
- Bought house; and
- Paid house off in seven years.

It wasn't rocket science, but it did require a strategy and financial discipline. To be clear, it wasn't as easy as it sounds. The journey didn't follow a straight line up; it was more like a jagged zigzag line that ran all over the place and then slowly inched northward.

It's also important to keep in mind that life will occasionally throw you a zinger, and everything doesn't always go according to your strategy. Sometimes the tactical details go awry. It doesn't mean you shouldn't have a plan, any more than you'd set out on a trip without a destination. Just be prepared to take the secondary roads at times.

Chapter Nine
Joy's Survival Blueprint

O ver the years of Joy's career, she handled a range of calls from the nonviolent, such as scams, thefts, etc., to the violent, such as sexual assaults, domestic violence, and robbery. During that time, women would always ask: "What can I do to avoid becoming a victim?"

This chapter describes the everyday practices that Joy puts to use to maintain her safety.

You may have heard some of these guidelines before and have gotten somewhat cavalier about practicing them, but Joy has seen countless women who could have avoided being victimized if they'd utilized these recommendations.

But even more important than the actual suggestions, however, the first thing you need to do is adjust your mindset. Just because you haven't been victimized yet doesn't mean that you won't be. You've just been lucky so far. And luck only goes so far.

A lot of women in dangerous situations get hung up by what is called normalcy bias, where your brain refuses to accept something because it hasn't seen it before. In other words, your response to a threat is delayed because you're so terrified that you can't believe it is happening.

We want you to make a commitment to yourself right now that you will act immediately on your own behalf if you need to. You'll thank yourself later. Predators count on your lack of awareness. You may be able to avoid many of these potentially dangerous situations by deploying Joy's strategies to keep your vulnerability to a minimum, using your safety intuition, and remaining persuasion-proof.

Let's start out with where you live.

Safety in Your Home

Joy has heard plenty of instructors tell women's safety classes that "your only safe space is in your home." It should be. But that is not always the case.

You should be in caution mode when you're out and about, and when you're home, you should be relaxed. Mainly because you know who's there or not there.

Certainly, you're often safer at home because you may control access, but as FBI profiler John Douglas notes in *The Killer Across the Table*, "Vulnerability, more than anything else, is likely to lead to someone's becoming a victim."

The goal of the predator is to maximize your vulnerability. Your job is to minimize it.

As we mentioned in Chapter 3, the biggest weapon that most predators have in their arsenal isn't a gun or a knife, it's their mouth. They *talk* their way into your home by getting you to just open the door. Predators are charming and personable; they *want* to make you comfortable, and they're experts at it. They've honed their skills as expert cons, so you must always be on alert when someone is trying to talk their way into your residence.

That's what you're up against.

But if they do temporarily get the best of you, here's the most important thing for you to always remember: You ain't no junkyard dog, and you can outthink some predator. Let's start by not getting into that type of scenario in the first place if it can be avoided. And many women just don't take those steps to minimize their own vulnerability.

The Stranger at the Door

Joy was visiting a neighbor's home a few months ago when the doorbell rang. Iris, the neighbor, immediately jumped up, like a game show contestant, hurrying to her door. Joy couldn't even finish warning her, "You don't need to open it. They can hear you through the door!"

"I don't want to be rude," Iris said as she flung it open.

Joy thought to herself, *You're a petite woman who could easily be overpowered, but it's more important to you not to be rude.*

The visitor turned out to be a man resembling a utility worker, wearing a company jacket with a corporate-looking logo. But in fact, his appearance was deceiving as he was allegedly soliciting for a solar panel company. Iris was about to give out personal information without realizing it, just by talking to a stranger.

The biggest mistake women make is opening their door to a stranger. Just because someone knocks at your door, it doesn't mean that you're required to open the door. If you're not expecting someone, don't open the door.

Opening the door to a stranger can open yourself up to danger.

In September 2017, Jennifer Folford of Winter Park, Florida, answered a knock at her door. She didn't know Scott Nelson, who used a ruse to get into the house. Nelson was a convicted felon who had a straightforward plan: kill someone that day. He murdered Jennifer in her home. Nelson was very cocky testifying at his trial. When asked how he gained access to the house, he sarcastically stated, "I knocked, and she let me in." He also noted that once he was in the home, the victim wasn't "very helpful."[1]

The second biggest mistake that people make is not locking their doors.

Yes, it still happens. We know them.

Richard Chase was a serial killer, cannibal, and necrophile who killed six people within the span of a month in the late seventies. Chase told the FBI that he heard voices that told him to kill someone, so he went down the street, rattling doors. If a door was locked, he wouldn't go in. However, if it was open, he'd enter and kill the occupants. When FBI profiler Robert Ressler asked Chase why he simply hadn't broken a door down, he replied, "If the door is locked, that means you're not welcome."[2]

The difference between life and a horrible death can be as simple as locking your door.

The following are suggestions to limit a stranger's access to your home. This can apply to utility/repair people, solicitors, or anyone that you don't know at your door.

- Be cautious of unannounced people at your door, including people wearing uniforms. Predators use this ruse all the time, e.g., flower deliveries, packages.

- Utility workers don't visit homes, even during a power outage. So that stranger is either trying to sell you something or they have something nefarious in mind.
- Even if a worker has previously been in your home in the course of their job, be wary if they show back up for no apparent reason. There was a case in Texas where a repair person who was employed by a well-known repair company completed work at a woman's house. He returned the following day in his work truck and wearing his work uniform. Because he was known to the woman, she let him in and was murdered. Tragically, the victim was duped.[3]
- Be particularly wary during the holiday season. Predators know that delivery companies hire extra help to deliver packages in unmarked vans and cars and can disguise themselves carrying a package. Have them leave it at the door and wait until you're sure they've left to retrieve your package. If anyone tells you they need a signature, meaning you need to open the door, don't believe it. You would know if you were receiving a special delivery package with a signature required. If you're still not sure if it belongs to you, ask them the sender's name (through the door).
- Predators have masqueraded as law enforcement officers to gain access into residences for years. If you're suspicious, ask them to identify the police department number, look up the phone number, call, and verify.
- Always check to verify a person's identification matches their picture ID.
- Don't let workers know that you live alone.
- Don't tell workers your schedule.

- Don't let a repair person go alone into a sensitive area (where jewelry or checkbooks are kept) alone. People aren't stupid; they know exactly where hiding spots can be.
- Have cash/checkbook on you if you know you will have to pay workers, so they don't see you go get it. Especially if you use them a lot. Workers talk about where they work or where they've been.
- Change the PIN on any lock after a repair person has learned the combination.
- Say no to outside workers (day laborers/ landscapers) using the bathroom if you are home alone. (They are accustomed to locating facilities to meet their needs.)
- Do not be in your home alone with a worker you're not familiar with if you can help it. Invite a friend over for coffee. Or have your cell on you and pepper spray handy. They should maintain a professional distance when talking to you. If you're uncomfortable, make an excuse that you have an emergency to handle and they need to leave.
- Never allow a worker you don't know into your home if you're incapacitated or physically impaired and alone.
- Use "we" when talking to delivery personnel or workers, so they don't assume you live alone. They don't ever need to know who lives with you or where anyone works. Someone is always home.

Also, keep in mind that many companies, including furniture and big-box companies, contract with third-party delivery services to deliver their products. These service delivery employees may or may not be screened for drug testing or criminal records.

Consider the following tragic incident where a delivery man inexplicably attacked and killed a Florida grandmother while delivering a washer and dryer.

On August 21, 2019, a third-party company delivered a washer and dryer to seventy-five-year-old Evelyn Smith Udell in Boca Raton, Florida. Jorge Dupre Lazacho was to instruct Udell on the use of the dryer while the delivery truck driver stepped outside to return phone calls. During that time, Lazacho fatally attacked Udell with a mallet and then set her on fire. Lazacho subsequently admitted to recently using cocaine and vaping marijuana prior to the incident. No motive was given.[4]

Udell's family subsequently sued Best Buy, J.B. Hunt Transportation Company, and X.M. Delivery Service, Inc., which employed Lazacho. The suit indicated that the three companies were negligent and had a responsibility to investigate their employees, even contractors.

Although companies may be negligent regarding your safety, you can and should take your own precautions. At the end of the day, those companies won't be at the receiving end of the attack. You will.

So how do you handle these types of situations? We've given you a lot of don'ts, but what can you do? Here are some suggestions:

- Keep your pepper spray, which is also referred to as OC spray (oleoresin capsicum because of the oily extract of pepper plants and the principal active ingredient causing the inflammatory response), in a pocket where you can easily access it.
- As mentioned before, when an installation/repair person will be at your home for an extended period, ask a friend to swing by or make it sound as if they will.
- Chat with a friend on the phone, letting the friend know that Acme Service is at your house doing some work.

- Do your chatting in the kitchen, close to an exit. Don't allow yourself to be trapped in a room with no escape, like an office or basement.
- If a worker shows up at your house unexpectedly "because they need to check on xyz," call their office before you open the door. If necessary, speak with a supervisor and advise them that the worker is at your door. Better to be safe.

Shopping

Many women let their guard down in crowded places such as shopping malls simply because there are so many people congregated there. They assume that there is safety in numbers. While that is generally true, there are also several situations that you may not have considered that can pose a danger to your life and property as you blithely enjoy your excursion.

And if you are depending on the kindness of strangers to keep you safe in a crowd, keep in mind that people in crowds are rarely willing to go out of their way to get involved. They may think that this is a domestic dispute or think that they will get attacked as well.

Do you lock your car door when you're shopping? Criminals also try car door handles and they can check dozens in a parking lot within a few minutes. Joy has handled so many burglaries of vehicles where the owners were surprised that their personal items were stolen. Lock it up when you're in it and when you're not.

Perps not only steal what they can, but they also hide and sleep in cars that they can access. Like something out of a horror movie scene, you wouldn't want to get into your car at night and have a voice talk to you from the back seat, telling you to drive. Joy has seen it happen.

Predators know that women tend to get in their cars after shopping and sit there while they check voicemail, text, or whatever. Be sure to lock your car with the windows up. If you need to make a call or check your messages, look up occasionally at your surroundings. When Joy is busy in her car, she starts it and locks it. This way, if a problem person comes up to her, she just backs away. You don't have to be startled by someone at your window and then try to start your car. You can back out immediately. They will move out of the way.

Before you encounter any of those situations, it's important for you to pay attention and use your safety intuition before a dangerous situation occurs. Your safety intuition will not only save your life but the lives of your family as well.

Safety Tips

Career predators and the young, new, up-and-coming ones are always out hunting for prey and easy marks or a quick cash score.

And that's exactly how they see you: prey.

It's up to you *not* to be the easy mark.

In addition to robberies and thefts, sexual predators are also seeking opportunity.

Always engage your safety intuition when you're outside. Be aware of people in your surroundings. Pay attention to your route to avoid avoidable surprises.

When the lions are hungry, the alert wildebeest in the middle of the pack live far longer than the outliers who are too distracted to pay attention.

The following are some suggestions to avoid being the easy mark:

- Parking garages: There are many opportunities for concealment. Keep your hand on your personal safety device; spray, taser, weapon, etc. Do not keep your hand on your phone.

If you're attacked, the only good a phone will do is help the police locate your phone.

- Be aware of who/what is parked around you. If you feel uneasy or suspicious, don't hesitate to move your car and ensure that you're not being followed.
- Don't keep your arms/hands too loaded with packages to respond to a threat. Keep your pepper spray in your hand.
- If you are holiday shopping and bring bags to your car to go back to the mall, move your car to another spot. Predators are always on the lookout for this scenario, prime for break-ins.
- Wear your purse cross-body, if possible. (You New Yorkers already know this.)
- Wear your purse in a bathroom stall or hold it. Don't put it on the floor.
- Avoid putting your purse on the floor of the bathroom while you're washing your hands. Wear it. Or hold it with your knees. Same goes for luggage. Keep it near.
- Never hang your purse on the back of your chair in a restaurant. Thieves from the next table can get into it (it's been done!). Or they can up and leave with it.
- Never entrust a stranger with your belongings in the airport, on the beach, or elsewhere while you go to the bathroom. People seem trustworthy, and then surprise! They walk away with your bags. Carry your own things.
- Never leave your purse unattended while you get a snack at the airport. Yes, it will get stolen. Joy could not believe how comfortable people felt just walking away from their seat, leaving their carry-on luggage, gifts, and purses while they ate at a restaurant or shopped. Public venues are not the same as

your home, so don't leave sensitive personal items out of your sight.

- Drive-up ATMs: Be cognizant of the car behind you. If you don't think it's a good idea to grab your cash in front of them, don't. Drive away and come back around. Better than having someone sketchy follow you, knowing you just got cash. Thieves wait in ATM lines with or without a car. They know the someone will leave the bank with money. This has been nicknamed "jugging," to follow someone after they get their money from the ATM and rob them.

- Don't ever leave a bank or store counting your cash and putting it in your wallet in the parking lot. Do that in the bank or at the cash register. Don't be a target.

- Check your hotel or cruise cabin with the door open to ensure that no one is hiding.

- Don't leave your sensitive or personal belongings out in the open in a hotel room or cruise cabin. Lock them in the safe.

- Don't put yourself in a secluded area while traveling in a hotel, on the beach, on a ship, or anywhere else you can avoid it. Carry your phone. There have been numerous incidents of attacks at resorts, on cruise ships, and of people alone on a beach at night. Predators are opportunistic.

- If you meet someone while traveling, be wary of providing too much personal information. Keep it friendly and very general.

- Do not give a stranger your phone number under any circumstances! Get their number if you're interested or if you want to do business with them.

- If you're uncomfortable because someone keeps pressing you for your phone number, and you're not able to shake them, get a Google Voice phone number. That way, they'll never know your real number. If they call the number while you're in front of them, it will ring through to your phone. We know a young woman who is a bartender and is constantly pestered for her number. The Google Voice phone number works well for her because every time she gives someone her number, she deletes it and gets a new one.

- When shopping, don't leave your purse in the grocery cart as you grab items from a shelf, or as you wander down the aisle to look at a sale. Thieves rove stores just to steal. It's an easy theft. They grab your bag and pass it to an accomplice who is out of the store in a flash. It has been done plenty of times. Joy has viewed it on stores' surveillance cameras while taking the report. Wear your bag.

- While in a checkout line, thieves tend to chat with you while they surreptitiously steal your wallet from a back pocket or from a purse. Keep your wallet in your hand or front pocket and keep your purse in front of you, not hanging on your shoulder on your side. Joy watched many videos of some crafty pickpockets. They are so good it's scary. Then when the person in line couldn't pay because they had no wallet, the thief walked away. Nobody sees the crime.

- After the store, when you're at your vehicle in the parking lot, don't leave your purse sitting on top of the grocery cart as you transfer your child into the car seat; it's easy for predators to grab 'n' go. Put the purse in the trunk first. Don't say, "Not in my neighborhood." When people are looking for a quick cash grab, a purse is #1.

- Pay attention to your surroundings in the grocery store parking lot when you're unloading a shopping cart into your car. Many abductions/carjackings occur when your car is open and you're busy. Put your purse/money in the trunk and then unload. See who's parked next to you. Turn around as you're rearranging your trunk so you're not surprised by an assailant.

- When you're walking to your car in a parking lot/parking garage, turn to your left before you open your door, in case someone quietly snuck up behind you. You would be prepared to spray them if you needed.

- If you're traveling with a child, be aware of what's around you as you transfer your child to/from the car seat. You are in a very vulnerable position during those moments. One mom Joy knows locks herself in her car while she's in the back seat transferring the baby. Good practice.

- Ensure that your computer and phone have a password enabled in the event that they are lost or stolen. Use any safety feature to prevent the loss of your data.

- Don't shout personal information over the phone while you're out in public. Joy has heard people yell out their credit card information at the gate in the airport. Thieves have ears. The public is not your friend.

- Don't use a debit card for payment if you can avoid it. The credit card company will cover you in the event of theft/fraud; the money from your debit card can take months to recover if you can be reimbursed.

- Don't tell Uber/Lyft/taxi drivers you live alone.
- If you're being robbed, hand over your money. Just do it.
- Keep a record in a secure place at home of your credit cards that you carry and make copies of your driver's license and any pertinent cards that you need that would take time to replace. This way, in case they're lost, you won't be as upset, wondering what you must replace. It's a stressful enough situation; don't make yourself a wreck over cards. Also, maybe pare down some cards from the wallet for everyday use.
- If you're held up and directed to get in the car or go to another location, do not do it. Run or fight. The secondary location will be isolated, and your chances of making it out alive will be lessened considerably. This is why Joy stresses the importance of having your personal protective device ready.
- Don't put all your personal information on your luggage tag, just your phone number.
- Don't leave your purse/wallet unattended on a plane when you go to the bathroom. Remember, as friendly as the stranger is, you don't know them.
- Keep your flight carry-on as close to you as possible on a plane. If you are sitting in the back, don't leave it in the front of the plane so you can grab it. Luggage gets stolen off planes all the time; much of it looks alike and if you're in the back, you can't see past eighty or more passengers that may be standing in front of you.
- Airport bins: Don't take off your watch and jewelry in front of people and plop it in the dishes in your bin. People watch that and when they are through security before you, they grab

what's in a bin near them. Once they're gone, it's difficult to find them. Hide your items before you get to security.

- Don't fill out a questionnaire with your personal information from someone holding a clipboard on the street or in front of stores. You can't be sure where that information goes. Same with credit card applications in stores. Apply online.

Safety Intuition

Safety intuition is the ability to identify and process information about your surroundings. Basically, it is paying attention to what is going on around you.

But here's the key: It isn't looking *for* things. It's looking *at* things.

If you focus on looking *for* things, you may be so focused that you miss important clues that your safety intuition may be trying to alert you to.

Awareness doesn't mean always being fearful. Unwarranted or constant fear works against you because you're focused on what *could* happen instead of what *is* happening.

Here's a famous experiment that illustrates this point: Go to YouTube and search for a video entitled "Selective Attention Test." Watch the video and then come back.

Right? The first time I saw the video, I would have sworn that I'd been tricked.

If you don't have time or network access to watch the video, here's the gist: It's a video about basketball players passing the ball. The video instructs the viewer to focus on counting how many times the players wearing white pass the ball.

In the middle of the video (while you're happily focused on your counting), a person in a gorilla suit walks into the group of players, saunters around, and then walks out of the scene.

Most people watching the video *don't ever notice the gorilla.* Myself included.

They are so focused on counting that they miss a huge disruption to the scene. So you are better served by remaining generally alert, calm, and curious about your surroundings—that's when you're more liable to be in tune with your safety intuition.

Active Shooter

Since 2015, *more than 19,000* people in the United States have been shot and killed or wounded in a mass shooting. In 2022 alone, over 600 people were killed, with over 2,700 wounded.[5] Mass shootings are defined as incidents involving four or more victims.

With these kinds of statistics, we want you to know what steps you can take to save your life.

Joy was involved in the aftermath of the mass shooting at the Fort Lauderdale–Hollywood International Airport on January 6, 2017. During that shooting, a lone gunman opened fire with a semiautomatic 9mm handgun in the baggage claim area of Terminal Two at the Fort Lauderdale–Hollywood International Airport (FLL) in Fort Lauderdale, Florida, immediately killing five innocent bystanders and wounding six others. Further carnage was halted when sheriff's deputies arrived in ninety seconds, overwhelming and apprehending the subject.

Approximately ten thousand passengers who were in the airport at the time were impacted. As you can imagine, pandemonium reigned as the Broward Sheriff's Office (BSO) tried to keep that many people safe while investigating whether the shooting was a terroristic attack and determining whether any other gunmen posed a threat.

This scenario is called an active shooter situation.

An active shooter is a person actively engaged in using firearms to kill people in a confined and populated area. These situations are unpredictable and develop rapidly. By far, it is one of the most terrifying events to encounter.

Typically, law enforcement is required to stop the shooter, but it takes time for law enforcement to arrive. Until then, you have to rely on yourself to reach safety.

But take a deep breath and stay calm because Joy is going to walk you through one of these scenarios and show you some steps you can take to increase your chances of getting through it safely.

Although active shooters have murdered people in many types of locations, we'll walk through a mall scenario as an example. Let's say that you and your family are out shopping at the mall, and you just walked out of Macy's, headed toward the food court. Suddenly, you hear shots ring out from the direction of the food court and people everywhere begin screaming. What do you do?

Finding Cover in an Active Shooter Scenario

Joy's 4-Step BARC© (Breathe, Assess, Run/Hide, Call 9-1-1) process will help you remember what to do in any mall emergency, including an active shooter scenario.

The steps will be discussed in more detail as follows, but before anything ever happens, always know your closest exit.

Where's Your Exit?

When you're wandering around the mall, looking for the sale rack or the biggest discount, periodically take a minute as you walk along and look for the nearest exit sign. That awareness could be just the lifeline that your brain needs in the event of panicked brain freeze.

Why? Because as author Amanda Ripley notes in *The Unthinkable: Who Survives When Disaster Strikes and Why*, "Under certain conditions, on burning planes, sinking ships, or even impromptu battlefields, many people cease moving altogether. . . . They shut down, becoming limp and still. This stillness descends involuntarily, and it is one of the most important and intriguing behaviors in the disaster repertoire. It happens far more often than, say, panic."

Ripley goes on to note that although this behavior remains a mystery, she offers a key observation: Those who didn't freeze in disasters seemed mentally prepared in some way—that they have in effect preloaded the data that they needed to take action.

She adds, "The National Transportation Safety Board has found that passengers who read the safety information card are less likely to get hurt in an emergency. In a plane crash at Pago Pago, all but five of the one hundred and one passengers died. All survivors had read the card and listened to the safety briefing."

She also notes other studies where passengers who had prelocated an exit sign on a flight were more likely to locate the exit in an emergency.

If it works on planes, it works in malls.

When you enter a shopping center, scan the directory with your phone so that you have the store layout and all the exits on your phone. Look it over before shopping so that you have a good idea of the map in your mind. If something goes down, your brain will probably freeze if it doesn't know what to do. But if you've primed it with the map, it will remember, and you'll be less likely to panic.

Also, if someone in your group has a handicap or disability, be mindful of their needs in the event that you all have to evacuate quickly. How can they get out safely?

Figure 9.1 on the next page illustrates the BARC steps to safety.

Figure 9.1: BARC steps to safety.

The Bang

Gunshots have a distinctive sound. Although they are loud, like other noises such as fireworks, the sound of gunfire is unique.

That said, inside a building with walls that echo, it may sound artificial. So assume that any bang or popping sound inside a building is gunfire and respond appropriately.

Do not run toward the sound to see where it came from.

The bang of gunfire carries quite far. Fired inside a large building like a mall, the sound waves will echo and bounce off the walls so loudly that it will be difficult to tell exactly how far away the shots were fired from.

So it's important that you stop exactly where you are as soon as you hear them.

If you see people running, do not assume that they have any clue what's going on. They may be running toward the gunshots; they may be running away. Truthfully, you don't know nor do most of them. *Do not follow the crowd. Head toward your exit.*

This is when the stress hormones will hijack your brain and your heartbeat may soar. You may have tunnel vision; you may temporarily lose your sense of hearing. Whatever physical symptoms you have, this is your body's normal response to an abnormal situation. *Don't panic. Instead, breathe deep.*

Breathe

Before you make any decision about the gunfire, let me first tell you what's going to happen to your body.

Lt. Col. David Grossman, US Army (Ret.), author of *On Combat: The Psychology and Physiology of Deadly Conflict in War and Peace,* notes that "warriors might experience impairments to vision, judgement, and hearing, or they might experience reduced motor skills— and they will likely experience all this during violence, unless the body and mind are integrated."

During an active shooter incident, you as a civilian are also a warrior engaged in deadly combat.

The stress hormones cortisol and adrenalin are going to slam you hard. They're supposed to because that's exactly why they're there. And when that happens, your heart rate is going to triple to rates approaching 180 to 220 beats per minute.

This is important: At that rapid rate, your heart will cause weird physical stuff to happen that will freak you out even further if you're not expecting it. Grossman calls this stress phenomena "condition black." On some of the symptoms of this condition, Grossman writes, "Cardiologists tell us that at a certain point an increased heart rate becomes counterproductive because the heart is pumping so fast that it cannot draw in a full load of blood before pumping it back out. As the heart rate increases beyond this point, the effectiveness of the heart, and the level of oxygen provided to the brain, steadily decreases." Your body becomes a fighting or running machine.

Your brain must immediately decide what to prioritize and what to neglect, so it goes into overdrive, giving your gross motor skills a huge jolt. But for every biologic gift that fear produces, it takes one away. Grossman goes on to describe the physical effects that this fear phenomena produces in the body.

> As you grow increasingly stressed and move into Condition Black, many people lose their peripheral vision, a condition commonly referred to as tunnel vision. The more stressed you become, the narrower the tunnel. There will also be a loss of depth perception, meaning that a threat looks closer than it really is, and a loss of near vision, meaning that you are going to have trouble seeing close things. . . . So, what does this loss mean? Consider the simple act of calling 9-1-1 on your phone . . . you won't be able to see the numbers.

You won't be able to see the numbers.

Which is why he wants you to practice calling 9-1-1 before you ever need to make that call. (More on that later.) Grossman continues, "As you enter Condition Black, your cognitive processing deteriorates, which is a fancy way of saying that you stop thinking. Your forebrain shuts down and the midbrain (the part of your brain that is like your dog's brain) reaches up and hijacks your forebrain."

You stop thinking.

Which means that you are unable to access your safety intuition. Just when you need it the most.

Is there a way to reengage this critical part of your brain immediately?

The answer is yes. And Grossman tells us how.

He calls it tactical breathing. But it is also called yoga breathing or Lamaze breathing. It is a simple yet powerful deep breathing technique that will slow your heart rate, enable you to back away from the abyss of panic, and reengage all parts of your brain. Grossman notes that it will "enable you to bathe yourself with a sense of calm and control."

In other words, by consciously slowing down your breath, you'll slow your pulse. That will enable you to take control of the primal fear response that will otherwise overwhelm you.

Joy has used this process many times during tense in-progress situations with perpetrators.

You can easily do it yourself, using the following steps. Try it right now.

1. Breath in through your nose to a slow count of four; expand your belly as you inhale;

2. Hold for a count of four;

3. Exhale through your lips to the count of four, collapsing your belly as the air is released; and

4. Hold your lungs empty for a count of four.

5. Repeat at least five times and adjust the timing of each step to

fit what works for you. It may be a count of three or five for each step.

As we mentioned earlier, preloading your brain with information will make it easier for you to react in an emergency. As Ripley notes in *The Unthinkable*, "The body's first defense is hard wired. The amygdala (in your brain) triggers an ancient survival dance, and it is hard to change. But we have an outstanding second defense: we can learn from experience."

She continues, "Fear is negotiable. So even civilians can benefit from some preparation. . . . The preparation will have increased their confidence, thereby decreasing their fear and improving their performance."

Just having this knowledge is a big step in your preparation.

Assess the Situation

While tactical breathing, assess your risk. If you're with your family or friends, calmly take command of the situation. (Moms, you already got this part.) The people that you're with may fall prey to that deadly "disaster freeze" that we mentioned earlier. So it will be up to you to snap them out of it.

In *The Unthinkable*, Ripley points out the effect that one leader in a group can have on survival: "On March 27, 1977, a Pan Am 747 awaiting takeoff at Tenerife Airport in the Canary Islands was sliced open without warning by a Dutch KLM jet that came hurtling out of the fog at 160 MPH. . . . Floy Heck, then seventy, was thrown forward and to the right, but seat belts held she, her husband and their friends in place. Seemingly frozen in place, Floy found that she could not speak or move. But her husband reacted immediately. He unbuckled his seat belt and started toward the exit. 'Follow me,' he told his wife.

Hearing him say that was enough to snap Floy out of her daze, she got up and followed him through the smoke."

If you're in an active shooter situation, ask yourself the following questions to help you to decide your next steps:

- Do you hear more shots? If not, the gunman may be reloading.
- Look around quickly. Do you see if the shooter(s) is coming in your direction?
- Are you in a safe/hiding place?
- Do you remember the last exit sign you saw?
- In a mall, the closest exit is the best. But if your last exit sign is too far away, run into the closest store or restaurant if you can. The main point is not to be out in the open. Every store in a mall establishment has a rear entrance for deliveries; keep this in mind in an emergency so you can make an exit. If you see the gunman coming in your direction, hide. Be quiet and throw yourself behind a counter in the back and low crawl out of the fire exit if it's possible.
- This is where your safety intuition will be your best friend.

Remember, while your conscious mind is on overload trying to process with its forty bits per second, your subconscious is humming away in the background like a boss with its eleven million bits per second. Your subconscious mind has the bandwidth available to process all this information, even as hectic as everything seems.

Run/Hide

Joy notes that in the catastrophic active shooter event at the Fort Lauderdale–Hollywood International Airport, passengers in the immediate area (baggage claim) of the shooter tried to do what they could quickly as there were limited areas for cover:

- There was no time to run, so they took cover behind whatever they could;
- They ensured that they were not the tallest object in the gunman's sight—hiding behind baggage carts and luggage, flattening themselves under and behind seats; and
- They focused on their personal safety and ignored their belongings.

In a rapidly evolving and dangerous situation such as that of an active shooter, how do you know whether to run or hide? In a situation like this, how would *you* determine the right thing to do?

Here are three quick rules of thumb to remember:

- If you don't see the gunman, move quickly away from the sound of gunfire. Leave your belongings behind, if you need to.
- If the gunman is visible or in your immediate vicinity, immediately take cover and hide.
- Turn down the volume on your phone. You don't want a ringtone to guide a shooter in your direction. If you're safe, text 9-1-1. Also, text a friend or family to let them know where you are and what's going on.

Note that if law enforcement or trained emergency personnel are available, always follow their directions.

The police may have already secured the building and locked it down. You won't know whether the gunmen has already been apprehended or whether they are still at large until law enforcement makes an announcement telling you it is all clear.

How would you know that it is really a policer officer telling people to come out? You could call 9-1-1 and ask if it's true. Officers would be on their radios looking for survivors, so there would be a significant number of officers and they are trained to get you out quickly.

Joy also notes that in the aftermath of a shooting, you could be detained for a considerable period while law enforcement secures the scene and interviews witnesses. She mentions that after the airport shooting, passengers were detained for up to ten hours as the Broward Sheriff's Office (BSO), the Florida Department of Law Enforcement (FDLE), and the FBI scoured the airport, parking garage, tarmac, and surrounding property to ensure that no additional gunmen were lurking. Passengers were confined on inbound and departing flights, all the terminal buildings were locked down, and the parking garage was secured as the area was cleared.

Mentally prepare yourself for this and do whatever you can to make yourself comfortable. This is a vital and necessary phase to ensure that everyone is safe and that as much evidence as possible is gathered without contaminating the crime scene.

Call 9-1-1

Don't assume that someone else has called 9-1-1.

Joy notes that people are sometimes embarrassed to call 9-1-1. They're afraid that they may have overreacted or think that they couldn't possibly have heard gunfire or have seen what they are seeing. As a result, there may be a delayed response on the part of emergency personnel during an emergency *simply because no one has called it in.*

Don't be afraid to call. Joy would always say that for a high-priority call, the calls just kept coming in. Dispatch answers them all. They will tell you what they can. And ask you if you're safe. Always call because what you heard scared you. Don't wonder if someone else is worried. Maybe they didn't hear it. Call and be the hero. You may have more detailed information about the situation or a more nuanced view than was previously known. Details that you may not consider important could be a matter of life and death. The unknown subjects (UNSUBs) may be using disguises; they may be changing shirts or hats to make themselves blend in more easily. The details that you provide could supplement existing information. You may have vital information that was previously unknown and could help in the apprehension of the perpetrator.

And when you do call them, be prepared to provide as much detailed information as possible about your own location, especially in the event of an active shooter. If you're hiding, tell the dispatcher exactly where you are. For example, if there are three of you hiding in a broom closet near the food court, provide the most accurate directions and information that you can.

Make sure that you tell the dispatcher whether anyone with you is armed. Ensure that you provide clear instructions to them that everyone's hands will be easily visible where the police can see them.

This information is vitally important as law enforcement is looking for an active shooter. Panicking and not listening to directions could have a devastating outcome for you, especially if the police have requested that no one move.

Also, if you see that people are injured, provide dispatch with as much detail as possible. How many are on the ground? Are any of them moving? Male? Female? All this information is vital in a crisis like this.

Have you ever noticed that when safety professionals talk about 9-1-1, they call it nine-one-one and *not* nine-eleven?

That's because when you are in an emergency, your brain locks up as it's immediately flooded with cortisol (your body's main stress hormone, which helps blood clotting in case of injury) and adrenaline (another stress-induced hormone that may cause your heartbeat to soar to over 200 beats per minute). And when that brain lock occurs, you'll have trouble even *navigating* your phone.

So if someone says, "Call nine eleven," your brain will look for eleven on the phone and freak out even more when it can't find it. That's why it's *always* "Nine. One. One."

Emergency SOS on Your Cell

Now *this* is a frustrating choice on the part of cell phone manufacturers, but you need to know about it so that you can train your brain.

Your cell is equipped to quickly call 9-1-1 for you. But it's *not* labeled *9-1-1*! It's labeled *Emergency call* (Android) or *Emergency SOS* (iPhone). What the what . . . ?

No matter what brand of phone you have, become familiar with its emergency features so that you don't have to figure it out under pressure. And when you get a new phone, make sure that you are familiar with all the features and that you still know how to access them.

Remember what we just mentioned about brain lock-up? This is going to be a *lot* for your brain to handle when you're jacked up on stress hormones! *But* if you train your brain to use this *before* you need it, your brain circuitry will be pre-wired, and it will follow the path of least resistance and remember its training. Which, by the way, is why military and law enforcement train so much, so that their brains and muscle memory revert to their training as an instinct in an emergency.

Text 9-1-1

In some locations, if you're in a situation where you're unable to speak or want to call quietly, you can also text a message to 9-1-1 in your messaging app to notify emergency personnel of your location, especially if you're hiding, so that you're not mistaken for the perpetrator; a text message sends your location to the police for what is occurring. Tell them if you are injured or have relevant info for dispatch, such as a description of the subjects, that will aid responding officers upon their arrival.

Keep in mind that this feature may not be available everywhere, so always call if you're able to.

If you follow these suggestions, you can save your life and the lives of others.

Chapter Ten

Shams, Scams, and Cons

Religion began when the
first scoundrel met the first fool.
—VOLTAIRE

The con is the oldest story ever told. Consider the story of Eve and Adam. As the story goes, God told the first two humans that they could eat freely of any fruit in the Garden of Eden except for that of one tree, the tree of the knowledge of good and evil. But a serpent persuades Eve that if she eats the fruit from the tree, she'll be like God. Convinced, she does and shares it with Adam.

So whether or not you're a fan of religious text, it is very interesting that the big opener is how two of the first humans were duped. Perhaps that's what caused Voltaire's observation.

And it's been going on ever since.

As opposed to a violent crime, such as a gun being held to your head, a scammer doesn't have to threaten you. No one forces you to do anything. Instead, the con artist persuades you to want to give them what they want, to participate in your own undoing, to being an accessory in a crime—against yourself.

Being the nice person you are, all you have to do is go along with it. And sometimes it may not be easy to *not* go along with it because some of them are so good, which is why they're called a con "artist." You have to be good to talk someone into doing something against their self-interest. Which is why you have to be good at detecting them, because not participating in becoming a victim is the part of the crime against yourself that you can control.

But no matter how convoluted any story gets, there are really only three components to being conned: liar, story, and victim.

The liar wants something (money, sex, world domination, whatever) that wouldn't be granted by the victim if they knew the truth. So the liar selects their victim and tells them a deceptive story. Now it's important to remember that victim selection isn't trivial. Because like law enforcement, liars are also profilers. They're looking for the easy mark, the one most likely to buy their bunk story. So you'll want to use your safety intuition to make sure that you're not the one they choose. But if you are, this chapter will show you how not to be taken advantage of.

And if you know what to look for, you'll almost laugh when you see a story coming at you and you'll recognize it from a block away.

"Hey, girl!" Joy turned around in aisle three. There stood Paula, her former neighbor. She hadn't seen Paula for a couple of years, but Paula still looked fab. A former hairdresser, Paula always looked as though she'd just walked out of the salon, Instagram filters be damned. But in a way, she seemed more subdued than Joy remembered.

"Hey! So good to see you!"

Then, to Joy's utter amazement, Paula flung herself into Joy's arms right there in the canned vegetable aisle and burst into tears.

It turned out that there'd been a fire in Paula's apartment building, and she'd lost everything except the few things she'd been able to salvage on the way out. Fortunately, her cat Bella was saved as well. Paula and Bella were staying with a friend, but for some reason, that arrangement would be short-lived.

It seemed like fate, because, as luck would have it, Joy was getting ready to call a real estate agent . . . the next day to rent her house out. They quickly checked out of Kroger's and immediately headed to Joy's rental. The deal was done within the hour. Paula was thrilled, and Joy felt that she had a good tenant as she'd known Paula for several years, so she gave Paula a small break on the rent and didn't charge a security deposit.

But two months in, Joy's cell buzzed. It was Paula.

She didn't have the rent check, but she did have a great story. And as Joy listened to Paula's long story of why she had no money and couldn't make the rent, she remembered a conversation with Paula, gushing about how much fun Paula's outings were at the casino as she's a "regular and gets freebies there all the time! You should go with me sometime!" Joy's safety intuition went off.

Paula, believing that she'd successfully sold the lie, concluded, "So you can see why it's impossible for me to meet the rent for a couple of weeks, as much as I'd like to."

Then Joy laughed out loud and said, "Good story. But unfortunately, if you can't make the rent, you'll have to move out. I have to pay my mortgage, so I'll have to find another renter."

Even though Paula finally paid, she couldn't be trusted anymore. Joy couldn't be sure that Paula wouldn't play another story in the future, so she was asked to move on. The lesson is that friends can be opportunistic too.

Joy was able to recognize a story when she heard one, because she heard them every day on the street. And if you think that someone wouldn't try to scam a cop, you'd be wrong, because chutzpah, or audacity, is an important part of the con.

And, as Paula demonstrated, fraud is an equal-opportunity crime. According to FBI statistics, 77 percent of violent crimes are committed by men, but anyone can be a scammer.

We hope that you begin to use your safety intuition to recognize a story and to remain persuasion-proof when you hear one. Because when you stand up for yourself and refuse to become part of the story, you'll avoid becoming a victim.

Grifters are going to grift, but you don't have to put out the welcome mat for them on your front door.

Characteristics of the Scam Artist

All successful liars basically have three key personality characteristics: charisma, chutzpah, and conceit.

Charisma: This is a big one. Scammers definitely need charisma of some sort, the ability to make someone like and trust them because they have to be able to sell the story. Hardly anyone will accommodate a person's request unless they trust that person and feel like they have a rapport or connection with them. And almost all of us fall for charisma, even when we know better. It's just that powerful.

At one time, Elizabeth Holmes was the world's youngest self-made billionaire. She was an unlikely candidate for the source of her wealth: a Silicon Valley start-up that promised world-class pharmaceutical companies a revolutionary biomedical device that would dramatically alter the medical industry forever. Her company, Theranos, was once valued at $10 billion and featured investments from the wealthiest and most connected people on the planet: Rupert Murdoch, the DeVos family, Robert Kraft of the New England Patriots football team, and more. Theranos's board also didn't lack heavyweights: former Secretaries of State Henry Kissinger and George Schulz, former US Senators Bill Frist and Sam Nunn.

All this available firepower would lead one to believe that Holmes had street cred a mile long to warrant all the world's elite lining up to associate with her and essentially writing her a blank check—especially as a woman in famously bro-culture Silicon Valley. But no. Holmes was a college dropout with zero professional health care or even science experience. No one in their right mind would throw money at her.

To the surprise of no one who was not involved, the story ended badly. The technology didn't work, patients were misdiagnosed, and investors lost their money. How did she pull it off in the first place? Elizabeth was a one-trick pony, but it was a powerful trick: charisma. In *Bad Blood: Secrets and Lies in a Silicon Valley Startup* by *Wall Street Journal* reporter John Carreyrou, we get a glimpse of her charismatic superpowers.

> Mosley had a weekly meeting with Elizabeth scheduled for that afternoon. When he entered her office, he was immediately reminded of her charisma. She had the presence of someone much older than she was. The way she trained her big blue eyes on you without blinking made you feel like the center of the world. It was almost hypnotic. Her voice added

to the mesmerizing effect: she spoke in an unusually deep baritone.

Holmes also had the other two characteristics of a hustler: chutzpah and narcissism.

Chutzpah: a Yiddish word for audacity. The perfect chutzpah scenario would be a person who has killed their parents and thrown themselves on the mercy of the court because they're an orphan. Chutzpah allows cons to get away with things the rest of us wouldn't even dream of, like Paula trying to scam a cop.

Narcissism or conceit: Grifters must have a self-centered streak a mile wide to devastate their victims' lives without a second thought to the carnage they leave in their wake. It's not that they think highly of themselves, or that they think often of themselves, but that they think only of themselves. Now, most of them may not admit it, even to themselves, but they couldn't do what they do to their victims otherwise. It never once occurs to them to give their victims a second thought. Even in prison, most criminals deny culpability, most insisting that they're the ones who've been victimized.

The series *Inventing Anna* details another scam by a female con artist. The series was based on a true story involving a fake German heiress calling herself Anna Delvey—but whose real last name was Sorokin—who conned New York's party people by pretending to have a $67 million trust fund in Europe. She used the claim of her trust fund as the basis for scamming not only rich socialites but well-known financial institutions such as Fortress and Citibank. Her ultimate goal was to get the institutions to loan her $22 million to establish a nonexistent arts foundation, using her fake trust fund as collateral. In reality, she actually didn't have a cent to her name.

In the midst of this scam, Sorokin's personal friends were not rich or influential. They were regular working people: a hotel concierge, a personal trainer, and a magazine photo editor. As the story unfolded, it turned out that Sorokin also tried to con these friends in different ways. Surrounded by the aura of success that Sorokin projected to lure potential investors, it was difficult for the friends to face the fact that Sorokin was actually a scammer, even when they actually saw evidence or experienced it in a way that couldn't be dismissed.

For example, Rachel DeLoache Williams was one of those "friends." Sorokin had invited her on a trip to Marrakech and then stuck her with the $70,000 hotel bill on her employer's credit card, telling her that she'd pay her back. Williams never would have agreed to take the trip had she known that Sorokin was actually broke. Over several months, as Williams gradually became more panicked due to her inability to pay off her company credit card, Sorokin continually claimed that she'd pay her back and belittled her panic. During those months, Williams kept believing in Sorokin and fell for lie after lie until it finally sunk in. In her 2019 book, *My Friend Anna*, DeLoache Williams described Sorokin as "a fraudster whose narcissism was despicable and whose scheming was indiscriminate."

She could have been describing every single scammer.

This goes back to our socialization. Women can shake up their "politeness" conditioning and understand that even seemingly nice people can dupe even the sharpest of women—right to their face.

Sadly, the scammer can even swing a red flag in front of you like a bullfighter, but many women fall for the scammer's persona and think that the red flag is a fashionable cape. When you hear a distressing story and the outcome suddenly becomes your problem to solve, stop the train right there. Be persuasion-proof.

How Liars Sell the Story

But how does the liar sell the story when it seems so obvious to see through? As an outsider, when we hear about a story that someone else has fallen for, like DeLoache Williams did, it is tempting to be condescending, priding ourselves that we would never allow ourselves to get into that situation. We would be able to see right through that load of rot. And every one of us tries to sell ourselves *that* story.

But that high horse is out to pasture somewhere when we're the victim.

Because the truth of the matter is that we're all susceptible to being fooled. We just have to want something badly enough to let our guard down. All the con must do is find out what it is that we want that badly and then sell it to us. Or rather, set the trap and allow us to sell it to ourselves.

How does it happen? Joy has observed that almost all wolves and liars basically use the same tactics to sell the lie and fool the lambs: persona, distraction, trust, rapport, and manipulation. The liar develops a persona, which is basically a distraction for their true motives. Then they use that persona to establish trust and rapport, and finally, manipulate the victim into giving them what they want. Victims are so bedazzled by the persona and so emotionally invested, because they trust the liar, that they never see the manipulation coming. Because if the con is really good, the victim will never even know it happened.

Which is why we may never know if a successful con was played on us. So if you find yourself on a high horse judging someone else who got played, you may want to remember that anyone can be conned.

Here's the takeaway: Just because someone appears to be successful, don't assume that they really are. As these stories show, once a person believes that you've successfully been sold on their story, that's when the con happens. And even though a scam may not be as violent as a robbery, the traumatic effect can be just the same. They have something of value that used to belong to you, but you wouldn't have given it to them if you knew the truth.

Although we've basically been discussing one-on-one cons, the technology revolution has made it possible for us to get defrauded from anywhere in the world. Federal Trade Commission (FTC) data shows that consumers reported losing almost $9 billion to fraud in 2022, an increase of more than 30 percent over the previous year.[1]

The only thing that technology has accomplished regarding scams is to make them far easier to proliferate. It's bad and getting worse. In *Scam Me If You Can*, Frank Abagnale, former con artist (who, before he was twenty-two, successfully assumed eight identities, including airline pilot, a doctor, and a lawyer) and current FBI consultant, notes, "At no other point in history has it been easier to be a con artist, or to be victimized by one. In the past decade, technology has completely transformed the landscape of scams, making them quicker, more global, more anonymous, and more interconnected than ever before."

Empowered by technology, scam culture is here to stay.

The most commonly reported category that the FTC reports are imposter scams.

An imposter is a criminal who adopts a persona: when someone pretends to be a trustworthy person so that you send them money.

These include:

- Tech-support scams;
- Investment scams;
- Social Security/IRS scams;
- Grandparent scam (where someone impersonates a grand-child needing funds);
- Jury duty scam;
- Sweepstakes/lottery scam (you won a prize, but you need to send money to get it);
- And many more.

And those are just the shams that are reported. An unknown number of people don't report being swindled, because they're embarrassed at being taken.

One of these unreported victims was our friend, Maria, who lost money in the tech-support scam. We suspect that she lost $30,000 (or more) in that scam. She didn't even want us to know that she'd been had, let alone notify law enforcement. We'll detail Maria's situation shortly.

Going back to the *Inventing Anna* series, two characters, both based on real people, are depicted as being taken by Anna Sorokin but were so embarrassed that they didn't tell anyone, not even law enforcement. Nora Radford is portrayed as a wealthy Manhattan businesswoman who loses hundreds of thousands of dollars to grifter Sorokin. Despite having so much money stolen, Nora declined to press charges because she was ashamed that she'd been scammed. Allen Reed in the series is a real estate attorney who fell for Sorokin's story and, based solely on her persona, checked the new client intake boxes, indicating that she had access to resources and wouldn't embarrass the firm. He then connected her with Citibank, Fortress, City National Bank, and others to arrange a $22 million loan.

Why would someone with Reed's street cred and cachet do that? Simple. He's already rich but wanted more. That man was flat-out greedy. The prospect of the recurring commissions that such a loan would generate caused that greed to get right into his eyes and blind him to his due-diligence obligation to the firm. He also was embarrassed at being bilked, although to be fair, this victim did contribute to his own bilking.

But why are the victims the ones who are embarrassed? Joy has observed that scammers are habitual and shameless, actually proud of how much they bilk. So if you don't have chutzpah and cruelty in spades, consider another occupation besides scamming people.

Some fraudsters find that they just can't get enough as solopreneurs, so they grow large, organized tentacles. Breast Cancer Research and Support Fund, Disabled Veterans Services, United States Firefighters Association. Wouldn't it be difficult to say no to charities that supported such worthy causes? But all these funds were operated by a group of umbrella companies with various names like Seven Sisters of Healing, Inc., Community Charity Advancement, Inc., National Community Advancement, Inc.

Prosecutors say that all these companies served one man: Douglas Sailors. They note that for almost a decade, as much as 98 percent of the donations collected supported Sailors's lavish lifestyle or was used to pay the lawyers and accountants to make the funds look legitimate.[2] Joy notes that Sailors is an example of a serial scammer. He was convicted of Medicare fraud in 1999, released in 2002. In 2007, he began setting up his series of fraudulent charities. Despite prosecutors seeking recovery of at least $22 million, he was released on just a $250,000 bond.

The 2022 FTC data shows that fraud is not a victimless crime. That year the FTC received 2.4 million fraud reports from consumers. How many good-hearted people turned their hard-earned cash over to Sailors? How many more Marias and Noras are out there, too ashamed of being taken to discuss or report it?

Scammers are extremely adept at using greed, sympathy, or fear to con their victims. And, as we'll discuss later, they use high-pressure tactics to manipulate their victims. If you become or have been the victim of fraud, be assured that it is nothing to be ashamed of, and for the love of yourself, report it to law enforcement, no matter how minor you think it is. Some cities, like Fort Lauderdale, Florida, make it easy for you and offer a scamming hotline. See if your area offers one.

Distraction

Like magicians, one of the primary tools of the con is distraction. Now you see your stuff, now you don't.

Laura was once having trouble getting a ticket in a Barcelona subway station when two very nice women came along and offered to help. In the middle of being distracted by the conversation, Laura glanced down and saw that one of the women had her hand in Laura's bag. Joy observed later that the pair must have been amateurs because they were caught in the act—the cardinal sin for a pickpocket.

Joy also notes that the same ploy is often used in airports, malls, and other busy locations. One person strikes up a conversation with the passenger or shopper while their accomplice switches luggage or quietly takes the passenger's bag or purse.

This is also true when people are in your home. One may ask to use the restroom (and search for valuables elsewhere in the home) while the other keeps you occupied in conversation.

But also, like magicians, many cons operate alone (who wants to split the cash?). Solo operators are usually very good. They can practically talk your money right out of your wallet (and this includes friends and family as well as strangers). Whenever you find yourself being talked into or out of something, use your safety intuition to ask yourself why the person is pushing you in this particular direction. Does it benefit you—or them?

Conning the Con

The most dangerous weapon of most predators isn't a gun or knife—it's their mouth. The story. But did you know that this is true on both sides of the law? Cops themselves aren't above sporting a wooly little guise and selling a story themselves, when necessary.

When you think of the police arresting a suspect, what comes to mind?

Usually, people think of an argument, a fight, and possibly weapons being drawn. And that would be true; the thought of jail or prison can bring out the worst in people. But fortunately, a good deal of Joy's arrests went down peacefully. Why? First, because she treated every suspect with respect, no matter what crime they were arrested for, no matter how despicable they seemed, no matter who they were. And a lot of them responded by apologizing for their behavior and admitting that it wasn't Joy's fault that they'd been arrested but, instead, acknowledged that the arrest resulted from their own actions.

But the biggest weapon she used against criminals was to create rapport with them. Prior to the arrest, she chatted with them and made them believe that she understood where they were coming from when they committed the crime. Once arrested, it was better to have an arrestee go willingly, preventing dangerous fights or a fleeing suspect. This is important because perps have already rationalized the crime within themselves, or they'd never commit it. Serial killer Donald Harvey could also have been talking about skilled cops when he mentioned being able to "talk a junkyard dog out of a garbage can." The perps that Joy arrested in those situations didn't realize that they were being scammed themselves, that they were being sold a story.

In other words, she conned the con.

Now this didn't happen 100 percent of the time, of course. It's a war zone out there, and not everyone wants to play nice. Some subjects, particularly if they're hopped up on something, want nothing to do with a conversation. They'll fight no matter what, especially the ones who swear that they'll never go back to prison.

In those cases, Joy had no other choice except to bring the hammer down. And that did happen 100 percent of the time if respect and rapport didn't work.

This same rapport building is used in almost every prisoner/jailer situation. It is the basis of the Stockholm syndrome, where kidnappers use it to build a relationship with their victims and get them to actually feel affection toward their captor. The North Koreans used it with American POWs to get them to falsely confess to war crimes that they didn't commit (as we discussed in Chapter 7), and it is the go-to technique of law enforcement interrogations of a crime suspect.

Why is this worth mentioning?

Because if the ability to make someone like and believe you is this powerful between known adversaries, imagine how persuasive it is when a woman has no idea that she's the mark. Which is why it's the basis of every sham, scam, and con. And rapport is based on trust.

Trust should be a commodity that you deal in sparingly. Instead of automatically trusting a person because they smile, are charming, or talk nicely to you, make them *earn* your trust. You can start small and then increase as time goes on. If the situation is a short transaction, you can be polite yet still use your safety intuition and remain persuasion-proof.

It is to the advantage of the con to make you believe that a transaction is a relationship. It isn't. It can be a pleasant transaction, but they aren't your friend, nor are they going to have anything to do with you once this transaction is done. If they persist, reread Chapter 5 to remind yourself how to be persuasion-proof.

The Currency of the Con

Joy looked at Laura as Carlo's frantic voice could be heard sobbing through the speakerphone. "Oh, my God. Help. Help! I don't know how much she's already given him!" Carlo's girlfriend, Maria, had a good job with a large medical firm. She was one of the top people in her field but knew next to nothing about technology. So when she got a call promising a lifetime guarantee to protect all her technology from scammers, including her work computer, she jumped on it. Carlo had called us in desperation after overhearing Maria promising to wire the mystery caller $30,000 for the "lifetime guarantee."

Joy advised Maria to call law enforcement, and Laura tried to explain to her that protecting her work laptop was her employer's responsibility, not hers. We never found out what Maria ultimately did, but it seemed doubtful that she contacted law enforcement. She seemed inclined not to listen to us, because the guy on the phone was "so nice."

We've all been Maria in that situation at some point in our lives. Every single one of us.

Why? Everyone can be swindled because humans are hardwired to trust. And trust is the currency of the con and the liar.

Trust and the Science of Deception

Humans are hardwired to trust. How do we know that, and what does it actually mean? Dr. Timothy Levine is distinguished professor and chair of Communication Studies at University of Alabama in Birmingham. Since 1984, Dr. Levine has specialized in effective communication, particularly focusing on deception, deception detection, and interrogation. In his book *Duped*, Dr. Levine cites the hundreds of deception experiments that he has run and the thousands that he's studied—and concludes that the best almost anyone can accomplish in discerning whether a person is telling the truth or not is approximately 56 percent—slightly better than chance.

How is this possible? Most of us consider ourselves pretty savvy consumers and a damn good judge of character. Residents from one state in the United States even pride themselves on their skepticism: "You'll have to show me. I'm from Missouri."

Sage was a sharp businesswoman who dressed well and enjoyed the good life. She met Micah, a Buffalo native, at a Pittsburgh hockey game. Seated next to each other, they good-naturedly argued whether the Penguins or the Sabres ruled the ice. Afterward, they continued their "debate" over an Iron City beer and met again the following night for dinner. Sage frequently dated but had been looking for a partner for quite a while and she really, really liked this guy.

An athlete since high school, she loved discussing sports with Micah so much that she didn't bother to find out much else about him. He told her that he worked for the electric company but was laid off for the winter so money was a little tight. Sage didn't mind; she also knew other guys who were in Micah's situation. Winter could be tough in a lot of ways if you worked outside in Pittsburgh. But money wasn't an issue for her. She'd had a good job for years and was financially secure. And although she'd frequented games often in the past, she began buying tickets to every sporting event and concert in town so that Micah could go and took him on lots of trips because it seemed as though he'd never been out of Pittsburgh. "Micah's never been there before" was her refrain.

She introduced Micah to her friends and became irritated when, one by one, they quietly informed her that she was getting scammed. It turned out that Micah only worked for the "power company" when the mood struck him for cash under the table. And the mood didn't seem to strike him that often anymore, especially with all the traveling and entertainment that he was rapidly getting used to. But Sage had fallen in love, quickly buying a house and moving Micah in from the government Section Eight housing that he shared with three other roommates.

Despite ultimately finding out that her friends were spot-on and that Micah was basically destitute, instead of breaking up with someone who basically used her for her money, Sage doubled down and also pretended that Micah had a job—while she paid the bills.

Dr. Levine provides us with part of the answer with his truth-default theory. Based on his life's work in deception detection, he postulates that when we communicate with each other, we basically assume that the other person is telling the truth. In *Duped*, Levine notes, "Most people lie infrequently. Most people are honest most of the time. There are a few people who lie often. Most lies are told by a few prolific liars." Therefore, based on the odds, our default is to perceive people to be honest, and basically don't assume lying until the evidence is overwhelming (and even then, but more about that later). In other words, it is human nature to believe that what people are telling us is true, which makes us vulnerable to being deceived by those who aren't.

Think about the truth in relationship to your own daily life: In the majority of your day-to-day encounters, you clearly find no evidence of fraud. The gas station reflects the price at the pump, the grocery store clerk accurately rings up the number of groceries you purchase, and your significant other tells you that tonight's dinner will be salad and pasta. You fill your car, get your groceries, and hope that the fettuccini isn't overdone. Because of the overwhelming number of things in our lives that we can count on, we live on autopilot for the most part.

So far, Dr. Levine is discussing everyone on the planet. But for women, this is only part of the answer, because it's even more complicated for us. But before we delve into the takeaways for women from Sage's situation, let's take a broader look at some of the ways that strangers and our less-intimate relations use us to line their pockets and why we fall for their foolishness.

Pro **TIP:**

It's no accident. It's all about the feeling of connection. You feel me?

What is it that makes us fall for their brazen lies, whether we know them or not?

The Story and Rapport

Stories are the oldest form of human diversion there is. Stories engage our feelings and create the sense of connection that we all need, which is why the story is the keystone of the con.

When we're interested in a story, we're almost hypnotized. Our rational mind goes on vacation, and our emotions go into overdrive. Just like the key to getting an audience to sit through a two-hour movie is to get them to let down their guard and suspend their disbelief, that same engagement occurs whenever we hear a story. It's like a siren song because our feelings are involved.

We can examine facts; we can agree or disagree about facts. But as Maria Konnikova points out in *The Confidence Game*, "Why is the emotional approach so important when it comes to the play (scam)? Simply put, because emotions cause us to act in a way that nothing else quite does—and action is just what the confidence artist wants. That is the con's entire endpoint."

Sometimes rapport and the story are created with just a few words.

"Hey, guy. How ya doing?"

Joy glanced in the squad car's rearview mirror at the suspect handcuffed in the back seat. He caught her eye in the mirror and burst into tears. He *should* have been crying. He'd just killed his wife in a domestic dispute. Joy had arrested him and was driving him to jail to be booked for murder. Joy tried to strike up a conversation with suspects if they weren't being a jerk to her. It kept them distracted and calm till she could get them booked.

"Hey." She continued, "It'll be okay. This will all get sorted out."

Those two sentences were all it took to sell the story to the suspect and to create rapport. He cried even harder and then confessed everything before they even arrived at the jail.

It *was* a story that Joy was selling. Because it is *never* going to be okay when someone gets murdered. And despite what she said, there was zero connection because Joy was personally revolted. But cons aren't the only ones who present with a persona. In law enforcement, when a crime is being investigated and crucial intelligence needs to be obtained from a perpetrator, tactics of conning the con can be used. This can be particularly crucial when time is of the essence.

Chapter Eleven

Women and Weapons

With the increase in violence in the world, women who never thought of arming themselves before are now asking the question: How can I protect myself?

We know many, many women who have been physically assaulted in some form or other. Some knew their attacker, some didn't. As a result, we urge you to ensure that you have some type of weapon at your immediate disposal as often as possible.

Your first level of protection is always your safety intuition because without it, you won't see the ambush coming until it's too late. But once you realize that an attack is imminent, you'll need some means of defending yourself, just because you could be easily overpowered.

There are many ways of doing so. You could take self-defense classes, and that is great if you have the funds and the time. But keep in mind that like anything, it takes time and practice to become proficient. An alternative (or supplement) is to use a weapon. Not all weapons are firearms, but a gun *is* the most lethal way to defend yourself. There are other weapons that can disable or incapacitate an attacker without physically harming them. In this chapter, we will cover considerations when choosing what type of weapon to arm yourself with.

Values

But before we get into the details of this weapon or that, let's discuss values for a moment.

Many people, especially women, have emphatically told us that they could not harm, let alone shoot, anyone. We take their statement at face value and respect their beliefs.

If that reflects your intrinsic value system and you haven't examined it, we invite you to revisit that philosophy. And here's why: In his excellent book, *Violence of Mind: Training and Preparation for Extreme Violence*, author Varg Freeborn puts it succinctly:

> Your values are the standards and personal principles that govern your behavior. How you see the world and treat others is based on your values and what you deem to be important in life. Do you always try to see the good in others? Do you try to be fair and honest, regardless of the other person's behavior? These values must be identified, and in some cases, separated from the decisions you use in violence. . . .
>
> If you were senselessly attacked in a violent way to the point that you or someone you care about is in mortal danger, then that attacker deserves no further consideration. This will be in stark contrast to the value system that you have lived with all of your life. If you do not directly recognize and address this, you will be in serious trouble during or after a conflict.

Read that again: If you or someone you care about is in mortal danger from a predator, *the attacker deserves no further consideration.* Neither of us were raised with that belief. We developed it from experience. In her law enforcement role, Joy was involved in hand-to-hand combat on almost a daily basis. And though Laura grew up in a violent home, encountering violence had not been her way of life as an adult. But being of petite stature has given predators the misconception that she would be an easy target. So she has had to fight off several attackers over the years. She has punched two men in the throat when they attacked her on two separate occasions. Though she was able to stop both attacks, she is aware that she might not be as fortunate a third time.

Being attacked once upset her. Being attacked the second time inflamed her. Even though Laura physically fought her parents growing up, being assailed by strangers changed her. Being assaulted by predators fundamentally changed her values—and her daily preparation for self-defense. Laura unconsciously internalized this way of thinking and living after the second attack but does so on a conscious level now. You may want to consider it as well.

If you are thinking that this mindset is a terrible way to live, let us reassure you that we're not extreme, we're just aware—and ready. Knowing that we're using our safety intuition, remaining persuasion-proof, and preparing for almost any encounter gives a feeling of freedom and of being at ease in the world.

The Big Question: Gun or No Gun?

As we mentioned earlier, when we use the term *weapon,* we don't always mean a gun or firearm. There are *many* weapons available. In fact, as you'll see shortly, almost anything can be a weapon. Some things make better weapons than others, but literally *anything* can be used. Including a pen.

A gun isn't for everyone.

Now before you gun owners go ballistic (pun intended), a gun *is* for you if you are confident that you can kill someone with it, have trained with the one that you'll use, and are comfortable handling it. That's why we urged you to consider your value system earlier.

If you can't say with 100 percent certainty that you could kill someone if your own or a loved one's life is in danger, then don't waste your money, because just having a gun won't do you one bit of good. In fact, being untrained and unfamiliar with its use could get you into a deeper mess at a time when you didn't think that things *could* get any worse.

Having and using a gun is a highly *personal* decision. Like sex and money, it's a choice that you and *only* you can make for yourself. And it should be a decision that should be made without undue pressure from family, friends, anyone, or anything with an agenda.

Full disclosure: We both own guns. As a law enforcement officer for almost thirty years, Joy has had comprehensive training and can shoot with great accuracy under almost every condition; she takes her safety seriously, so she is always armed with a firearm and other weapons. Laura has also trained extensively, including under less than optimum conditions, to develop her ability to react under stress. They both practice on a regular basis to keep their skills sharp.

But before you go out and buy a gun or even pick one up, answer the following questions:

- Do you know how to check if it's loaded?
- Will you examine it yourself to see if it's loaded?

- Do you know how to use it right now (unless you are in a class)?
- Have you trained, or will you train enough to use it when you're under stress/attack? When your body has done an adrenaline dump, your hands are shaking, and you're too panicked to think clearly?
- Are you fully prepared to use it to incapacitate an attacker or to end someone's life if they intend to harm you or someone you love? (Note—*to save a life,* not to protect your money.)

If you answer no to any of these questions, then carefully back away from the gun.

Some people, especially women, just aren't comfortable with guns. It's *not* our mission to change your mind. It is our mission to encourage you to consider several scenarios in which you could be attacked and how you would defend yourself if you were.

Because if you have at least considered your options, you'll be less likely to freeze and more likely to have the mental ability and a weapon to defend yourself against a predator.

Let's look at both sides.

Pro-Gun Argument

The biggest argument for guns is that they are the alpha personal weapon, the most powerful self-defense tool you can have. This gives you several advantages:

- **The gun is the top of the weapon food chain.** A good example is an iconic scene from the first Indiana Jones movie from back in the day: Harrison Ford as Indiana is fleeing from a pack of goons and comes face-to-face with a swordsman. The swordsman brandishes his sword with some fancy moves to intimidate Ford, so Ford just pulls out his gun from thirty feet away and simply shoots him with a minimum of fuss.

- **Guns level the playing field.** In a physical fight, most men can overpower most women. So you obviously want to stay as physically far away from a perpetrator as you can and also keep them from coming anywhere near you. Nothing says, "Don't come any closer," better than a gun does. Even the biggest, fastest human can't outrun a bullet. Caveat: Don't scream out, "I have a gun!" They may respond, "Me too."

- **Guns stop the attacker if you hit and disable the person.** Intimidation factor—if someone is trying to break into your house or your bedroom, nothing will make that person change their mind like a gun will. Even the sound of a gun will stop a perpetrator right then and there. An urban legend in South Florida is that in the aftermath of Hurricane Andrew, the Category Five hurricane that left many in their homes without power for months, gangs were going from house to house to see what they could loot—whether the homes were occupied or not. The sound of a shotgun being racked on the other side of a door stopped that shit right in its tracks.

All these are powerful arguments for having a gun. So when *isn't* having a gun a good idea for you?

No-Gun Argument

There are some people who just should not own a gun or try to use one. Owning a gun is a serious responsibility that demands training, a clear head, and self-control at all times. A gun is not the best choice of defense if you:

- Could be attacked and not use it, even if you are able to;
- There is one in your house, but you don't know how to use it;
- Have a gun "just to have it" in your bag.

Keep in mind many accidental deaths have occurred at home from someone cleaning a gun and not using proper safety or from good Samaritans who have been killed by trying to help because responding police saw a person with a gun and thought that the Samaritan was the subject they were called on. Most deaths that occur in the home from firearms are caused by improper handling, and the homeowner was killed. These guns tend to be left unsecure at home, where they're stolen, or children find a gun and then turn it on family members (intentionally or accidentally). Lately, kids of all ages are finding that gun and taking it to school, where inevitably someone gets killed. Today, with active shooters on the rise, if you're armed and plan to take out the shooter, be aware of some factors: innocent bystanders could get hurt, or you may be advertising your hiding place to the shooter(s).

Moving Ahead with a Gun for Defense

Okay, you've thought about the considerations, and you've decided to choose a gun as one of your defensive options. So many women ask Joy: What kind of gun should I get? The answer is: it varies from person to person, depending on your hand and grip strength to hold the gun.

Ask your friends, family, co-workers, or neighbors if they are knowledgeable about various firearms. If they are, ask them to go with you to a firing range. But make your own decision. It's like buying a car; take it for a test drive on the range. You should get some training and rent some guns at the range during that training. The classes aren't free but are well worth it for your safety and to build experience. Would you buy a pair of shoes without trying them on?

Then visit a gun store. If this is your first time, be aware that it may not be what you think. Many stores not only carry guns—pun intended—they also stock clothes, purses, carry bags, alternative weapons, and cases. There are men and women salespeople, in case you feel more comfortable speaking with a woman. Also, the gun range areas have glass enclosures so you can watch people shooting without having to be on the firing line. This is important if you're not ready for that yet. Going to the gun range will also give you an idea of what the new larger guns sound like. If you've never heard gunfire before, go to a range so you hear how that sound makes you feel. Practice your four-point breathing steps if you get overwhelmed. Also, take advantage of the concealed carry classes that some gun stores offer. The classes will give you an overview of the laws in your state.

There's always something new on the market that is being advertised as "the best" and only thing you should carry. But keep in mind that women's self-defense needs are different from those of men.

Not all women's hands are as large as men's, so if you're buying a gun, you need to have an expert at the gun store fit you properly. It's not as easy as buying it online and being done. All firearms may look the same, but some of the features, such as the safety or trigger, might be difficult for some women's small hands to manipulate. Also, the weight of many handguns is deceiving without the ammunition added. Another important factor in buying a gun is the recoil. This is the force that occurs when the gun is fired. Some women have difficulty controlling a gun with a powerful recoil. That issue can cause you to injure yourself, or to not be able to shoot the attacker. If the attacker sees that you can't stabilize the gun, they'll feel emboldened to grab it from you. There are different calibers. It's best to start with a small caliber and then work your way up.

Semiautomatic guns eject the spent bullet cartridge. The following are semiautomatic pistols that have a magazine of bullets inserted in the bottom of the grip.

- **9mm:** This caliber is probably the most popular. It's manufactured by many companies, so you have a large selection to choose from. Ammunition is always available for this type of caliber. It's a great gun for women for self-defense.
- **.40 and .45:** These calibers have more stopping power than the other calibers but tend to be heavier and difficult to conceal. They also have a bigger recoil.
- **.380 Automatic Colt Pistol (ACP):** This is a small, inexpensive, lightweight, and easy-to-conceal gun for self-defense. It's not as powerful as the other semiautomatic pistols, but it is capable of stopping an attacker.

A revolver is different than the semiautomatic pistols. Its spent bullet cartridge stays in the gun's chamber. Some revolvers include:

- The .38 is a good choice because it is easy to use and maintain. They have a small ammunition capacity of six rounds and are concealable on yourself or in your bag.
- Revolvers can also come in larger models, such as .44 Magnum, which can contain more bullets and larger ammunition rounds. In the *Dirty Harry* movies, the feared inspector was

known for carrying a .44 Magnum, known at that time as the most powerful handgun in the world. It's still up near the top. It is actually too heavy for concealed carry but is an excellent choice for home use.

There are also a lot of things that may look great when you first see them, but unfortunately, like so many other cool things you have with dust on them stored away and forgotten about, if they aren't something you'll use every day, they are useless to you and a waste of money.

Gun Ownership

Remember, if you're a gun owner, you should be proficient with it, keeping your skills sharp with practice. If you carry your gun with you all the time, you should find a training facility that lets you draw from where you carry the gun. If you need to draw quickly, you'll need muscle memory to get the gun out of the holster—from your bag, leg, or belt area. Practicing builds that muscle memory. You do not want to be in a position where you'll need your gun, only to suddenly realize that the zipper on your bag sticks, or that you have trouble getting it out of the holster in the small of your back. It's little things like this that will loom large in an emergency. These are also the things that can inadvertently cause injuries to you or an unintended person.

If you have a gun because you got it as a gift, or want to purchase a firearm, go to a gun range in your area and ask about lessons. Test out different guns until you feel comfortable there under an instructor. Then you can do your price comparisons and see which kind works for you. Guns are only similar in the fact that when the trigger is pulled, a potentially life-ending bullet is propelled.

Even if you're a long-time gun owner and you already know all this, remember that you do lose dexterity in your hands as you age. The gun you've had for years may now be hard to load and difficult to shoot. If you have had an injury or arthritis, that old gun might need to be traded in for the newest model that is easier for you to use in an emergency. Joy also reminds you that we all need to practice.

If you do want to have a variety of guns in your possession for the family, sometimes it's easier to keep them all the same caliber, so that all of them use the same ammunition. Also, in the event of a threat and a family member needs to load a gun, they won't have to worry about finding the right bullets, especially if it's dark in the house at the time.

Make sure that you haven't gone lax on gun safety in the home. If you use the same bag for traveling as you do to take your gun equipment to the range, you might want to invest in a designated bag for firearms. Joy has encountered many professional and weekend warriors who forgot to take their firearms out of their carry-on bag from the range and were the unlucky person who got pulled aside at the airport for carrying a gun in their bag at the checkpoint! It's jail time and a costly event. Always check your bags, coat pockets, purses, briefcases, and laptop bags for weapons of any kind before you leave your house.

Because this is so important, we want to recap the key things you should remember before you buy a gun: Know that when you purchase a firearm you need to be responsible for it. Know where it is all the time (because it should be in the same place all the time, but that isn't always the case). You must have a mindset that if you need to protect your life or your family's, there's a good chance someone won't live. Life-changing thought. But if your home is broken into or you're attacked outside somewhere, that's a conversation you need to have with yourself. If you own a gun and used to practice at a range, go back to refresh your skills.

Remember, accidents happen. Don't say, "It will never happen to me."

It can happen to *anyone*.

Shooting Scenario

If you are in a life-or-death situation, follow the shooting pattern as shown in Figure 11.1. Start with the groin and shoot upward. You'll be nervous and full of adrenalin; this will give you a pattern to focus on, keeping your brain engaged. It will also give you a better chance of disabling the attacker, increasing the odds of hitting a vital organ. Even law enforcement knows that sometimes the attacker can still get up and charge at you! You may not have hit a vital organ or nerve center, so the attacker is injured, but they can still function. Be cautious.

The important thing to remember is shoot to stop the attacker if they keep advancing on you. For one thing, when you're panicked and scared because your stress hormones kicked in, your aim won't be good, so always try to shoot for the center of the torso, not an extremity like an arm or leg while the perp is moving at a high rate of speed. When law enforcement must defend themselves from a deadly encounter, the public tends to ask, "Why couldn't they shoot them in the leg?" It's a life-or-death situation, and law enforcement trains to aim for the large center mass, not the smallest body part running toward you, or the hand holding the firearm. So when you draw a gun, aim for the torso.

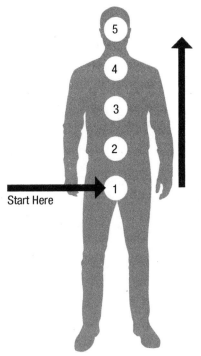

Start Here

Figure 11.1: Shooting Pattern to Disable Attacker.

At this point, it is not up to you to check on them. They may get a surge of adrenaline and resume the attack, and if you're too close, they'll succeed. If you have fired your gun at the perpetrator or hit them, here is how to engage law enforcement:

- Get yourself to safety and call 9-1-1 immediately!
- Give a location first and tell the dispatcher that you shot an attacker.
- Wait for the police but don't wait near the attacker; they may be pretending to be dead or injured.
- When the police arrive, keep your hands away from your gun.
- When they ask where the gun is, just point to it.
- Keep your hands visible and remain calm. Do your four-point breathing.

Other Weapons

Guns are one option, but they aren't your *only* option. There are alternative weapons. Although most people think of guns as synonymous with weapons, they are not. This section gives you a breakdown of the variety of self-defense weapons available. Whether or not the weapon is effective depends on the situation and often on your will to use it. As mentioned earlier, even a pen can be used as a weapon. It can be used to drive into someone's windpipe, ear, or eye. We carry tactical pens made from steel that are designed for multiuse survival situations. It is a sleek-looking refillable pen with a steel tip for glass breaking and defending against an attacker. Also mentioned earlier, Laura punched people in the throat. Her success in doing so lay in the element of surprise, which is also the only time you'd count on a pen to save you.

Predators profile their victims like lions profile zebra on the Serengeti. They pick the one that they believe will offer little resistance and therefore is easy to pick off. Laura was incorrectly profiled as a weak target. Both times, she had no other weapon available (including a pen). But instead of thrashing and screaming as they expected, she immediately went limp, then drove for the throat with her fist. Helpful tip: When counterattacking like that, drive as hard as you can toward the spine to increase damage to the windpipe. Since they weren't expecting it, Laura was fortunate that she was able to escape.

Women, if you're not comfortable with firearms, there are *nonlethal* options available! Some are listed as follows.

Taser: Energy Weapons with Projectiles

This is the brand name of an electronic weapon that resembles a gun in shape but is distinguishable by the neon color on the device. It's made of a durable polymer, and at eight ounces, it's easy to hold and use. Law enforcement uses a professional model series, but the ones for civilians are just as effective. Once you strike the subject, the Taser's cartridge affixed to the front of the weapon shoots a two-pronged barbed projectile that attaches to the subject's body. Once contact is made, you can press the trigger so that the Taser delivers a continuous shock to the attacker from fifteen feet away. The difference between a Taser and a stun gun is the proximity to the attacker: stun guns require contact with the attackers while Tasers allow you to maintain your distance.

It can immobilize an attacker for about thirty seconds. More than enough time for you to get away.

- They're affordable, ranging from around $400 to $1,300, and easy to use;
- Effective from a distance of fifteen feet, so you can safely keep your distance; and
- Can be effective against some attackers, depending on their clothing and body type.

Mini Stun Guns

Though the terms are often used interchangeably, a stun gun is different from a Taser. These are small—about the size of a flashlight—handheld devices that deliver an electric shock to the attacker when you press the device *against their body*. It causes their muscles to contract and they fall to the ground. Sometimes, it causes them to go unconscious. And although the effects don't last long, the immobilization of the attacker will provide enough time for you to flee.

- They are inexpensive and easy to use.
- They have an optional flashlight, so you can see in the dark.
- Some are disguised as other objects, such as phones and cigarette boxes, so the attacker may not realize what you are actually holding.
- They are battery operated.

Larger-Model Stun Guns

These larger models are handheld plastic or polymer devices that deliver an electric current to an attacker by pressing the button and holding it against the person's body. Similar to the "mini," it gives a powerful shock, causing the muscles to contract and the subject to fall to the ground in pain. The subject may also be disoriented by the shock.

- These larger models have a charger.
- These are great but may not be effective on intoxicated subjects or people high on drugs.

Bear Spray

Next to a gun, this is our second favorite weapon. Yes, even if you don't live in bear country. Its benefits? It can shoot a stream of pungent capsaicin for about thirty feet! It's easily aimed, and the smallest residual amount left in the air is enough to cause eye irritation, violent coughing, and respiratory issues for a while. Great if you're walking the dog or by yourself in an uncomfortable area.

Bear spray is a concentrated pepper formula in a larger, handheld canister. The effects are intense but temporary, and no lasting damage is done to the animal or to a human.

Joy had gotten the spray online to deal with several dogs in the neighborhood who sometimes escaped from their homes when the owners opened the door to walk outside. Several dogs had attacked other dogs and residents in the past, and although no serious damage had been done yet, it was obvious that they were intent on protecting their territory and meant business.

We were walking our dogs a few years ago on a pleasant fall evening. Suddenly, a large dog escaped from the front door of its home and headed straight toward us with bared teeth. Fortunately, Joy was carrying bear spray and sprayed the dog while it was twenty feet away. It stopped the attack momentarily, then lunged again. She sprayed again to stop the second attack, and it was done. The dog limped to a nearby lawn and rolled its face in the grass, trying to get pepper spray out of its eyes.

Then we calmly went on our way.

If it works against bears (and certainly large dogs), it will also work against human predators. Keep in mind that the goal is to keep the predator as far from you as possible to minimize the damage that it can inflict.

Bear spray fits that bill. You'll ideally want to aim for the eyes and face to maximize its impact. However, as noted below, a less than ideal aim will still enable the spray to do its job. You can feel confident that it will fend off an attacker.

The downside to bear spray lies in its size. To accommodate enough accelerant to propel the pepper stream as far as it does, it needs to be packaged in 8 oz. or 9 oz. canisters, as opposed to the personal-size pepper sprays. The canisters make it easy to deploy the spray when you need it, but the size makes it difficult to conceal. Although, if you're riding a bike outside, this fits great in a water bottle holder or bike bag. Don't go anywhere without some form of defense protection.

And, as with any weapon, you should be familiar with the use and deployment of sprays. You extend your arm and spray from side to side. This way if you don't hit the target directly, you have a field of mist that will be like a wall against the attacker. If the attacker is still coming closer, spray again. On a side note, do not try out any pepper spray in an enclosed environment. Breathing and seeing can be difficult if it is deployed, and it can take up to several hours for it to dissipate from the area.

Personal Pepper Spray

An all-time favorite of Joy's! It comes in many sizes and various colored cannisters, even with a Velcro holster to wear. A big advantage of this weapon is that it is legal in all fifty states. What's great about pepper spray is that you can conceal it in your hand and spray someone quickly in the face if they surprise you from behind. There are four types: mist, stream, gel, or foam.

- You can spray the mist type from approximately ten feet away in the direction of an approaching attacker. This will slow them down because it will impact their vision and respiration.
- The stream version shoots farther than the mist and is effective up to twenty feet.
- One of the most effective models is Sabre Red Pepper Gel. It has a range of about eighteen feet, and the effects can last from fifteen to forty-five minutes, depending on the attacker's stamina.

- The foam version is excellent to use up close. It covers the attacker's face with what looks like shaving cream, but it is red, and the attacker can feel the capsaicin (made from chiles) working as a burning sensation.

Mace is the brand name of the oldest kind of chemical spray, which is actually a lighter version of tear gas. The difference in pepper sprays is the strength of capsaicin, the active ingredient. Joy recommends buying a couple of them and using one as a tester. Try it out before you carry it to see how far it shoots. Also, if you try it out in your backyard and get a bit in your face, you'll know how to handle it and not freak if you spray yourself while fending off an attacker.

If you get it on your face and in your eyes, cold water and cool compresses will make you feel better shortly. You don't need eye drops, either. Just keep using cool compresses. You won't need to go to the emergency room unless you experience breathing difficulty or if the effects are bothering you for more than a couple of minutes. You be the judge of how you feel. But at least you'll know how you will react if the wind blows the spray back at you.

It's important to be aware of these trade-offs when choosing what spray to carry when. There are different brands of pepper spray. Joy recommends the pepper spray that also contains tear gas and ultraviolet (UV) marking dye. It is available online or at any sporting goods store. The attacker would be easily identifiable by the public and law enforcement. Like the dye packs the banks use when they're robbed, it gets on their face, and they stick out like a sore thumb when trying to get away.

The best feature of the spray is that the perp can be incapacitated immediately, and they'll be momentarily blinded and gasping for air.

Suddenly, they aren't interested in you, and that's your time to *run*! Is it foolproof? No. But it will immobilize the attacker.

One final note: remember that you can't take any pepper spray or Mace products in your luggage (even checked baggage) on a flight.

Knives

Nothing wrong with carrying a knife (remember to empty out your carry-on bags when traveling).

It could help you out of an up-close situation if you had access to it and were mentally prepared to stab or slash the offender. Those are also the big drawbacks to using a knife. You must be very close to the attacker, and you could be overpowered. In addition, stabbing someone is a very personal and violent thing to do. So you have to be able to visualize yourself doing so and be ready to do it, if needed.

If you choose to carry a small knife in your purse, bag, or pocket, it should be easy to open with one hand and have a grip on it, so it won't slide. Carry it concealed in your strong hand while walking alone to your car in a parking garage or on campus.

Practice opening a small knife with each hand in case you need to use your nondominant hand in an emergency.

Just showing it to the attacker will not work well for you. Never "show your cards" to an attacker. Hey, they might have one too, or it may cause them to pull a gun. But if you keep a small one concealed on yourself, you would be ready if someone grabbed you by surprise.

The advantage of using a knife is that most assailants won't expect you to have or use a knife on them, so you'll have the element of surprise. A knife is good to have in your purse or vehicle as an emergency go-to weapon. Consider situations where an attacker forces themselves in your car or tries to drag you into their car. You may not be able to access your gun but could access your knife. It could be useful to stab someone's hand as they attempt to grab you. You should know where it is at all times or get one with a clip and wear it.

Like any weapon we've discussed, make sure that you are comfortable with it in your hands before you need to use it. Try some scenarios with a friend (without the knife in the open position, or the blade exposed). Just bring it out of where you keep it hidden and prevent the attack. At least you'll have primed your brain and muscle memory, and you'll know what can work if you or a friend encounter an actual threatening situation.

Finally, a knife or all-in-one survival tool is good to keep in your car in case you need to cut yourself out of your seat belt. Always think ahead for safety.

Small Weapons

A lot of small weapons that can be hung on your keychain or key fob are good for lifesaving hand-to-hand fighting, if you could get it out of your purse or navigate through the car's center console of junk.

Here's a few that are out there and some pluses and minuses of each one:

- **Cat Ears:** (Yep, looks like a cat head, and it has pointed ears.) It's for slipping on your fingers and punching/stabbing an attacker. Could it work? Yes. But it might be difficult to use in a frantic moment. You need to have it in your hand, or the attacker will grab it or knock it out of your hand.
- **Kubaton:** (6-inch-long cylindrical tool you would grip to poke your attacker in soft tissue.) It's made from steel or hard plastic. It's meant to be used up close, on an attacker's face or throat, anywhere sensitive that you can stab them to

temporarily disable them. You want to buy time to free yourself and get away. On a somewhat sarcastic note, you might need a tissue when you realize how you need to strike the right area for it to be effective. Will it work? Yes, but you need to have practiced with it, so you don't lose it fighting.

- **Concealed self-defense rings:** A modern minimalist idea for wearing a weapon for quick access and ease of use, the downside of it is that the hand holding it could be restrained. Otherwise, it's always there on your fist ready to strike, slice, and punch.

- **Personal safety alarm:** These are usually small devices that emit a high-pitched sound when activated. They are excellent to deter an attacker and draw the attention of others. Used at night, the sudden noise and bright light will deter and disorient an attacker, giving you time to get away safely. However, keep in mind that it isn't an actual weapon.

These items are an excellent choice to add an extra layer of safety to your personal arsenal.

But like we say, be prepared. At the very least, we encourage you to carry personal self-defense spray.

No matter which option is right for you, keep in mind that you'll want to consider your self-protection plans carefully—before you need to. Use the following in your everyday life:

- Always walk with purpose and confidence;
- Glance around at your surroundings wherever you are; and
- If you detect suspicious behavior, in someone you know, from strangers, no matter who it is—pay attention—that's your safety intuition alerting you to be cautious. You may not get another notice.

Chapter Twelve
Call to Freedom

There are two ways you can learn: the easy way or the hard way. The easy way is the shortcut: learn from someone else's experience. The hard way is to find out for yourself. Hopefully, this book has provided you with the easy way.

Some of the things in here may have scared you. If so, it could be because you haven't faced the reality of predators and violence against women before. It is in society's best interest to keep the threats to our safety in the background as an implicit threat and, at the same time, tacitly assure us that it's just the way it's always been. Our lot as women: keep us afraid and thereby controlled.

The other threat is that if we dare to speak out, we'll be silenced. The world tries to silence survivors. It happened to the domestic violence movement and to #MeToo. But despite the challenges to our security, our sanity, and even our lives, women's safety is not hopeless. In fact, far from it—because our safety intuition is our natural gift and always has been. When we listen to ourselves, to our bodies, to our natural instincts, we can protect ourselves and stop living in fear.

And when we're not afraid, we can't be controlled. We are free.

The world fears free and unfettered women more than anything else, which is why so much is invested in suppressing and controlling us.

But our freedom doesn't mean that we don't care about others. It doesn't mean that we're not compassionate. Because it isn't either/or. It isn't a zero-sum game, which means that if one wins, the other loses.

We can do both. We can be independent and inclusive. But to really do that, we have to heal from trauma first.

Trauma Recovery

Helen Keller noted, "Although the world is full of suffering, it is full also of the overcoming of it."

We can attest to that.

With the growing awareness of trauma comes new discoveries of modalities that can shorten the road to wholeness.

For many years, endless repetition of talk therapy was the only tool available, sitting on a therapist's sofa and rehashing the past, hoping for a glimmer of insight. That therapeutic model certainly has its place but also its limitations. As many trauma experts have noted, trauma impacts both the mind and the body, so recovery of trauma involves both. Dr. Candace Pert, noted neuroscientist, pharmacologist, and discoverer of the opiate receptor in the brain, once remarked, "The body can't get well without the mind and the mind can't get well without the body."

After a lot of searching, we found several tools that proved helpful for us. This is by no means an exhaustive list of trauma recovery tools. It doesn't include psychotropics, psychedelics, or other medications that have proven helpful with some trauma sufferers. And there are other modalities that we're probably not even aware of.

- Meditation;
- Hypnosis;
- Breathwork;
- Rebirthing;
- Eye movement desensitization and reprocessing (EMDR);
- Cognitive behavioral therapy (CBT);
- Anger body work;
- Psychodrama;
- Biofeedback; and
- Neurofeedback.

Community

An important and often overlooked component of trauma recovery is a sense of community because trauma thrives in isolation. And, as we saw in Chapter 7, domestic abusers and captors seclude their victims so that they must rely on their capturers to define their reality. Laura's own mother rarely left her home in almost twenty years. Her world became so small that it could only be viewed by what was happening within her house—a life defined entirely by domestic violence.

Worst of all, our society shames victims, somehow convincing them that had they just done something, anything, differently, they could have avoided the tragedy that befell them. Being involved in a community can help you overcome that sense of shame by providing you with the antidote: support.

Trauma's death grip on your mind and soul cannot be sustained when you are connected to a supportive community. Knowing that you're not alone and that other people support you is a large part of twelve-step groups. No matter what you've done or have experienced, other people have done similar or had worse happen to them.

Community is the bond that breaks the bondage.

More groups such as churches, temples, and other support organizations can offer similar support. If you are unable to leave your house, there are hundreds of thousands online. And you are always welcome in our free online Facebook community as well (https://www.facebook.com/streetsmartsafety/).

Relying on a community can provide a sense of family. It can be the type of healthier family that you may have always wanted. By being there for you, a community may help you find yourself.

Trauma as Transformative

The world breaks everyone, which is why trauma is a fact of life.

And if we recognize that trauma can be overcome, then as Dr. Levine points out in *Waking the Tiger: Healing Trauma*, it doesn't have to be a life sentence.

Better yet. It can be transformative.

Post-traumatic growth is a burgeoning field that describes the positive growth that some people achieve after working through their trauma. Not only can we survive trauma, not only can we recover from it, but it can also be the springboard to launch you into a new existence.

An existence that you maybe never even dreamed of.

We aren't talking some woo-woo mystical jargon. We are talking about real-life, better-than-ever awesomeness!

Transforming trauma is a choice. A difficult task but not impossible—we have done it.

Auschwitz survivor and psychologist Dr. Edith Eva Eger says that we can choose. In *The Choice: Embrace the Possible*, Dr. Eger notes, "I can celebrate your choice to dismantle the prison in your mind, brick by brick. You can't change what happened, you can't change what you did or what was done to you. But you *can* choose how you live now. My precious, you can choose to be free."

When you choose freedom, you choose yourself, perhaps for the first time in your life.

It's been sixteen years since Laura chose vanilla extract over sobriety. She then fought back and chose recovery again. The second round of fifteen continuous clean years have been transformative. If you do the work, you also can transform trauma.

We hope you do.

You can be there for others and still kick ass.

But most of all, be there for yourself.

This isn't some "You can have it all if only you try hard enough" drivel.

It's "You don't have to attend to others, even strangers on the street, before you listen to yourself" straight talk.

You can reduce your chances of being the victim of a crime. Practice your safety intuition. Be persuasion-proof. Keeping your safety top of mind doesn't make you paranoid, it makes you confident enough to walk away or to defend yourself, if needed. And by doing so, you can also be there for others—when *you* want to.

Your safety intuition is your natural gift, your birthright. It is powerful; it is there to protect you. Don't override it. For anyone. That is why we want you to be persuasion-proof.

Don't override it wanting to be nice. Don't override it wanting to be loved. Don't override it because society tells you that you are nothing if you are not with someone.

When you honor your safety intuition, you can move through the world differently.

You are free.

Appendix One
Survival Tips

1. Never open your car window to talk to a stranger (male or female). You can speak to them through a closed window. Once you open the window or locked door, you endanger yourself.

2. "Help me!" is a term that predators may use to get you to leave your area with them, or to have you come with them to a parking lot or location where it's not busy. Then you're robbed or assaulted. Call 9-1-1 and report what you hear or are being told in case someone needs assistance.

3. Lock your car doors while pumping gas if you are alone. Predators check for unlocked doors and slide into cars to steal valuables or to hide in the back to abduct you when you get in.

4. Do not watch the TV on the gas pump while you are pumping; it is too distracting.

5. While walking outside, use the mirrored view of store windows to see if someone is following you.

6. Turn off the door lock feature on your car that unlocks all doors. This will prevent a predator from jumping into your car from the passenger side or a back door.

7. Do not immediately open a hotel or cruise cabin door to someone just because they say that they're security or staff. Call the desk to verify the person's name. Predators use this trick to gain access to travelers.

8. If any person or situation makes you uncomfortable, leave immediately! That's your safety intuition talking to you! Listen!

9. If you're not traveling alone, take your friend with you to use a convenience store bathroom. Many abductions happen near bathrooms because they're out of sight. If you are alone, carry your personal pepper spray.

10. Never let children go to the restrooms in convenience stores or department stores alone. Predators tend to look like regular patrons to them, and they can be easily overpowered, assaulted, or abducted.

11. When a male tries to get you to stop by saying, "Excuse me, miss," it is usually a ploy that predators use to get you to stop for them. Then they can attack because you're closer to them. Look at them; if they can't tell you what they want, keep going.

12. When you're traveling or going out for the evening, be sure that your phone is fully charged.

13. Keep some personal safety device of any kind, such as a Taser, pepper spray, stun gun, etc., hidden in rooms of your house, so that you are always prepared.

14. When entering your hotel room or cruise ship cabin, prop the door open, grab a hanger from the closet, and look around to

make sure that no one is concealed. Use the hanger to look under the bed or behind the curtains.

15. Don't leave windows or sliding doors open or unlocked if you're in another room and can't monitor that area, or aren't home. Use battery-operated sonic alarms for doors and windows. And use screw-on window locks to keep the windows from being pushed open.

16. Once you get into your car, do not linger in a parking lot. Predators watch for you to be alone and distracted. Get in your car and leave immediately.

17. Keep your bedroom door locked at night. Good protection in case of a fire and in case an intruder is in the house. You can be secure, hide, and call the police.

18. Have a safety plan to get out of your home if an intruder has entered. If you are on a higher floor, get a rollup ladder that you can use to exit from a window. Practice with a family member or friend.

19. When staying in a hotel, bring your own security lock (available online) for extra protection.

20. Get a video door alarm. You can view the immediate area in front of your door or home to ensure that no one is lurking. You can also answer that type of doorbell on your phone, so the person at the door doesn't know if you're not there.

21. Do not hire someone to work around/in your house if they just showed up at your door with a sob story for needing cash. Verify people and companies online.

22. Don't leave your garbage in front of your house when you are leaving on a trip and garbage day is not for a few days. Ask a

neighbor if you can leave it with theirs. That is an obvious sign you are not home.

23. When you pull into your garage, especially at night, look behind you to be sure no one pulled up behind you. Predators follow people home to rob or assault them.

24. Always look behind you before opening the driver's side door in a parking lot. Many carjackers and kidnappers sneak up behind or start talking to women at their car door to be able to force themselves inside.

25. If you're ever grabbed around the neck from behind, turn your head quickly right or left, so your chin is over the bend in their elbow. You will be able to breathe. You will be able to punch them in the face, by surprising them. You can kick their kneecap backward. As soon as they are in pain, they release their grip. Try it with a friend. If you do not turn immediately, you will pass out from carotid artery pressure.

Appendix Two
Dating Red Flags

1. Does the person prefer to communicate with you online as opposed to speaking on the phone or even meeting in a public place? They may be catfishing.

2. Did the relationship online get hot and heavy too fast? Did he pressure you into sending intimate pics after only chatting via computer for a brief period?

3. Have you caught the person in excessive lying?

4. Have you found them to be enamored with violent video games by themselves or online with strangers?

5. Does he have a substance abuse problem he's not willing to work on?

6. Has your dating partner shoved, hit, or physically hurt you?

7. Have you received expensive gifts after a few dates or way too early in the relationship? Perhaps love bombing?

8. Did you find out he is concealing an arrest history after you asked if he was ever arrested?

9. Has he pressured you for sex?

10. Have you observed inappropriate anger issues, such as road rage, blowing up at someone for an accidental issue, anger at an opposing team player, or for imaginary issues?

11. Has he shown that he's possessive by being obsessed with your ex?

12. Has he repeatedly told you that you would look better with a different hair color, larger breasts, a face-lift, or weight loss?

13. Does he insult or demean you, publicly and/or privately?

14. Is he affiliated with extremist/hate groups while telling you he is against that type of behavior?

15. Does he always want to spend more time partying with his pals than having quality time with you? Has he told you that he was stalked by an ex?

16. Have you asked him to take responsibility for his actions?

17. Do you feel you are being isolated from your family and friends?

Acknowledgments

None of us can accomplish anything without community and love. The authors thank their community and especially the following for their feedback and support: Elizabeth and Mark Wilson, Linda Friedman and Jill Bulmash, Mike Martinelli, Alison Levins, Cindi Koulax and Lorraine Ferrini, Angela Love, Jennifer Mills, Sam and Christina Parmarter, A. J. Harper, Laura Stone, the community of Top Three Books, Jill Caugherty, Stephen Gold, PhD, Stephen Karpman, MD, Teri Bunetta, LMHC, ACHT, Domestic Abuse and Intervention Programs, our editor, Darcie Abbene, and HCI Books.

Notes

Introduction

1. UN Women, "Facts and Figures: Ending Violence Against Women," accessed April 2, 2023, https://www.unwomen.org/en/what-we-do/ending-violence-against-women/facts-and-figures.

2. Ibid.

3. Judy Kurtz, "Angelina Jolie Makes Emotional Plea for Violence Against Women Act," *The Hill*, February 9, 2022, https://thehill.com/blogs/in-the-know/in-the-know/593578-angelina-jolie-makes-emotional-plea-for-violence-against-women.

4. Chantal Molop, "It's Time to Stop Normalizing Violence Against Women," *Newsweek*, February 10, 2022, https://www.newsweek.com/its-time-stop-normalizing-violence-against-women-opinion-1678066?fbclid=IwAR1_Q26lrq1rDKWQ_2SfbxXM5dKinlZS4KVmc3jm5hlXDJEyvGe7TzdNras.

5. FBI Crime Data Explorer, National Incident-Based Reporting System (NIBRS) Details Reported in the United States, accessed April 6, 2023, CDE (cjis.gov).

6. Ibid.

7. Rape, Abuse & Incest National Network, "Scope of the Problem: Statistics," accessed April 5, 2023, https://www.rainn.org/statistics/scope-problem.

Chapter One
Design for Defensive Living

1. Radu Danescu, "Detecting Micro-Expressions in Real Time Using High-Speed Video Sequences," *InterTech Open Access Books,* November 2, 2017, https://www.intechopen.com/chapters/60579.

2. Paul Ekman, "What Are Microexpressions," accessed April 5, 2023, https://www.paulekman.com/resources/micro-expressions/.

3. "Janice Ott and Denise Naslund Go Missing from Lake Sammamish State Park," *Lubbock Avalanche-Journal,* July 24, 1974, https://www.newspapers.com/clip/31115003/janice-ott-and-denise-naslund-go/.

4. Phyllis Armstrong, *Biography, Ted Bundy: Falling for a Killer,* Amazon Mini-Series, accessed April 6, 2023, https://www.imdb.com/name/nm11292444/bio?ref_=nm_dyk_trv#trivia.

Chapter Two
Victimization and Trauma

1. FBI, "Coping with Crime Victimization," fbi.gov, accessed April 25, 2023, https://www.fbi.gov/how-we-can-help-you/victim-services /coping-with-victimization.

2. Anushka Pai, "Posttraumatic Stress Disorder in the DSM-5: Controversy, Change and Conceptual Considerations," National Institute of Health, National Library of Medicine, February 13, 2017, https://www.ncbi.nlm.nih.gov/pmc/articles/PMC5371751/#B1 -behavsci-07-00007.

3. Bessel Van der Kolk, *The Body Keeps the Score: Brain, Mind, and Body in the Healing of Trauma* (New York, NY: Penguin Books, 2014), 20.

4. Bureau of Justice Statistics, "Family Violence Statistics: Including Statistics on Strangers and Acquaintances," US Department of Justice, accessed April 11, 2023, https://bjs.ojp.gov/content/pub/pdf/ fvs02.pdf.

5. Steven Karpman, "The New Drama Triangles," USAA/ITAA conference lecture, August 11, 2007, https://karpmandramatriangle .com/pdf/thenewdramatriangles.pdf.

Chapter Three
Can You Recognize a Predator?

1. FBI Crime Data Explorer, National Incident-Based Reporting System (NIBRS) Details Reported in the United States, accessed April 6, 2023, CDE (cjis.gov).

2. Samuel Samenow, *Inside the Criminal Mind*, rev. and updated ed. (New York: Broadway Books, 2014).

3. Dr. Robert C. Barkman, "Why the Human Brain Is So Good at Detecting Patterns," *Psychology Today,* May 19, 2021, https://www .psychologytoday.com/us/blog/singular-perspective/202105/why -the-human-brain-is-so-good-detecting-patterns.

4. Martha C. White, "Madoff Exploited Weak Oversight, but Did Regulators Learn Their Lesson," *NBC News,* April 14, 2021, https:// www.nbcnews.com/business/business-news/madoff-exploited -weak-oversight-did-regulators-learn-their-lesson-n1264094.

5. Dobson Digital Library, "A Serial Killer Warns the World About Pornography," accessed April 7, 2023, https://dobsonlibrary.com/ resource/article/cfeb58f0-967e-4bd5-afbe-7e12206d5ffb.

6. PBS News, "Elizabeth Holmes Gets More Than 11 Years in Prison for Theranos Scam," *PBS Newshour,* November 18, 2022, https:// www.pbs.org/newshour/economy/elizabeth-holmes-gets-more -than-11-years-in-prison-for-theranos-scam.

7. Chrissy Callahan, "Where Is Anna Delvey Now? 'Inventing Anna' Subject Is Released from Prison," *Today,* November 22, 2022, https://www.today.com/popculture/tv/anna-delvey-now -rcna15204.

Chapter Four
Technology Terror

1. Clarence Page, "Jim Bakker's Sentence Is Too Harsh," *Chicago Tribune,* October 29, 1989, https://www.chicagotribune.com/news/ ct-xpm-1989-10-29-8901260441-story.html.

2. This Day in History, "President Clinton Impeached, 1998," accessed April 7, 2023, https://www.history.com/this-day-in-history /president-clinton-impeached.

3. Joe Palazzolo, "Donald Trump Played Central Role in Hush Pay-offs to Stormy Daniels and Karen McDougal," *Wall Street Journal*, November 9, 2018, https://www.wsj.com/articles/donald-trump-played-central-role-in-hush-payoffs-to-stormy-daniels-and-karen-mcdougal-1541786601.

4. Ashley Johnson, "Overview of Section 230: What It Is, Why It Was Created, and What It Has Achieved," Information Technology and Innovation Foundation, February 22, 2021, https://itif.org/publications/2021/02/22/overview-section-230-what-it-why-it-was-created-and-what-it-has-achieved/.

5. Ibid.

6. Statista, "Most Popular Websites Worldwide as of November 2022, by Total Visits," accessed April 8, 2023, https://www.statista.com/statistics/1201880/most-visited-websites-worldwide/.

7. Worldometer, "Current World Population," accessed April 8, 2023, https://www.worldometers.info/world-population/.

8. Cat Zakrzewski, "Tech Companies Spent Almost $70 Million Lobbying Washington in 2021 as Congress Sought to Rein in Their Power," *Washington Post*, January 21, 2022, https://www.washingtonpost.com/technology/2022/01/21/tech-lobbying-in-washington/.

9. Ibid.

10. Jeff Horowitz, "The Facebook Files: A *Wall Street Journal* Investigation," *Wall Street Journal*, September 13, 2021, https://www.wsj.com/articles/the-facebook-files-11631713039?mod=series_facebookfiles.

11. Jeff Horowitz, "Facebook Says Its Rules Apply to All. Company Documents Reveal a Secret Elite That's Exempt," *Wall Street Journal*, September 13, 2021, https://www.wsj.com/articles/facebook-files-xcheck-zuckerberg-elite-rules-11631541353?mod=article_inline.

12. Aaron Schaffer, "Meet the Tech Trade Group Outspending Trump on Facebook Ads," *Washington Post*, January 10, 2022, https://www.washingtonpost.com/politics/2022/01/10/meet-tech-trade-group-outspending-trump-facebook-ads/.

13. Sue Halpern, "The Facebook Whistleblower's Testimony and the Tech Giant's Very Bad Week," *New Yorker*, October 7, 2021, https://www.newyorker.com/news/daily-comment/the-facebook-whistle-blowers-testimony-and-the-tech-giants-very-bad-week.

14. John Arlidge, "The Dirty Secret That Drives New Technology: It's Porn," *The Guardian*, March 2, 2002, https://www.theguardian.com/technology/2002/mar/03/internetnews.observerfocus.

15. Dr. Natalie Purcell, *Violence and the Pornographic Imaginary: The Politics of Sex, Gender and Aggression in Hardcore Pornography*, (New York: Routledge, 2012), 91.

16. Boston University School of Medicine, "Young Adults Say Porn Is Their Most Helpful Source of Information About How to Have Sex," accessed April 8, 2023, https://www.eurekalert.org/news-releases/817870.

17. Maria Ahlin, "Let's Talk Porn," TEDxGöteborg, June 21, 2019, https://youtu.be/DBTb71UzPmY.

18. Ibid.

19. Hannah Bowes, "Getting Away with Murder? A Review of the 'Rough Sex Defence,'" *Sage Journals,* June 29, 2020, https://journals.sagepub.com/doi/full/10.1177/0022018320936777.

20. Itsaso Biota, "Analyzing University Students' Perceptions Regarding Mainstream Pornography and Its Link to SDG5," National Library of Medicine, June 30, 2022, https://pubmed.ncbi.nlm.nih.gov/35805712/.

21. Nicholas Kristof, "The Children of Pornhub," *New York Times,* December 6, 2020, https://www.nytimes.com/2020/12/04/opinion/sunday/pornhub-rape-trafficking.html.

22. Theresa Braine, "Pornhub Deletes More Than Two-Thirds of Its Content After Being Dropped by Mastercard, Visa," *New York Daily News,* December 14, 2020, https://www.nydailynews.com/news/national/ny-pornhub-purges-millions-user-uploaded-unverified-videos-20201214-krjdkoftvncz7ig3jnr4etcobu-story.html.

23. Michael Robb, PhD, "Teens and Pornography," *Common Sense Media,* January 10, 2023, https://www.commonsensemedia.org/research/teens-and-pornography.

24. Jim Waterson, "Porn Survey Reveals Extent of UK Teenagers' Viewing Habits," *The Guardian,* January 31, 2020, https://www.theguardian.com/culture/2020/jan/31/porn-survey-uk-teenagers-viewing-habits-bbfc.

25. Dakin Andone, "Josh Duggar Arrested, Indicted on Child Pornography Charges," *CNN,* April 30, 2021, https://www.cnn.com/2021/04/30/us/joshua-duggar-arrest-child-pornography/index.html.

26. Sukwhant Dhaliwal, MD, "The Links Between Radicalisation and Violence Against Women and Girls," London Metropolitan University, June 2020, https://cwasu.org/wp-content/uploads/2021/04/radicalisation_and_vawg.pdf.

27. Andrew Theen, "Umpqua Community College Shooting: Killer's Manifesto Reveals Racist, Satanic Views," *Orgeonian*/Oregonian Live, September 8, 2017, https://www.oregonlive.com/pacific-northwest-news/2017/09/umpqua_community_college_shoot_3.html.

28. Tammy Waitt, "Violent Actors in the Periphery of the Incel Movement," *American Security Today,* October 31, 2019, https://americansecuritytoday.com/violent-actors-in-the-periphery-of-the-incel-movement-multi-video/.

29. CourtTV, "FL v. CRUZ: Parkland School Shooter Penalty Phase," CourtTV, July 18, 2022, https://www.courttv.com/news/fl-v-cruz-parkland-shooter-penalty-phase/.

30. Sukwhant Dhaliwal, "The Links Between Radicalisation and Violence Against Women and Girls," London Metropolitan University, June 2020, https://cwasu.org/wp-content/uploads/2021/04/radicalisation_and_vawg.pdf.

31. United States Secret Service, "Hot Yoga Tallahassee: A Case Study of Misogynistic Extremism," March 2022, https://www.secretservice.gov/sites/default/files/reports/2022-03/NTAC%20Case%20Study%20-%20Hot%20Yoga%20Tallahassee_0.pdf.

32. Tim Stelloh, "Ohio 'Incel' Who Plotted to 'Slaughter' Women Pleads Guilty to Attempted Hate Crime," *NBC News,* October 12, 2022, https://www.nbcnews.com/news/us-news/ohio-incel-plotted-slaughter-women-pleads-guilty-attempted-hate-crime-rcna51812.

33. Matthew Weaver, "Plymouth Gunman: A Hate-Filled Misogynist and 'Incel,'" *The Guardian*, August 13, 2021, https://www.theguardian.com/uk-news/2021/aug/13/plymouth-shooting-suspect-what-we-know-jake-davison.

34. Darlene Powells, "Self-Proclaimed 'Incel' Charged with Pepper Spraying Women in Orange County Arrested in Northern California," *CBS Los Angeles*, September 28, 2022, https://www.cbsnews.com/losangeles/news/self-proclaimed-incel-recorded-himself-pepper-spraying-women-orange-county-arrested-northern-california/.

35. Ashley Judd, "How Online Abuse of Women Has Spiraled Out of Control," TEDWomen 2016, https://www.ted.com/talks/ashley_judd_how_online_abuse_of_women_has_spiraled_out_of_control?utm_campaign=tedspread&utm_medium=referral&utm_source=tedcomshare.

36. Guy Raz, "Ashley Judd: How Can We—as a Society—Heal from Sexual Violence," *TED Radio Hour*, February 1, 2019, https://www.npr.org/transcripts/689946997.

37. UN Women, "Accelerating Efforts to Tackle Online and Technology Facilitated Violence Against Women and Girls (VAWG)," accessed April 8, 2023, https://www.unwomen.org/sites/default/files/2022-10/Accelerating-efforts-to-tackle-online-and-technology-facilitated-violence-against-women-and-girls-en_0.pdf.

38. International Center for Research on Women, "Technology-Facilitated Gender-Based Violence," accessed April 8, 2023, https://www.icrw.org/issues/tech-gbv/.

39. UN Women, "Accelerating Efforts to Tackle Online and Technology Facilitated Violence Against Women and Girls (VAWG)" accessed April 8, 2023, https://www.unwomen.org/sites/default/files/2022-10/Accelerating-efforts-to-tackle-online-and-technology-facilitated-violence-against-women-and-girls-en_0.pdf.

40. Suzie Dunn, *The Emerald International Handbook of Technology-Facilitated Violence and Abuse,* 1st ed. (UK: Emerald Publishing Limited, 2021), 45.

41. Jennifer Smith, "US TikTok Star, 15, Reveals How Ex-Cop Father Shot Dead Stalker, 18, Who Turned Up at Their Home to KILL Her After Buying Her Cell Number from Her Friends, Dad Is Free Under Florida's Stand-Your-Ground Law," Dailymail.com, February 17, 2022, https://www.dailymail.co.uk/news/article-10524573/Teenage-TikTok-stars-ex-cop-father-shot-dead-stalker-turned-home-trying-kill-her.html.

42. Apple, "What to Do if You Get an Alert That an AirTag, Find My Network Accessory, or Set of AirPods Is with You," Apple.com, accessed April 8, 2023, https://support.apple.com/en-us/HT212227#:~:text=If%20an%20AirTag%20that's%20separated,AirTag%20Found%20Moving%20With%20You.

43. Insider Intelligence, "US Video Gaming Industry in 2023: Gaming Devices & Video Game Content Viewership Trend," *Insider Intelligence,* January 24, 2023, https://www.insiderintelligence.com/insights/us-gaming-industry-ecosystem/.

44. Eric Griffith, "Here's What Parents Really Think About Their Kid's Online Activity," *PC Magazine,* July 11, 2022, https://www.pcmag.com/news/heres-what-parents-really-think-about-their-kids-online-activity.

45. Josh Campbell, "Arrest Made in 'Sextortion' Case Police Link to Teen's Suicide," CNN.com, December 20, 2022, https://www.cnn .com/2022/12/20/us/california-ryan-last-sextortion-scam -arrest/index.html.

46. Ekō, "Metaverse: Another Cesspool of Toxic Content," Ekō.org, May 2022, https://www.eko.org/images/Metaverse_report_May_ 2022.pdf.

47. Jamillah Bowman Williams, "Five Years On, Here's What #metoo Has Changed," *Politico*, October 14, 2022, https://www.politico .com/newsletters/women-rule/2022/10/14/five-years-on-heres -what-metoo-has-changed-00061853#:~:text=The%20%23Me Too%20movement%20did%20not,Sexual%20Harassment%20 Act%20of%202021.

Chapter Five
Persuasion-Proof

1. Adrian Chen, "Working at the Apple Store Is a Real Nightmare," *Business Insider*, June 16, 2011, https://www.businessinsider.com/ working-at-the-apple-store-is-a-real-nightmare-2011-6.

Chapter Six
Dating the Wolf

1. Jeff Truesdell, "The True Story Behind Dirty John: A Mom-of-4's Whirlwind Romance Reveals Shocking Lies & Violence," *People*, December 16, 2018, https://people.com/crime/the-true-story -behind-dirty-john-meehan/.

2. Meta Minton, "Jury Finds Man Guilty of Raping Woman He Met at Lake Sumter Landing," *Villages-News,* October 12, 2022, https://www.villages-news.com/2022/10/12/jury-finds-man-guilty-of-raping-woman-he-met-at-lake-sumter-landing/.

3. FBI Crime Data Explorer, National Incident-Based Reporting System (NIBRS) Details Reported in the United States, accessed April 9, 2023, CDE (cjis.gov).

4. Robin Hattersly, "The Sexual Assault Statistics Everyone Should Know," *Campus Safety Magazine,* March 5, 2018, https://www.campussafetymagazine.com/safety/sexual-assault-statistics-and-myths/.

5. Daniel Modesto, "There's a Huge Sense of Fear: Discussion of Date-Rape Substance Use Increased During the Last Two Terms, Students Say," *The Dartmouth,* May 24, 2022, https://www.thedartmouth.com/article/2022/05/theres-a-huge-sense-of-fear-discussion-of-date-rape-substance-use-increased-during-the-last-two-terms-students-say.

Chapter Seven
Just a Domestic

1. UN Women, "Facts and Figures: Ending Violence Against Women," unwomen.org, accessed April 9, 2023, https://www.unwomen.org/en/what-we-do/ending-violence-against-women/facts-and-figures.

2. UN Women, "Measuring the Shadow Pandemic: Violence Against Women During COVID-19," data.unwomen.org, 2021, https://data.unwomen.org/sites/default/files/documents/Publications/Measuring-shadow-pandemic.pdf.

3. Brad Boserup, "Alarming Trends in US Domestic Violence During the COVID-19 Pandemic," *American Journal of Emergency Medicine*, December, 2020, https://ajemjournal-test.com.marlin-prod.literatumonline.com/article/S0735-6757(20)30307-7/fulltext.

4. UN Women, "Measuring the Shadow Pandemic: Violence Against Women During COVID-19," https://data.unwomen.org/sites/default/files/documents/Publications/Measuring-shadow-pandemic.pdf.

5. Julia Felsenthal, "American Crime Story and the Vindication of O.J. Simpson Prosecutor Marcia Clark," *Vogue*, January 28, 2016, https://www.vogue.com/article/american-crime-story-marcia-clark-interview.

6. Leslie Morgan Steiner, "Why Domestic Violence Victims Don't Leave," TEDx Ranier, January 25, 2013, https://youtu.be/V1yW5IsnSjo.

7. Kellianne Costello, "Update on Domestic Violence and Traumatic Brain Injury: A Narrative Review," National Library of Medicine, January 12, 2022, https://www.ncbi.nlm.nih.gov/pmc/articles/PMC8773525/.

8. D. J. Summers, "Which States Have Mandatory Arrests for Domestic Violence? What Are Their Impacts?" *KDVR News*, updated May 13, 2022, https://kdvr.com/news/data/which-states-have-mandatory-arrest-dv-laws-and-what-impact-do-they-have/.

9. Adolphe A. Berle, "Symposium on Communist Brainwashing," *New York Public Radio*, November 7, 1957, https://www.wnyc.org/story/symposium-on-communist-brainwashing/.

10. Editors of *Encyclopedia Britannica,* "Brainwashing," updated March 25, 2023, https://www.britannica.com/topic/brainwashing.

11. Berle, "Symposium on Communist Brainwashing." *New York Public Radio,* November 7, 1957, https://www.wnyc.org/story/symposium-on-communist-brainwashing/.

12. Terry Gross, "The CIA's Secret Quest for Mind Control: Torture, LSD and a 'Poisoner in Chief,'" *National Public Radio,* September 9, 2019, https://www.npr.org/2019/09/09/758989641/the-cias-secret-quest-for-mind-control-torture-lsd-and-a-poisoner-in-chief.

13. Stephen Kinzer, *Poisoner in Chief: Sidney Gottlieb and the CIA Search for Mind Control,* illustrated ed. (Henry Holt and Company, 2019), 86.

14. Ibid., 168.

15. Albert D. Biderman, "Symposium on Communist Brainwashing." *New York Public Radio,* November 7, 1957, https://www.wnyc.org/story/symposium-on-communist-brainwashing/.

16. Albert D. Biderman, "Communist Attempts to Elicit False Confessions from Air Force Prisoners of War," *Bulletin of the New York Academy of Medicine,* September 1957, https://www.ncbi.nlm.nih.gov/pmc/articles/PMC1806204/pdf/bullnyacadmed00378-0046.pdf.

17. R. Renick, "Power and Control Comparison," National Network to End Domesic Violence, 1994, rev. 2012, https://nnedv.org/wp-content/uploads/2019/06/Power-and-Control-Comparison-2012.pdf.

18. Ann Silvers, "Brainwashing in Abusive Relationships," Psych-Central, September 14, 2015, https://psychcentral.com/blog/brainwashing-in-abusive-relationships#1.

19. Domestic Abuse Intervention Programs, "Wheel Information Center," Power and Control Wheel, accessed April 10, 2023, https://www.theduluthmodel.org/wheels/.

20. Domestic Abuse Intervention Programs, "The Duluth Model," Definition of Duluth Model, accessed April 15, 2023, https://www.theduluthmodel.org/wp-content/uploads/2017/11/Definition-of-Duluth-Model-June-2015.pdf.

21. Adolph A. Berle, "Symposium on Communist Brainwashing." New York Public Radio, November 7, 1957, https://www.wnyc.org/story/symposium-on-communist-brainwashing/.

Chapter Eight
Financial Security Is Key to Your Safety

1. Pham LeBach, "When Could Women Have a Bank Account? A Short History of Financial Gender Equality and the Financial Road Ahead," *Spiral,* April 22, 2021, https://www.spiral.us/blog/when-could-women-have-a-bank-account-a-short-history-of-financial-gender-equality-and-the-financial-road-ahead.

2. Martha J. Bailey, "Fifty Years of Family Planning: New Evidence on the Long-Run Effects of Increasing Access to Contraception," National Library of Medicine, Spring 2013, https://www.ncbi.nlm.nih.gov/pmc/articles/PMC4203450/.

3. Robin Saks Frankel, "History of Women and Credit Cards: 1970s to Present," *Forbes,* December 2, 2022, https://www.forbes.com/advisor/credit-cards/when-could-women-get

-credit-cards/#:~:text=1974%3A%20The%20Equal%20Credit%20
Opportunity%20Act&text=1974%20at%20a%20time%20
when,name%2C%20regardless%20of%20marital%20status.

4. National World War II Museum, "Research Starters: Women
in WWII," accessed April 10, 2023, https://www.nationalww2
museum.org/students-teachers/student-resources/research
-starters/research-starters-women-world-war-ii#:~:text=More
%20than%20six%20million%20women,200%2C000%20
served%20in%20the%20military.

5. New York City Department of Consumer Affairs, "From Cradle
to Cane: The Cost of Being a Female Consumer," December 2015,
https://www.nyc.gov/assets/dca/downloads/pdf/partners/Study
-of-Gender-Pricing-in-NYC.pdf.

6. Stuart Anderson, "Trade Reports Find Tariffs Hurt Consumers,
Particularly Women," *Forbes,* November 3, 2022, https://www.
forbes.com/sites/stuartanderson/2022/11/03/trade-reports-find
-tariffs-hurt-consumers-particularly-women/?sh=2720d75c6b32.

7. CBS News, "CBS News Goes Undercover to Reveal Gender Price
Discrimination," January 25, 2016, https://www.cbsnews
.com/news/price-discrimination-gender-gap-cbs-news
-undercover-dry-cleaners/.

8. Mindy Isser, "The Grooming Gap: What 'Looking the Part' Costs
Women," *In These Times,* January 2, 2020, https://inthesetimes
.com/article/grooming-gap-women-economics-wage-gender
-sexism-make-up-styling-dress-code.

9. US Bureau of Economic Analysis, "Why Isn't Household Production Included in GDP?," US Bureau of Economic Analysis, April 15, 2018, https://www.bea.gov/help/faq/1297.

10. Claudia Goldin, *Career and Family: Women's Century-Long Journey toward Equity* (Princeton, NJ: Princeton University Press, 2021), 8.

11. Editors of *Encyclopedia Britannica,* "Gross National Product (GNP)," Britannica Money, updated March 20, 2023, https://www.britannica.com/money/gross-national-product.

12. Federal Reserve Economic Data, "GNP," St. Louis Federal Reserve, accessed April 16, 2023, https://fred.stlouisfed.org/series/GNP#.

13. Sarah Jane Glynn, "Connecting the Dots: 'Women's Work' and the Wage Gap," US Department of Labor Blog, March 14, 2022, https://blog.dol.gov/2022/03/15/connecting-the-dots-womens-work-and-the-wage-gap#:~:text=In%202020%2C%20the%20latest%20year,every%20dollar%20paid%20to%20men.

14. Abha Bhattarai, "What Does It Cost to Raise a Child?," *Washington Post,* October 13, 2022, https://www.washingtonpost.com/business/interactive/2022/cost-raising-child-calculator/.

15. Daniel De Visé, "More Adult Children Are Living with Their Parents. Parents Are Not Pleased," *The Hill,* December 16, 2022, https://thehill.com/policy/finance/3777185-more-adult-children-are-living-with-their-parents-parents-are-not-pleased/.

16. Aden Barton, "A Gender Gap at Harvard?," *Harvard Crimson,* November 14, 2022, https://www.thecrimson.com/article/2022/11/14/barton-men-in-higher-ed/.

17. Nick Kolakowski, "Do You Need a Degree to Work for a Big Tech Company Like Google?," *Dice,* April 27, 2022, https://www.dice.com/career-advice/do-you-need-a-degree-to-work-for-a-big-tech-company-like-google.

Chapter Nine
Joy's Survival Blueprint

1. Fox 35 Orlando, "Jurors Hear Detective's Interview with Scott Nelson," *Fox 35 Orlando,* June 26, 2019, https://www.fox35orlando.com/news/jurors-hear-detectives-interview-with-scott-nelson.

2. Robert Ressler, *Whoever Fights Monsters: My Twenty Years Tracking Serial Killers for the FBI* (St. Martin's Press, 2015), 1.

3. Amritpal Kaur Sandhu Longoria, "Cable Company Ordered to Pay $7 Billion to Family of Texas Woman Murdered by Repairman," *USA Today,* July 28, 2022, https://www.usatoday.com/story/news/2022/07/28/texas-jury-awards-7-billion-woman-killed-charter-cable-repairman/10158999002/.

4. Hannah Phillips, "Family Wants Boca Grandmother's Killer to Suffer After 2019 Beating, Burning," *USA Today,* April 5, 2023, https://www.usatoday.com/story/news/crime/2023/04/05/murder-of-boca-raton-grandmother-earns-life-sentences-for-delivery-man/70080392007/.

5. Everytown Research, "Mass Shootings in the United States," Everytown Research, updated March 2023, https://everytownresearch.org/mass-shootings-in-america/.

Chapter Ten
Shams, Scams, and Cons

1. Federal Trade Commission, "New FTC Data Shows Consumers Reported Losing Nearly \$8.8 Billion to Scams in 2022," February 23, 2023, https://www.ftc.gov/news-events/news/press-releases/2023/02/new-ftc-data-show-consumers-reported-losing-nearly-88-billion-scams-2022.

2. Lukas I. Alpert, "Prosecutors Say Douglas Sailors Used an Elaborate System of Shell Companies and Phony Administrators to Hide That Millions of Dollars Was Going to Him," MarketWatch, November 8, 2022, https://www.marketwatch.com/story/florida-charity-king-charged-with-raising-millions-for-firefighters-veterans-and-cancer-survivors-but-keeping-the-cash-for-himself-11667935186.

About the Authors

JOY FARROW is a retired deputy sheriff with twenty-eight years of experience, who worked as a police officer for the Pompano Beach Police Department in Pompano Beach, Florida, and faced every situation imaginable. Joy later worked as a deputy sheriff for the Broward Sheriff's Office, in Ft. Lauderdale, FL. After the attacks on 9/11, Joy transferred to the Fort Lauderdale–Hollywood International Airport with the Broward Sheriff's Office to focus on the safety of air travelers. She also assisted in the aftermath of the 2017 mass shooting at the Fort Lauderdale–Hollywood International Airport. She has saved many lives over the course of her career. Joy was one of the featured speakers at the TEDx Eustis conference and speaks on women's safety.

LAURA FROMBACH was introduced to technology in the US Army while working on Pershing nuclear missiles. She has spent much of her career as a technologist and engineer with IBM, HP, FedEx, Coca Cola Enterprises, Lenovo, and others. A turning point in Laura's life was the 'aha' moment when she correlated her mother's mental illness to domestic violence. She speaks on behalf of local domestic violence shelters.